D0468749

Off the
Beaten Path®

NINTH EDITION

virginia

A GUIDE TO UNIQUE PLACES

JUDY COLBERT

INSIDERS' GUIDE®

GUILFORD, CONNECTICUT
AN IMPRINT OF THE GLOBE PEQUOT PRESS

To Harry and Bernice Mudrick,

who started me on my way.

The prices, rates, and hours listed in this guidebook
were confirmed at press time. We recommend,
however, that you call establishments to obtain
current information before traveling.

To buy books in quantity for corporate use
or incentives, call **(800) 962–0973, ext. 4551,**
or e-mail **premiums@GlobePequot.com.**

INSIDERS'GUIDE®

Copyright © 1986, 1989, 1993, 1995, 1998, 2001, 2002, 2005, 2007 by Judy Colbert

Insiders' Guide and Off the Beaten Path are registered trademarks of Morris Book
Publishing, LLC.

Text design by Linda Loiewski
Maps created by Equator Graphics © Morris Book Publishing, LLC
Illustrations by Carole Drong, based on photographs by Judy Colbert
and the Virginia Division of Tourism
Spot photography throughout © James P. Blair/Getty

ISSN 1539-8110
ISBN-13: 978-0-7627-4215-8
ISBN-10: 0-7627-4215-1

Manufactured in the United States of America
Ninth Edition/First Printing

Contents

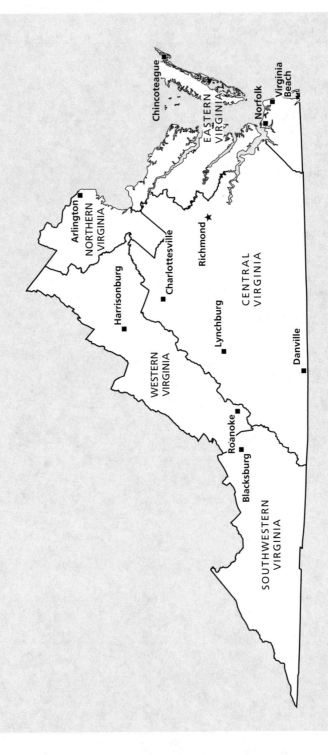

VIRGINIA

Introduction

Virginia is having a party. Lots of parties. Communities across the state are celebrating the 400th anniversary of its founding in 1607 at Jamestown, and the observances have already started. Check www.jamestown2007.org for a calendar listing such events as an exhibit in Covington of 31 WPA photos from the 1930s categorized as "unidentified," a Charter Day Ball celebrating the 200th anniversary of the City of Salem, kayaking the Captain John Smith Trail on Virginia's Eastern Shore out of Cape Charles, and the sailing of the *GodSpeed,* a newly commissioned replica of one of the ships that landed on Virginia's shores. Those who only dream of visiting Virginia can see the ship in Baltimore, Maryland, Philadelphia, Pennsylvania, Newport, Rhode Island, and Boston, Massachusetts.

Among the many "firsts" of Virginia, one of the most recent is the establishment of a statewide birding and wildlife trail so visitors can view some of the 400 species of birds, 250 species of fish, 150 species of terrestrial and marine mammals, 150 species of amphibians and reptiles, and who knows how many aquatic and terrestrial invertebrates. There are three guides you can request: a 200-page Mountain Area (everything west of U.S. Route 29), an 84-page Piedmont Area (central portion), and the 100-page Coastal Area (eastern Virginia and the Eastern Shore). It's a partnership between the Department of Game and Inland Fisheries and the Virginia Tourism Corporation. In promoting Mother Nature's fall foliage fashion show, the VTC joined with the Virginia Department of Forestry and Virginia State Parks.

Remember, whatever you love in a vacation you can find in Virginia.

Whatever frame of mind you're in, there's a place for you in Virginia. From mountains to beaches, from cosmopolitan to country, from great dining and fine lodging to down-home cooking and rustic campsites, look to Virginia for a special time in your life.

What's meant by Virginia's famed tourism slogan, "Virginia Is for Lovers"? It means that Virginia is for lovers of mountain climbing, catching some rays, or seeing innovative modern architecture and log cabins from a previous century. It means that Virginia is for lovers of horseback riding, auto racing, outlet shopping, covered bridges, gristmills, great wineries, and just about anything else you can imagine. Okay, so it's not great for extreme skiing, but you *can* downhill and cross-country ski.

You can find the most bodacious BBQ and a library designed by noted postmodernist architect Michael Graves. Varieties of tomatoes and cantaloupes are grown here that are grown nowhere else. Smithfield ham can only come from Smithfield, Virginia.

Virginia is the fourth largest South Atlantic state and thirty-sixth in size among all the states. It extends 200 miles from north to south and almost 440 miles from east to west. It's the twelfth most populous state in the country, with nearly three-fourths of the population living in cities. Within its woodlands are twelve varieties of oak, five of pine, and two of walnut, as well as locust, gum, and poplar. Its indigenous mammals include the white-tailed Virginia deer, elk, black bear, bobcat, woodchuck, raccoon, opossum, and nutria.

Operation Wildflower is a combined program of the Virginia Department of Transportation and the Virginia Federation of Garden Clubs Inc. that has grown from twenty-five plots of wildflowers planted in 1976 to hundreds of acres of assorted species planted along state highways today. From April through October, you'll see (seasonally) black-eyed Susans, New England asters, oxeye sunflower, New York ironweed, butterfly weed, lance-leaved coreopsis, purple coneflower, tickseed-sunflower (all native to Virginia), Indian blanket (central United States), plains coreopsis (southern United States), sulphur cosmos and mixed cosmos (Mexico), and corn poppy (Europe). If you don't know a sunflower from an aster, pick up a *Wildflowers Color Virginia* brochure at a welcome station; or call (804) 371–6825 or (800) 774–3382.

Drink to Me Only with Thine Eyes

There are nearly one hundred wineries in Virginia. You're invited to visit, learn about wine making, and attend special events. The Virginia Wine of the Month Club can help highlight individual wines for you. (800) 826–0534 or (434) 985–9709; www.vawineclub.com. A free wine festival and tour guide is available by calling (800) 828–4637 or through the Internet at www.virginia wines.org.

As this is a guide to unique places, there's not much emphasis on the major tourism destinations and sites. To find those roads more traveled, call (800) 847–4882 (VISIT–VA) for a Virginia vacation guide, or write to the Division of Tourism at 901 East Byrd Street, Richmond 23219. The tourism division (804–786–4484; www.virginia.org) can also provide more specific information about a particular area. They have many special-interest brochures that will help you in your search for the perfect bed-and-breakfast, African-American and Hispanic sites and events, and other destinations.

Much of Virginia is old, and many buildings were constructed before handicapped accessibility was a public concern. For specific information about public accessibility, request the *Virginia Travel Guide for Persons with Disabilities* brochure. Be sure to call any place you plan to visit to determine whether the facility is accessible to people in wheelchairs or if there are special provisions for those who have visual or hearing impairments. (The TDD number is 804–371–0327.)

Virginia has 95 counties, 40 independent cities, and 189 incorporated towns. This can be a little confusing, particularly when trying to locate and visit an independent city that's located within a county. You'd probably do well to avoid trying to figure the difference between Fairfax County, Fairfax city, Alexandria, Arlington, etc. Just plug the information into your GPS or find an online map. Persevere, please.

By the way, Virginia is a commonwealth—first used in Jamestown in 1619—not a state. Kentucky, Massachusetts, and Pennsylvania also use the term commonwealth.

Many thanks to the Virginia Division of Tourism, Martha Steger in particular, and to all the wonderful Virginians who have taken time to assist me in researching and updating *Virginia: Off the Beaten Path*.

The prices and rates listed in this guidebook were confirmed at press time. We recommend, however, that you call establishments before traveling to obtain current information.

Virginia Tourism Resources

VIRGINIA TOURISM

Virginia Tourism Corporation, 901 East Byrd Street, Richmond 23219; (804) 545–5572 or (800) 732–5827 or (800) VISIT–VA (847–4882); fax (804) 371–0327; TTY/TTD (804) 371–0327; www.virginia.org

VIRGINIA REGIONAL TOURISM COUNCILS

Northern Virginia

Alexandria Visitors Center, Ramsey House, 221 King Street, Alexandria 22314; (703) 838–5005 or (800) 388–9119; www.funside.com

Arlington County Visitors Center, 1301 South Joyce Street, Arlington 22202; (800) 677–6267; www.stayarlington.com

Chesapeake Bay/Potomac Gateway Visitors Center, 3540 James Madison Parkway, King George 22485; (540) 663–3205; www.northernneck.org

Fairfax City Visitors Center, 10209 Main Street, Fairfax 22030; (800) 545–7950 or (703) 385–7862; www.fairfaxva.gov/museumvc/mvc.asp

Fairfax County Visitors Center, 8180-A Silverbrook Road, Lorton 22079; (703) 550–2450 or (800) 732–4732; www.fxva.com

Fredericksburg Visitor Center, 706 Caroline Street, Fredericksburg 22401; (800) 678–4748 or (540) 373–1776; www.visitfred.com

Loudoun County Visitors Center, 222 Catoctin Circle Southeast, Suite 100, Leesburg 20175; (800) 752–6118 or (703) 771–2617; www.visitloudoun.org

Manassas Visitor Center, 9431 West Street, Manassas 20110; (703) 361–6599 or (877) 848–3018; www.visitmanassas.org

Prince William County, Manassas Tourist Information Center, 14420 Bristow Road, Manassas 20112; (703) 792–4254 or (800) 432–1792; www.visit pwc.com

Spotsylvania County Visitors Center, 4704 Southpoint Parkway, Fredericksburg 22407; (877) 515–6197 or (540) 891–8687; www.spotsylvania .va.us

Warrenton–Fauquier County Visitors Center, 33 North Calhoun Street, Warrenton 20186; (540) 341–0988 or (800) 820–1021; www.fauquiertourism.com

Chesapeake Bay

Assateague Island National Seashore, Toms Cove Visitor Center, 8586 Beach Road, Chincoteague 23336; (757) 336–6577; www.nps.gov/asis

Chincoteague Chamber of Commerce and Visitor Center, 6733 Maddox Boulevard, Chincoteague 23336; (757) 336–6161; www.chincoteaguechamber.com

Eastern Shore Visitors Center and Tourism Commission, P.O. Box 460, Melfa 23410; (757) 787–2460; www.esvatourism.org

Hampton Visitors Center, 120 Old Hampton Lane, Hampton 23669; (800) 800–2202 or (757) 727–1102; www.hamptoncvb.com

Newport News Tourist Information Center, Newport News Park, 13560 Jefferson Avenue, Newport News 23603; (888) 493–7386 or (757) 886–7777; www.newport-news.org

Norfolk Visitors Information Center, 9401 Fourth View Street, Norfolk 23503; (800) 368–3097 or (757) 441–1852; www.norfolkcvb.com

Portsmouth Visitors Information Center, 6 Crawford Parkway, Portsmouth 23704; (800) PORTS–VA (767–8782) or (757) 393–5111; www.portsva.com

Smithfield and Isle of Wight Visitors Center, 335 Main Street, Smithfield 23431; (800) 365–9339 or (757) 357–5182; www.smithfield-virginia.com

Suffolk Visitor Information Center, 321 North Main Street, Suffolk 23434; (866) SEE–SUFK (733–7835) or (757) 923–3880; www.suffolk-fun.com

Virginia Beach Visitor Information Center, 2100 Parks Avenue, Virginia Beach 23451; (800) 822–3224 or (757) 437–4919; www.vbfun.com

Williamsburg Area Convention and Visitors Bureau, 421 North Boundary Street, Williamsburg 23187; (800) 368–6511 or (757) 253–0192; www.visit williamsburg.com

Central Virginia

Appomattox Visitor Information Center, 5 Main Street, Appomattox 24522; (434) 352–2621; www.appomattox.com

Ashland–Hanover Visitor Information Center, 112 North Railroad Avenue, Ashland 23005; (800) 897–1479 or (804) 752–6766; www.townashland.va.us

Bedford Area Welcome Center, 816 Burks Hill Road, Bedford 24523; (540) 587–5691 or (871) HI–PEAKS (447–3257); www.visitbedford.com

Charlottesville–Albermarle County Visitors Center, 100 South Street NE, Charlottesville 22902; (877) 386–1102 or (434) 293–6789; www.charlottesville tourism.org

Culpeper Visitors Center, 109 South Commerce Street, Culpeper 22701; (540) 825–8628 or (888) CULPEPER; www.visitculpeperva.com

Danville Tourism Division, 645 River Park Drive, Danville 24540; (434) 793–4636; www.dpchamber.org/VisitorInfo.cfm or www.visitdanville.com

Hopewell Visitor Center, 4100 Oaklawn Boulevard, Hopewell 23860; (800) 863–TOUR (863–8687) or (804) 541–2461; www.ci.hopewell.va.us

Lynchburg Visitors Center, 216 Twelfth Street at Church, Lynchburg 24504; (800) 732–5821 or (434) 732–5821; www.discoverlynchburg.org

Madison County Chamber of Commerce, 110 North Main Street, Box 373, Madison 22727; (540) 948–4455; www.madison-va.com

Nelson County Visitors Center, 8519 Thomas Nelson Highway (US 29), Lovingston 22949; (800) 282–8223 or (434) 263–6823; www.nelsoncounty.com

Orange County Visitors Center, 122 East Main Street, Orange 22960; (877) 222–8072 or (540) 672–1653; www.visitocva.com

Petersburg Visitors Center, 425 Cockade Alley, Petersburg 23803; (434) 733–2400 or (800) 368–3595; www.petersburg-va.org

Pulaski County Visitor Center, 4440 Cleburne Boulevard, Dublin 24084; (540) 674–1991; www.pulaskicounty.org

Richmond Region Visitor Center, 401 North Third Street, Richmond 23219; (800) 370–9004 or (804) 783–7450; www.richmondva.org

Smith Mountain Lake Visitors Center, 16430 Booker T. Washington Highway, Unit 2, Moneta 24121; (800) 676–8203 or (540) 721–1203; www.visit smithmountainlake.com

South Hill Tourist Information Center, 201 South Mecklenburg Avenue, South Hill 23970; (800) 524–4347 or (434) 447–4547; www.southhillchamber.com

Western Virginia

Alleghany Highlands Travel Council, 241 West Main Street, Covington 24426; (540) 962–2178; www.ahchamber.com

Buena Vista Regional Visitor Center, 595 East Twenty-ninth Street, Buena Vista 24416; (540) 261–8004, www.lexingtonvirginia.com

Front Royal–Warren County Visitor Center, 414 East Main Street, Front Royal 22630; (800) 338–2576 or (540) 635–5788; www.ci.front-royal.va.us

Harrisonburg Tourism and Visitor Services, 212 South Main Street, Harrisonburg, 22801; (540) 434–8935; www.harrisonburgtourism.com

Lexington and the Rockbridge Area Visitor Center, 106 East Washington Street, Lexington 24450; (877) 453–9822 or (540) 463–3777; www.lexington virginia.com

Luray–Page County Chamber of Commerce, 46 East Main Street, Luray 22835; (540) 743–3915 or (888) 743–3915; www.luraypage.com

Roanoke Valley Visitor Information Center, 101 Shenandoah Avenue NE, Roanoke 24016; (800) 635–5535 or (540) 345–8622; www.visitroanokeva.com

Rockfish Gap Tourist Information Center, 20 Afton Mountain, Afton 22920; (540) 943–5187; www.waynesborova-online.com

Salem Visitors Center, Salem Civic Center, 1001 Roanoke Boulevard, Salem 24153; (888) VA–SALEM (725–2536) or (540) 375–4044; www.visitsalemva.com

Shenandoah Valley Travel Association, 277 West Old Cross Road, New Market 22844; (877) VISIT–SV (847–4878) or (540) 740–3132; www.shenandoah.org

Staunton Tavel Information Center, 1290 Richmond Road, Staunton 24401; (800) 332–5219 or (540) 332–3972; www.stauntonva.org

Waynesboro Department of Tourism, 301 West Main Street, Waynesboro 22980; (866) 253–1957 or (540) 942–6644; www.waynesboro.va.us/tourism .html

Winchester–Frederick County Visitors Center, 1360 South Pleasant Valley Road, Winchester 22601; (877) 871–1326 or (540) 542–1326; www.visit winchesterva.com

Southwestern Virginia

Abingdon Visitors Center, 335 Cummings Street, Abingdon 24210; (800) 435–3440 or (276) 676–2282; www.abingdon.com/tourism

Blue Ridge Plateau Regional Visitor Center, 235 Farmers Market Road, Hillsville 24343; (276) 730–3100; www.visittheblueridge.com

Bristol Convention and Visitors Bureau, 20 Volunteer Parkway, Bristol, TN 37620; (423) 989–4850; www.bristolchamber.org/bristolvisit

Grayson County Tourist Information Center, 107 East Main Street, Box 336, Independence 24348; (276) 773–3711; www.graysoncountyva.com

Lonesome Pine Tourist Info Center, 619 Gilley Avenue East, Box 236, Big Stone Gap 24219; (276) 523–2060; www.bigstonegap.org

USEFUL WEB SITES

Metropolitan Washington Airports; www.metwashairports.com
National Park Service; www.nps.gov
Virginia Tourism Corporation; www.virginia.org

MAJOR NEWSPAPERS

Bristol Herald-Courier/Virginia-Tennessean, 320 Morrison Boulevard, Bristol 24201; (276) 669–2181; www.tricities.com

Charlottesville Daily Progress, 685 West Rio Road, Charlottesville 22901; (434) 978–7200; www.dailyprogress.com

Culpeper Star-Exponent, 122 West Spencer Street, Culpeper 22701; (540) 825–0771; www.starexponent.com

The Daily News Leader, 11 North Central Avenue, Staunton 24402; (540) 885–7281 or (800) 793–2459; www.newsleader.com

Daily Press, Main Office, 7505 Warwick Boulevard, Newport News 23607; (757) 247–4600; www.dailypress.com

Danville Register & Bee, 700 Monument Street, Danville 24541; (434) 793–2311; www.registerbee.com

Eastern Shore News, Tasley 23441; (757) 787–1200

Free Lance–Star, 616 Amelia Street, Fredericksburg 22401; (540) 374–5537; www.freelancestar.com

Lynchburg News & Advance, 101 Wyndale Drive, Lynchburg 24501; (434) 385–5440 or (800) 275–8830; www.newsadvance.com

Manassas Journal Messenger, 9009 Church Street, Manassas 20110; (703) 368–3101; www.manassasjm.com

News Leader, 11 North Central Avenue, Staunton 24401; (540) 885–7281; www.newsleader.com

The News-Virginian, Waynesboro 22980; (540) 949–8213 or (540) 886–3400; www.newsvirginian.com

Richmond Times Dispatch, 300 East Franklin Street, Richmond 23219; (804) 649–6000; www.timesdispatch.com

Roanoke Times, 201 Campbell Avenue SW, Roanoke 24070–2451; (540) 981–3100 or (800) 346–1234

Washington Post, 1150 Fifteenth Street NW, Washington, D.C. 20071; (202) 334–6000; www.washingtonpost.com

PUBLIC TRANSPORTATION

Amtrak, (800) USA–RAIL; (800) 872–7245 or (888) 268–7251 or (888) AMTRAK1; www.amtrak.com

Norfolk International Airport, Norfolk 23502; (757) 857–3351; www.norfolk airport.com

Ronald Reagan National Airport, Arlington 22210; (703) 417–8600; www .metwashairports.com

Newport News–Williamsburg International Airport, Newport News 23602; (757) 877–0221; www.nnwairport.com

Richmond International Airport, Richmond 23231; (804) 226–3000; www .flyrichmond.com

Roanoke Airport, Roanoke 24011; (540) 362–1999; www.roanokeregional airport.com

Virginia Railway Express (VRE), (703) 684–0400 or (800) RIDE–VRE (743–3433); www.vre.org

Washington Dulles International Airport, Herndon 22204; (703) 572–2700; www.metwashairports.com

Fast Facts about the Old Dominion

Area (land): 39,598 square miles; rank: 35

Capital: Richmond

Largest city: Virginia Beach, population 425,257

Number of counties: 95

Highest elevation: 5,729 feet, Mount Rogers

Lowest elevation: sea level, at the Atlantic Ocean

Population: 7,567,500 (2005 estimate)

Population distribution: 88.5 percent in urban areas, 11.5 percent rural

Institutions of higher education: 97

Median family income: $57,598

Statehood: June 25, 1788; the tenth state

Nickname: Old Dominion

State flower: dogwood flower

State tree: dogwood

State motto: *Sic Semper Tyrannis* ("Thus Always to Tyrants")

State bird: northern cardinal

State shell: oyster shell

State dog: American foxhound

State drink: milk

State insect: Tiger Swallowtail butterfly
State folkdance: square dancing
State boat: Chesapeake Bay Deadrise
State fish: brook trout

Climate Overview

Virginia's weather depends on the region and the season. The Tidewater area is relatively mild in the winter but can be quite humid in the summer. Northern Virginia also has hot, humid summer days but receives an average 20 inches of snow each winter. The mountains can receive severe winter storms but enjoy delightful summer days.

Famous Sons and Daughters of Virginia

Richard Arlen, actor
Arthur Ashe, tennis champion
Stephen F. Austin, Texas founder
Pearl Bailey, singer
Russell Baker, columnist
Warren Beatty, actor
George Bingham, painter
Richard Evelyn Bird, naval officer/explorer
Jeff Burton, NASCAR driver
Willa Cather, novelist
Roy Clark, country music artist
William Clark, soldier/explorer
Henry Clay, orator and statesman
Patsy Cline, singer
Joseph Cotten, actor
Ella Fitzgerald, jazz singer
William Henry Harrison, U.S. president
Patrick Henry, statesman
Sam Houston, political leader
Thomas Jefferson, U.S. president
Henry "Light-Horse Harry" Lee, public official
Robert E. Lee, Confederate general
Meriwether Lewis, explorer
Shirley MacLaine, actress
James Madison, U.S. president

John Marshall, U.S. chief justice
Cyrus Hall McCormick, inventor
James Monroe, U.S. president
Opechancanough, Powhatan leader
John Payne, actor
Pocahontas, Indian princess
Walter Reed, army surgeon
Matthew Ridgway, army chief of staff
Joseph Jenkins Roberts, first president of Liberia
Bill "Bojangles" Robinson, dancer and actor
George C. Scott, actor
Sam Snead, golfer
James "Jeb" Stuart, Confederate army officer
Thomas Sumter, army officer
Zachary Taylor, U.S. president
Nat Turner, leader of slave uprising
John Tyler, U.S. president
Booker T. Washington, educator
George Washington, U.S. president
James E. West, inventor
Thomas Woodrow Wilson, U.S. president
Tom Wolfe, journalist

Northern Virginia

Poor Northern Virginia. Other than those who follow Civil War history, there probably aren't many visitors who say, "Oh, I'm going to Northern Virginia for my vacation." They say they're going to Washington, D.C., and decide to stay in the neighboring state across the Potomac River. That's all well and good for the restaurants and hotels—their managements love it. But it's not fair to the visitor who could be missing a spectacular Virginia museum, an unusual spot to get away from it all for a few hours, or a significant link to history.

Visit an old gristmill, see where the George Washington cherry tree fable originated, or check out an apothecary that seems frozen in time. All of these wonders and curiosities are within a short drive of our nation's capital; you can go out, have your adventure, and be back in just a few hours.

Arlington

If you aren't a local resident, the chances are good that you flew into National Airport (although Dulles International Airport and Baltimore-Washington International Airport are almost as convenient), so our visit will start in Arlington.

NORTHERN VIRGINIA

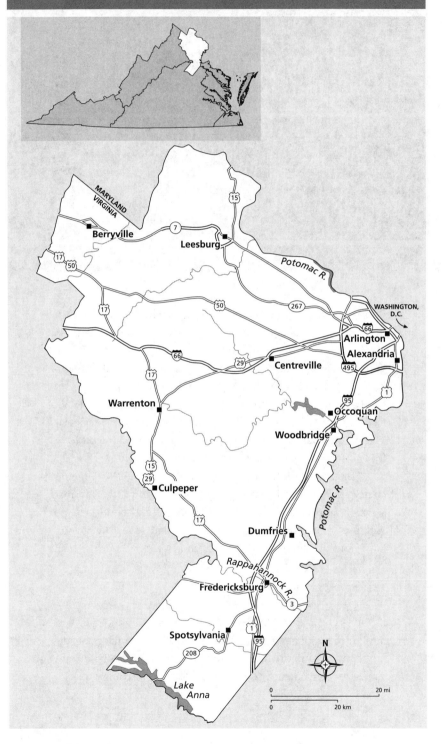

MARYLAND
VIRGINIA

Berryville

Leesburg

Potomac R.

WASHINGTON,
D.C.

Arlington

Alexandria

Centreville

Warrenton

Occoquan

Woodbridge

Culpeper

Potomac R.

Dumfries

Rappahannock R.

Fredericksburg

Spotsylvania

Lake
Anna

N

0   20 mi

0   20 km

For brochures and specific information, contact the ***Arlington County Visitors Center,*** 1301 South Joyce Street, Arlington 22202 (1½ blocks from the Pentagon City Metro station), which is open seven days a week from 9:00 A.M. to 5:00 P.M. except for Thanksgiving, Christmas, and New Year's Days; (703) 228–5720 or (800) 677–6267; www.stayarlington.com.

Near Arlington National Cemetery, the Iwo Jima Memorial, and the Netherlands Carillon is ***Fort Myer,*** home of the oldest military division in the United States, the Third U.S. Infantry Division. This is the ceremonial unit for Arlington Cemetery.

The caissons, stables, and the ***Old Guard Museum*** in the fort are often open to the public on weekdays. Blackjack, the riderless horse whose symbolism was so moving during the funerals of Presidents John F. Kennedy and Dwight D. Eisenhower as well as more than 150 other funerals, is buried on the marching grounds. Look for the plaque and flowering bushes marking his grave. A stable has been dedicated as a museum to him. The rest of the museum, which is the only U.S. Army museum in the Washington, D.C., area, is dedicated to the regiment that began its history in 1784.

For additional information, contact the Old Guard Museum, Building 249, Sheridan Avenue, Fort Myer, Arlington 22211. The museum is open Monday through Saturday 9:00 A.M. to 4:00 P.M. and Sunday from 1:00 to 4:00 P.M. Admission is free. Call (703) 696–6670 before your arrival to schedule a forty-minute guided tour.

It's a Photo Moment

I'm always looking for that perfect or unusual photo, particularly when it comes to views of Washington. If you didn't see enough of the Washington skyline as you landed (perhaps you came in from the south approach or you were on an inside seat, or maybe you drove), there are some great spots with amazing views of downtown Washington, with its marble monuments and greenery. Try Freedom Park; J.W. Steakhouse on the fourteenth floor of the Key Bridge Marriott at Rosslyn; the Iwo Jima Memorial; Arlington House at Arlington Cemetery; the revolving Skydome Lounge, atop the Doubletree Hotel in Arlington; and the Vantage Point Restaurant and Lounge at the Holiday Inn Rosslyn. The George Washington Masonic National Memorial, the most visible sight in Alexandria, also provides a most spectacular view of the city and of Washington, D.C., 6 miles away. You'll want to bring your widest and longest camera lenses to shoot from the observation tower of this 333-foot building.

AUTHOR'S FAVORITES IN NORTHERN VIRGINIA

Annual Historic Garden Week, April, statewide, (804) 644–7776

Chocolate Lovers Festival, February, Fairfax, (703) 385–8179, www.chocolate festival.net

Easter Sunrise Service, March/April, Arlington, (202) 685–2851

Eighteenth-century craft fair, September, Mount Vernon, (703) 780–2000, www.mountvernon.org

Fauquier County Fair, July, Warrenton, (540) 788–9549, www.fauquierfair.org

Great Falls National Park, Great Falls, (703) 285–2966

Holiday Train Show, December, Fairfax Station, (703) 425–9225, www.fairfax-station.org

Hot Air Balloon Festival, August, Bealeton, (540) 439–8661

International Children's Festival, September, Wolf Trap Farm Park for the Performing Arts, Vienna, (703) 938–2404

Juneteenth Commemoration, June, Alexandria City, (703) 838–4356, www.alexblackhistory.org

Strawberry Festival, May, Sky Meadows State Park, Delaplane, (540) 592–3556

U.S. Marine Corps War Memorial (Iwo Jima Memorial), Arlington

Wolf Trap Farm Park for the Performing Arts, Vienna, (703) 938–2404

Free concerts by the U.S. Army Band and guest artists are held on a regular schedule in Brucker Hall. For more information call (703) 696–3399 (a recorded concert hotline), or visit www.army.mil/armyband.

Women in Military Service for America Memorial, located at the ceremonial entrance to Arlington National Cemetery, is dedicated to all military women—past, present, and future. The views from the memorial are impressive (that's Arlington House above it as you're approaching the memorial), and just listening to the stories of the battles fought to create the memorial, particularly the architectural ones, is almost as impressive as learning about the battles these women fought for more than two centuries, from Revolutionary days to the present. You can search for women who have served, either in person or online. There's a gift shop; rotating exhibits of artifacts, photographs, documents, memorabilia, and uniforms; a film, *In Defense of a Nation;* a comput-

star-shine

Sandra Bullock, Katie Couric, Roberta Flack, Shirley MacLaine, Warren Beatty, and 1996 Olympic swimming gold-medalist Tom Dolan are among the celebrities raised in Arlington.

erized register with the stories of some 350,000 military women; and a monthly children's program. The Women's Memorial is open daily from 8:00 A.M. to 5:00 P.M. October through March; to 7:00 P.M. April through September, closed

December 25. Children are welcome, and it's wheelchair accessible. Women in Military Service for America Memorial, Department 560, Washington, D.C. 20042-0560; (800) 222–2294 or (703) 892–2602; www.womensmemorial.org.

It seems there's a museum for and about everything, and now there's one about drugs—not pharmaceuticals meant to save your life, but dope drugs. It's the *Drug Enforcement Administration's Museum and Visitors Center* at DEA headquarters (700 Army-Navy Drive, Arlington 22202-4222; 202–307–3463; www.deamuseum.org) in Pentagon City (across from the Pentagon City Metro stop).

On display are 150 years of drug and alcohol abuse paraphernalia, including bent spoons, bongs, hash pipes, hookahs, marijuana, photos, and old syringes. It also follows the history of the DEA and its predecessors, starting in 1906 when the government began regulating drugs. The display, contained in a narrow 2,200-square-foot room, is fairly small, and there is a gift shop, run by the Association of Former Federal Narcotics Agents Foundation. Just as the Mint doesn't give samples of the paper money it prints, the DEA museum doesn't offer drug samples. But you can pick up a DEA sweatshirt, coffee mug, miniature lapel badge, badges in Lucite, pens, key chains, or a Beanie bear with a DEA shirt. The museum is open Tuesday through Friday from 10:00 A.M. to 4:00 P.M.

If you stop by the seventeen-acre *Lyndon Baines Johnson Park* off the George Washington Memorial Parkway, you will find white pine, dogwoods, numerous flowering bushes, and a tape recording of Lady Bird Johnson's remarks at the dedication ceremony in 1976. Her speech is played through an outdoor speaker installed at one end of the footbridge that connects the grove to the Pentagon parking lot. There is also a forty-three-ton obelisk that was brought in from Marble Falls Quarry, near the LBJ Ranch in Johnson City, Texas. If it looks

funfacts

rough, that's because it has been sculpted to give it a rugged look.

There are no quotations or citations proclaiming Johnson's victories while in office. There are just peace and tranquility and natural beauty signifying the Johnsons' contribution to our national park system and the highway beautification program. For additional information, call the National Park Service, (703) 289–2553; www.nps.gov/lyba.

The *Upton Hill Regional Park Mini Golf Course* is where you'll find the longest minigolf hole in the world. The 140-foot hole is part of the course designed by Jim Bryant, one of the world's foremost designers of miniature golf courses. These holes have more exotic themes than you find in your normal miniature golf course.

The course is open daily from Memorial Day to Labor Day and weekends during the spring and fall. The charge for the minigolf is $5.50 for adults (13–59) and $4.50 for children and seniors. All-day play is $8.50 per person.

The pool is open Memorial Day Weekend through Labor Day. The minigolf and batting cages are open March to November. The rest of the park is open year-round; 6060 Wilson Boulevard, Arlington; (703) 534–3437; www.nvrpa.org/minigolfupton.

To get away from museums and traffic, stop by Arlington's *Bon Air Park and Memorial Rose Garden,* with its selection of roses (more than 157 varieties, of which 32 have been awarded the American Rose Society's "E" award for Excellence), azaleas, ornamental tree garden, and wildflower area. The park isn't huge, but it's nice, and there are benches for sitting and enjoying the gardens. It is located at Wilson Boulevard and North Lexington Avenue, Arling-

Good Things Come in Small Packages

Arlington is the smallest county in the United States that is self-governing. New York County, New York (22 square miles) is smaller, but, as the borough of Manhattan, it is not a separate jurisdictional entity. Established March 13, 1847, as Alexandria County, the name was changed to Arlington on March 16, 1920. The county is named for the estate where George Washington Parke Custis lived before he built the house currently known as Arlington House in Arlington National Cemetery. The estate had been named to honor England's Earl of Arlington.

Precious Stones

The 15-foot pinkish granite archway monument at 540 South Washington Street in Falls Church honors two African Americans, Joseph Tinner and Edwin B. Henderson, who started the fight for civil rights in 1915. They founded what was the first rural NAACP branch. Tinner worked in a quarry, and the stone excavated there was used for the foundations of many Falls Church buildings. As they were demolished, local residents claimed the old stone and used it in their gardens. When the monument was approved, the residents gave up their stones to the tune of sixteen tons from twenty-six different sites. Future plans for honoring these leaders include constructing a replica of the house where Tinner lived, on the then-called Tinner Hill, to be used as a black history museum.

ton, and is open from sunrise to one half hour after sunset. For more information call (703) 228–6525 or visit www.arlingtonva.us/Departments/Parks Recreation/parksrecreationMain.aspx.

Clarendon—a small corner of north Arlington, which until 1846 was the rest of the diamond shape of the District of Columbia—was named in 1899 for the Earl of Clarendon (1609–1674). Catch the subway (orange line) to Clarendon Station under the intersection of Fairfax Drive, Washington Boulevard, and Wilson Boulevard. Wander out to see the American Legion War Memorial monument, or go to the Court House stop and enjoy the variety of restaurants, pubs, coffeehouses, Stein's Theatrical, and shops reflecting the multiethnic (Japanese, Chinese, Korean, Moroccan, Indian, Cuban, Greek, Peruvian, Persian, Mexican, Irish, Salvadoran) population of the area. Not far from the Virginia Square Station is the Arlington Arts Center, home of exhibits, classes, and live theater.

The **Ball-Sellers House,** a log house built around 1742, is Arlington's oldest residence and is believed to be typical of the way many early settlers lived in Colonial Virginia. John Ball built the one-room house on a 166-acre land grant, along Four Mile Run, from Lord Thomas Fairfax. It has a loft and an attached lean-to room at the rear that has its original logs, clapboard roof, and pegged floorboards. Ball, his wife, and

metrofacts

The Franconia-Springfield subway, the seventy-fifth station in the Metro system, opened on June 30, 1997, and cost $175 million to construct. With 5,069 parking spaces, it serves about 8,500 travellers a day. The station, on the Metro's blue line, was the last one to be completed in Virginia from the original plan, and it connects with a Virginia Railway Express station. www.wmata.com.

Daisy, Daisy

The **W & OD Trail** is 45 miles of rails-to-trails path from Arlington to Purcellville for bikers, hikers, and others. It's accessible in Falls Church, Vienna, Reston, Herndon, and Leesburg. You may walk, hike, jog, bike, or in-line skate along the trail. Or horseback riders may use a bridle path that parallels the trail for 32½ miles from Vienna to Purcellville. www.wodfriends.org. For more biking information about the Rock Creek Trail (in Washington), the Capital Crescent Trail (from Georgetown to Silver Spring, Maryland), and special events, call the Potomac Pedalers Touring Club (they organize about a thousand local and regional tours a year) at (202) 363–8687 (www.bikepptc.org), or the Washington Area Bicyclist Association, publishers of *Greater Washington Area Bicycle Atlas: 67 Scenic Tours in the Mid Atlantic Region* at (202) 628–2500 (www.waba.org).

their five daughters lived here, until Ball's death in 1766. It was donated to the Arlington Historical Society in 1975; it's open from 1:00 to 4:00 P.M. on Saturday from April through October and by appointment. There's no admission charge, but donations are appreciated; 5620 Third Street South, Arlington; (703) 379–2123; www.arlingtonhistoricalsociety.org/learn/sites_properties/ball-sellers/index.asp.

Alexandria

The **Ramsay House Visitor Center** (Alexandria Convention & Visitors Bureau) is the place to start your Alexandria touring. It's open daily 9:00 A.M. to 5:00 P.M. seven days a week except Thanksgiving, Christmas, and New Year's days. The visitor center is at 221 King Street, Alexandria 22314. For more information call (703) 838–4200 or (800) 388–9119; www.funside.com.

If you enjoy walking tours and ghost tales, call **Alexandria Colonial Tours** for their "Ghosts & Graveyards" tour, presented from the first weekend in April through November. During the tour you'll hear legends, folklore, and twisted tales, starting with George Washington's time, and you'll end up in a cemetery! Tours are presented by colonial-clad guides. A history tour of Alexandria also is available. Group reservations are required for the Ghosts and Graveyards and the history tour. Tours start by the garden of the visitor center, at the corner of King and Fairfax Streets. Call (703) 519–1749 for additional information; or write P.O. Box 20485, Alexandria 22320.

As you wander around the historic section of town, you'll notice cobblestone streets (the 100 block of Prince Street and the 600 block of Princess Street), brick sidewalks, and vintage streetlamps. You can see the narrowest houses in Alexandria in the 400 block of Prince Street and the 500 block of Queen Street. These were alley houses built between two other houses. Sometimes they were called "spite houses" or "mother-in-law houses."

Alexandria features an architectural style that may be unique, called a Flounder house. A typical house was cut in half the long way, was usually much taller and narrower than normal, and was probably built to satisfy a provision of the sale of the lots that the property would be improved within two years. People who envisioned building something grander started with the Flounder, which became a minor wing when the larger front part was constructed. The original section usually was built without windows because of taxes on glass. Besides the Flounder house, you can find examples of Georgian (starting about 1700 and ending around the time of the Revolutionary War), Federal (late eighteenth century), Greek Revival (late 1840s), Victorian (1860–1900), Gothic Revival, Italianate (1820–1885), Second Empire (1885–1900), Richardson Romanesque (1880–1900), and Queen Anne (1880–1910) architecture.

More than six million patents are kept on file in the U.S. Patent and Trademark Office in Crystal City. You can research an idea or the history of invention here, but you can also visit the *United States Patent and Trademark Museum,* in the atrium of the Madison Building, 600 Dulany Street, Alexandria, which was established in 1955. As secretary of state, Thomas Jefferson issued the first patent in 1790 to Samuel Hopkins, who invented a way to make potash, an ingredient of soap.

Four permanent exhibits present information on intellectual property and how it's protected; the history of the Patent Office and some patent models; Thomas Alva Edison, America's most prolific inventor (with 1,093 patents to his credit); and trademarks found on ancient and modern items. This probably is the most interesting exhibit, for it

hungry?

If you have to be near the Fairfax Courthouse, you may as well have a bite where it seems most of the courthouse regulars do, at the **Havabite Eatery,** 10416 Main Street, Fairfax; (703) 591–2244. No, you don't have to be in a suit to eat here; come in your jeans if you wish. The Eatery is praised for its steak-and-cheese sandwich (or cheesesteak, depending on your place of origin) as well as its spanakopita and moussaka.

areacodes

All telephone calls from northern Virginia must include the area code (but not a "1"), even if you're calling across the street or next door. Area code 571 was overlaid on the original 703 area code. In other words, both area codes will coexist within the same geographic region.

ready,action,shoot

Motion pictures set and filmed in and around Arlington include *Deep Impact* with Téa Leoni and Robert Duvall, *No Way Out* with Kevin Costner, and Francis Ford Coppola's *Gardens of Stone*. The television show *Scarecrow and Mrs. King* was set largely in Arlington, and the area has been the site of many inexplicable occurrences on *The X-Files*.

shows more relevance to our daily lives (and shopping) than the inventions do.

Other rotating exhibits might focus on types of patent art and technologies and inventions by African Americans or women. A gift shop is open Monday through Friday from 9:00 A.M. to 5:00 P.M. and Saturday from noon to 5:00 P.M.; (703) 306–0455; www.invent.org.

One of the most widely imitated art forms is the transformation of an old factory into an arts center. One of the first was the ***Torpedo Factory Arts Center*** (a 1918 factory where torpedo shell cases were manufactured), housing more than 160 artists in three floors of studio space. You can buy original artwork (weavings, paintings, musical instruments, pots, prints, sculptures, jewelry, glassworks, and photographs), talk with the artists, attend lectures, take art classes, and take part in a variety of other activities. You can also see an MK-14 torpedo on display on the first floor. An annual jury for studio space is held each March. All artists working in fine arts and fine crafts are eligible. The Torpedo Factory Arts Center, 105 North Union Street, Alexandria, is open 10:00 A.M. to 5:00 P.M. daily except major holidays; (703) 838–4565; www.torpedofactory.org.

The ***Alexandria Archaeology Museum*** and research lab (105 North Union Street #327, Alexandria) are located on the third floor of the Torpedo Factory Arts Center. In addition to the rotating exhibits on the archaeological history of the area, they might have a Family Dig Day where children, their families, and friends enjoy hands-on experience with the past while screening for artifacts on an excavation site. Two weeklong day camps are held in the summer for twelve- to fifteen-year-olds. The museum is open Tuesday through Friday 10:00 A.M. to 3:00 P.M., Saturday 10:00 A.M. to 5:00 P.M., and Sunday 1:00

Public Art

Two Metro stations in Northern Virginia feature public arts projects. At the Huntington Station (yellow line), you'll see "Metropolitan Scene," a painted mural about urban congestion and mass transit efficiency, by David Chung, installed in 1990. The Rosslyn station (orange and blue lines) has another David Chung–painted mural that's 88 feet by 4 feet portraying stylized images of local architecture, installed in 2000.

Shirley You Jest . . .

Shirley Memorial Highway (Interstate 95 and 395) runs from U.S. 1 (at the southern end), north of the Occoquan River to US 1 (at the northern end) near the Pentagon in Arlington. It was named for Henry G. Shirley, the head of the Virginia Department of Highways (now Virginia Department of Transportation) from 1922 to 1941. Shirley was a leader in national highway policy and oversaw the creation of the state's extensive highway system. The first section opened in October 1943 and the highway was completed in 1952.

to 5:00 P.M. There is no admission fee. Call (703) 838–4399 for more information; or visit www.alexandriaarchaeology.org.

The *Alexandria Farmers' Market,* on the south plaza of City Hall at 301 King Street, was established in the original lot sale of July 1749, when two lots were designated for the purpose. The farmers' market started in 1753 and is said to be the nation's oldest continually operating market. George Washington, born near Fredericksburg, spent his young adult life in this area and is said to have sent produce here to be sold. The market moves indoors during winter to the lobby of City Hall. Farmers come early, about 5:30 A.M., as do wise shoppers. You might see notices that it's open until 10:30 A.M., but by that time your selections will be slim, if any. For more information call (703) 838–5006; www.alexandriava.gov/market.farmersmarket.

John Gadsby was an Englishman who operated a tavern and an inn in the late eighteenth century. What is now *Gadsby's Tavern* was the center of all that was political, social, and commercial. Meetings, dances, and theatrical and musical presentations all found a home here. Dentists treated their patients here, and merchants sold their wares. It's said that even George Washington recommended it.

The buildings were used as a tavern and hotel until the late nineteenth century and then housed a variety of businesses, eventually falling into disrepair and near-demolition. Fortunately the American Legion Post 24 bought and saved the buildings in 1929, but it wasn't until 1972 that they were given to the city of Alexandria.

Both structures, restored to their late-eighteenth-century manner, are open for inspection, and an Early American–style restaurant serves visitors in three of the tavern rooms.

The *Gadsby's Tavern Museum* is open 10:00 A.M. to 5:00 P.M. Tuesday through Saturday and 1:00 to 5:00 P.M. on Sunday, April 1 through September 30. Guided tours are given at quarter past and quarter of the hour, with the last

funfacts

Gadsby's Tavern Museum was the site of George Washington's last two birthday celebrations.

tour starting at 4:15 P.M. From October 1 through March 31, the museum is open from 11:00 A.M. to 4:00 P.M. Tuesday through Saturday and 1:00 to 4:00 P.M. on Sunday, with tours at quarter past and quarter of the hour. The last tour starts at 3:15 P.M. Admission is $4.00 for adults, $2.00 for students ages eleven through seventeen, and free for children ten and younger with a paying adult. The museum is located at 134 North Royal Street, Alexandria; (703) 838–4242; http://oha.ci.alexandria.va.us/gadsby.

Locals and foreigners alike will talk about the jelly cake from **Shuman's Bakery** as though it rates five stars in anyone's restaurant guidebook. It may not actually compare to a fine repast, but you might want to make the taste test yourself. The buttery pound cake is split and filled with red currant jelly, cut into diamond shapes, and dusted with powdered sugar. The bakers at Shuman's have been doing this for more than a hundred years, and as many as 4,000 will be sold during the holiday season, so you know they're doing something right. Shuman's Bakery is open from 7:00 A.M. to 6:00 P.M. Monday through Saturday, 430 South Washington Street, Alexandria; (703) 549–0128.

History buffs will delight in visiting **Fort Ward Museum and Historic Site.** Because Virginia was definitely a Southern state, Union troops occupied Alexandria and Arlington Heights at the beginning of the Civil War. They began construction of 162 earthen forts around Washington, with Fort Ward the fifth largest of the fortifications and supply bases. Named for Commander James Harmon Ward, the first Union naval officer to be killed in the war, the fort had thirty-six guns mounted in five bastions.

Major preservation work started on the fort in 1961 as part of a Civil War Centennial project. The Northwest Bastion was restored, with a reconstructed ceremonial gate marking the entrance to the fort. Young soldiers can let their imaginations go wild with the defenses displayed here. A reconstructed Offi-

Let It Snow

Although the D.C. area, including northern Virginia, normally receives 16 to 18 inches of snow during a winter, there are times when all of it comes in one day. That's the time to take your sled to the grounds of the Masonic Temple and have a ball. One side of the lawn is for beginners and wannabes; the other is for more advanced sledders. This is not necessarily an authorized Masonic Temple activity, but it's a great place for snow fun.

cers' Hut represents a typical fort dwelling of that time.

Exhibits on a number of Civil War subjects are in the museum, which was opened in 1964. Interpretive programs, tours, and lectures are offered throughout the year.

The museum is open Tuesday through Saturday 9:00 A.M. to 5:00 P.M. and Sunday noon to 5:00 P.M. It is closed on Monday, Thanksgiving, Christmas, and New Year's Days. The historic site is open daily 9:00 A.M. to sunset. There is no admission charge, but donations are accepted.

Fort Ward is located at 4301 West Braddock Road, between King Street (State Route 7) and Seminary Road, east of I–395, Alexandria; (703) 838–4848; http://oha.ci.alexandria.va.us/fortward.

The Americana in the ***Collingwood Library of and Museum on Americanism*** deals with patriotism, and the collection includes copies of the U.S. Constitution, a Sioux chief's headdress, presidential china, and a library of about 7,000 books on military history. The books are available for research.

Originally part of George Washington's farm, the estate eventually was divided for a streetcar line and then Mount Vernon Parkway, built in 1932. It was converted into this library and opened in 1977. It is named for British Admiral, Lord Cuthbert Collingwood, the hero of the Battle of Trafalgar.

The museum is located at Collingwood on the Potomac, 8301 East Boulevard Drive, Alexandria. It is open 10:00 A.M. to 4:00 P.M. on Monday and Wednesday through Saturday, and 1:00 to 4:00 P.M. on Sunday. There is no admission charge. Guided tours are available and last as long as you're interested. The museum is accessible to people in wheelchairs. Call (703) 765–1652 or visit www.collingwoodlibrary.com for additional information.

The George Washington Masonic National Memorial houses a collection about Washington's life from his days as a surveyor to his first inauguration. Over the front doors is a frieze of Washington in profile. The main lobby features two 46-by-18-foot murals by Allyn Cox, one depicting the laying of the cornerstone of the United States Capitol in September 1793 and one of General Washington at a religious service on St. John's Day 1778 in Christ Church, Philadelphia. There's a 17-foot-3-inch bronze statue of George Washington in the Memorial Hall and a collection of Washington memorabilia, including the clock that stopped by itself when he died, the family Bible, and sabers used at his funeral. The auditorium is surrounded by granite columns and bronze medallions of the U.S. presidents who have been Freemasons. The Parade Room contains an elaborate display of a mechanical parade of miniature uniformed Shrine Units.

The memorial is open 9:00 A.M. to 5:00 P.M., with free thirty-minute tours (donations accepted) offered daily (except Thanksgiving, Christmas, and New Year's Days) at 9:30, 10:30, and 11:30 A.M. and 1:00, 2:00, 3:00, and 4:00 P.M.

There's plenty of free parking, and it's also within walking distance (uphill) of the King Street Metro station. Although it is not accessible to the disabled, Masons visiting the shrine will be helped by the brothers. The memorial is at 101 Callahan Drive, atop Shooters Hill at the west end of King Street, Alexandria; (703) 683–2007; www.gwmemorial.org.

funfacts

Those who enjoy such games as Rush Hour, Smart Mouth, Word Sense, and Pet Hunt (and with millions of these games in American households, there are a lot of you) should know they're produced by an Alexandria company, *Think Fun* (formerly Binary Arts). 1321 Cameron Street, Alexandria; (703) 549–4999; www.thinkfun.com.

Still another viewpoint of the area can be found along the *Mount Vernon Trail,* which parallels the George Washington Memorial Parkway from Mount Vernon to Theodore Roosevelt Island in the Potomac River. Starting south at the Arlington Memorial Bridge (dedicated in 1932 to symbolize the union of the North and South following the Civil War and connecting the Lincoln Memorial to the Lee home), you'll go past the Lyndon Baines Johnson Memorial Grove in Lady Bird Johnson Park; the *Navy-Marine Memorial* (the Ernesto Begni del Platta statue honoring Americans who served at sea, dedicated in 1934); Gravelly Point, which is a terrific place to view the takeoffs and landings at Reagan National Airport; Old Town Alexandria; Jones Point Lighthouse (in service from 1836 to 1925); and Dyke Marsh (a 240-acre wetland where more than 250 species of birds have been sighted). You can catch a look at Fort Washington (on the Maryland side) and end at Mount Vernon.

You can walk, jog, or bike the length of this 18½-mile trail or just parts of it. There are at least two or three places in Alexandria where you can rent a bike for an hour or a day. Check with the visitor center for more information. (Three areas are quite steep and might be a little strenuous for new bikers.) There are plenty of places to picnic and to enjoy nature and history, and a physical fitness course helps you vary the type of exercise you're doing. Call (703) 289–2500 or visit www.nps.gov/gwmp/mvt.

Among the numerous Alexandria cemeteries is the *African-American Heritage Park.* There are six identified headstones of about twenty-one burials that took place here. The wetlands part of the cemetery is a home for mallards, painted turtles, beavers, and crayfish. *Truths that Rise from the Roots Remembered,* a bronze sculpture of trees by Jerome Meadows, is a tribute to the contribution of African-Americans to Alexandria. A number of other statues are placed throughout the cemetery.

The park is located at 902 Wythe Street and is open during daylight hours. The museum is open from 10:00 A.M. to 4:00 P.M. Tuesday through Saturday. For more information about this park and the African-American contributions to Alexandria and the area, contact the Alexandria Black History Resource Center, 638 North Alfred Street, Alexandria; (703) 838–4356; http://oha.alexandriava.gov/bhrc/.

It isn't often that you can see what a Quaker pharmacy of 200 years ago looked like, but at the **Stabler-Leadbeater Apothecary Shop** you can. Edward Stabler opened his shop in 1792, when Alexandria was a bustling port city with about 300 homes. The family operated the business through the War of 1812, an 1821 yellow fever epidemic, the Civil War, the Spanish-American War, and World War I, before succumbing to the Great Depression and closing the store in 1933.

---

blastfromthepast

Nostalgia buffs might want to visit the *Tastee 29* diner in Fairfax, built in 1947 and listed on the National Register of Historic Places. Clad in blue and silver porcelain enamel and stainless steel, the interior is complete with a marble counter and terrazzo floor. Blue Naugahyde seats, tile, and Formica highlight the decor. The diner is open twenty-four hours a day, seven days a week, and is located at 10536 Lee Highway, Fairfax; (703) 591–6720; www.29diner.com.

Designer Library

Virginia has a Michael Graves–designed library—quite a difference from the structured architecture of Old Town Alexandria, and one you're sure to remember. The **Charles E. Beatley Jr. Central Library** (named after the city's longest-serving mayor, who died in December 2003) is located at the intersection of Duke and Pickett Streets, south of the Old Holmes Run Channel. At 60,200 square feet, it's more than twice as large as the Barrett Branch, which had been the central library. Special features include a full-service library for the blind, speaking computer terminals with OptiVoice artificial speech and enlarged type capabilities, and dataports at carrels for personal laptops. The precast stone clock on the south side, the Duke Street facade, weighs five tons. The library is at 5005 Duke Street, Alexandria; (703) 519–5900; www.alexandria.library.va.us/branches/beatley.

Fortunately, Stabler was a master pack rat; miraculously, more than 8,000 herbs, potions, pill rollers, mortars and pestles, drug mills, medical glassware, documents, journals, letters, and paper labels are still around. Volunteers have gone through the boxes of deteriorating books and letters, finding a note from Martha Washington, a letter to Robert E. Lee, prescriptions for curing everything from gout to hams, and much more. Among the changes that took place over the lifetime of the apothecary are the introduction of prescription forms, the hypodermic needle, pills, and controlled-substance regulations. This is the only old apothecary museum in the country where the shop sold retail, wholesale, and manufactured products.

The apothecary is at 105–107 South Fairfax Street, Alexandria (703–836–3713; www.apothecarymuseum.org) and is open Monday through Saturday 10:00 A.M. to 4:00 P.M. and Sunday 1:00 to 5:00 P.M. There is a small admission fee of $2.50 for adults and $2.00 for students; children ten and under free.

George Washington's Mount Vernon Estate and Gardens is one of the more popular "off the beaten path" sites in Northern Virginia.

Frequent special events make a visit even more interesting and delightful. Here are just a few:

In February you can have "breakfast with George" on the weekend around his birthday. His favorite breakfast is said to have been "hoecakes swimming in butter and honey," and you can sample this delicacy (while supplies last) and then participate in "America's Smallest Hometown Parade" in the afternoon. Enjoy a fife and drum corps, eighteenth-century music, and wish the "General" a happy birthday. Admission is free if you're named George or if your birthday is February 22. Yes, if your name is Martha or you were born on June 2, you also receive free admission on that day.

Sealed with a Kiss

If you collect postage stamps or like some of the unusual designs, chances are you're familiar with the work of Howard Paine of Delaplane. Paine was involved in the design or as art director for such stamps as the one dedicated to Raoul Wallenberg, the flowering trees, songwriters, big bands, peaches and pears, American Holly, United Nations, Milton S. Hershey in the Great Americans stamp series, and the winter scene postal card. Paine designed, among others, the Leonard Bernstein commemorative stamp issued on July 10, 2001. The first U.S. postage stamp to honor the favorite pastime of cruciverbalists was issued in February 1998 as part of the Celebrate the Century series. The stamp was issued to commemorate the publication of the first crossword puzzle and is in the sheet for the decade of 1910 to 1919. Paine designed this stamp also.

Mrs. Washington is available for photographs on Mother's Day in May and shares her thoughts on motherhood in the late eighteenth century.

As noted elsewhere, there are almost one hundred wineries throughout Virginia, and more than a dozen of them are featured at the Spring Wine Festival and Sunset Tour in mid-May. Samples are offered, accompanied by live jazz music, and the rarely opened wine cellar can be toured. Another wine festival is held in the fall.

Another annual May event is a naturalization ceremony where one hundred people receive their American citizenship. Dignitaries abound, and the Marine Band and the National Men's Choir perform music.

adayinthelife

The *Claude Moore Colonial Farm* at Turkey Run, a small tenant farm from Colonial times, is the only privately operated park in the National Park System. If you and your family want to know what life was like in those days, you may participate in chores alongside the eighteenth-century "farm family," portrayed by staff and volunteers. It's $3.00 for adults and $2.00 for senior citizens and children (3–12). Open Wednesday through Sunday, April through October, 10:00 A.M. to 4:30 P.M., 6310 Georgetown Pike, McLean; (703) 442–7557 or (703) 847–0710; www.1771.org.

July Fourth, as can be imagined, is a daylong celebration with patriotic music, a reading of the Declaration of Independence (by "George" himself), a band concert, and birthday cake (while supplies last).

By far, the annual eighteenth-century Craft Fair, held in mid-September, is one of the highlights of the year. Not only can you watch Colonial-attired crafters create baskets, leather goods, woodcarvings, paper cuttings, and other items from the period, but you can buy them for a most unusual souvenir.

Mount Vernon is a constantly changing destination, so if you saw it ten or twenty years ago, it's different now. The latest project started in September of 2005 with the laying of the cornerstone for the restoration of Washington's distillery, adjacent to the Gristmill (see below) and a national distillery museum scheduled to open in fall 2006.

Mount Vernon is open daily from 8:00 A.M. to 5:00 P.M. April through August; 9:00 A.M. to 5:00 P.M. March, September, and October; and 9:00 A.M. to 4:00 P.M. November through February. Adult admission is $13.00, senior tickets are $12.00, and children six through eleven (with an adult) are $6.00; (703) 780–2000 or (703) 799–8121 (TDD); www.mountvernon.org.

Washington's Gristmill is a reconstruction of George Washington's 1772 stone mill on Dogue Creek, built when the creek was still navigable. Located in the George Washington's Gristmill Historic State Park, it's in a beautiful scenic setting, just 3 miles from Mount Vernon. The mill has a 16-foot waterwheel and millstones that weigh a thousand pounds each. The foundation cornerstone of Washington's mill is shown at the beginning of the tour. During the careful excavation, part of the wheel, bearings for the wheel, part of the trundlehead, complete wheel buckets, and other items were found. Open daily 8:00 A.M. to dusk Memorial Day through Labor Day, the mill is at 5514 Mount Vernon Memorial Highway, Mount Vernon. Call (703) 780–3383 for more information in the summer, (703) 550–0960 the rest of the year. You can buy a joint Mount Vernon and gristmill ticket for $2.00 more for adults and $.50 for children.

As you head west toward Dulles International Airport, you travel past a lot of shopping centers (areas that were corner grocery stands just a few years ago) and thinktanks. But you can spend a day at **Colvin Run Mill Park** and not begin to realize you're only moments away from the hustle and bustle of the commercial Tysons Corner area. This is a particularly good place to bring pre-schoolers on puppet show day, where the docent will speak of the Little Red Hen who took her grain to the miller; you'll meet Marvin the Miller, Fred the Farmer, Matilda the farmer's wife, and Alvin the Apprentice and discuss where grain comes from and how it's ground into flour.

The restored early-nineteenth-century mill usually is in operation (call to make sure, if that's the primary reason for your visit), and you can tour a miller's house (built by Philip Carper), walk through a dairy barn, and stop to buy a few things from the general store.

Programs include grain grinding on the first and third Sundays of October and November noon to 2:00 P.M., blacksmithing demonstrations on Saturday

Drink, drink . . .

On September 28, 2005, the cornerstone was laid to authentically restore George Washington's distillery. The cornerstone comes from a sandstone block used in the original 1793 U.S. Capitol, and is from the same vein of sandstone Washington used to build his distillery in 1797. Archaeologists have determined, after six years of digging, that our Founding Father was also the most successful distiller of his time. As part of the ceremonies, master distillers from some of the world's best-known liquor brands handcrafted a limited edition George Washington's Distillery Vatted American Whiskey on an eighteenth-century pot still over an open fire under a special license from the U.S. Government and the Commonwealth of Virginia. The distillery is adjacent to the gristmill just down the road from the Mount Vernon mansion. The "brew" was made from barrels of Jack Daniels, Jim Beam, Makers Mark, Wild Turkey, George Dickel, Virginia Gentleman, and others that had been aging at an "undisclosed location" on the mansion grounds. Guests were allowed to sample the spirits, and the remains were auctioned to benefit the Mount Vernon educational mission.

Colvin Run Mill Park

11:00 A.M. to 2:00 P.M., ghost tales around Halloween time, spring and fall dulcimer concerts, and fall scarecrow making.

There are also beautiful picnic grounds and ducks to feed.

Colvin Run Mill Park is located off Leesburg Pike (Route 7) at 10017 Colvin Run Road, Great Falls 22066, 5 miles west of Tysons Corner. It's open daily except Tuesday, 11:00 A.M. to 5:00 P.M.; closing at 4:00 P.M. in January and February. The tours cost $5.00 for adults, $4.00 for students sixteen years and up with ID, $3.00 for seniors and children younger than sixteen. For more information call (703) 759–2771, or visit www.co.fairfax.va.us/parks/crm.

Okay, **Dulles International Airport** isn't exactly off the beaten path, unless you're coming from the Maryland side of the Potomac. Millions of people use this airport every year. The Eero Saarinen–designed terminal was doubled in size just a few years ago, and you can see the airport in lots of movies (it even doubled as Kennedy International in *Forces of Nature*).

However, thousands more are now flocking to the Chantilly site to see the Smithsonian Institution's National Air and Space Museum's new museum for the display and preservation of its collection of historic aviation and space artifacts. Named the **Steven F. Udvar–Hazy Center** (in honor of its major donor), this new space provides display room for a lot of things that couldn't be included in the Smithsonian's National Air and Space Museum on the Mall in Washington, D.C. It opened in December 2003 in honor of the one-hundredth anniversary of the Wright brothers' first powered flight.

There are more than eighty aircraft and dozens of space artifacts here, including the Space Shuttle *Enterprise*, an SR-71 Blackbird reconnaissance aircraft, the Dash 80 prototype of the Boeing 707, the Superfortress *Enola Gay,* and a DeHavilland Chipmunk, which is an aerobatic plane.

You can walk among the artifacts on the floor and look into space or stroll along skyways to see the hanging displays. Some of the airliners, engines, helicopters, rockets, satellites, ultralights, and experimental flying machines are on display for the first time in a museum setting. There's also the Donald D. Engen Observation Tower (164 feet high) and an IMAX theater.

Eventually, there will be more than 200 aircraft and 135 spacecraft on display. In the meantime, in the not-too-distant future, you'll be able to watch restoration specialists work on air and space objects.

If you've contributed to this museum, you should be able to find your name on a permanent memorial at the entrance.

There is no admission fee to the museum, which is open daily from 10:00 A.M. to 5:30 P.M. except December 25. There is a fee for the IMAX films; tickets can be purchased online. Parking is available for $12 a car. (202) 633–1000; www.nasm.si.edu.

If you'd like a really nice meal but don't want to go into downtown Washington, then head toward Tysons Corner and Bob Kinkead's **Colvin Run Tavern.** Kinkead's downtown eatery is one of the best, if not the best, in Washington, so you know you're in for a treat in this suburban location with chef de cuisine Jeff Gaetien (formerly sous chef at Kinkead's). Start a wintery day by warming yourself in front of a nice fire in the foyer, and set your sights on some tasty roast beef, served from a silvery cart. There are plenty of seafood, shellfish, and poultry options for those who don't care for red meat. Squid and crab Napoleon are definitely among the signature dishes. To stay in your Virginia state of mind, eat in the Shenandoah room or aim for one of the other areas, including the Charleston and the Nantucket.

A Town of Firsts

Clifton, a town of about 200 people (although other residential areas nearby have glommed onto the Clifton zip code for its cachet) located at the junction of the railroad tracks and Route 645, southwest of Fairfax, was the first community in the area to have electricity—from the Bull Run Power Company—in 1925. It also had the first high school whose students commuted by train from other parts of Fairfax County.

The Susan Riviere *Hetzel House,* one of thirty-three stops along a walking tour of historical buildings, is named for Susan Riviere Hetzel (1846–1908), who organized the National Society of the Daughters of the American Revolution. The Hetzel House is located at 7151 Pendleton Avenue at Chapel Road, 1 block east of Main Street; (703) 830–2844.

Who Woulda Thought?

Virginia's minerals and indigenous botanicals inspired the products used in treatments at Spa Min-Rale (min-er-al) at the Lansdowne Resort, Lansdowne (not too far from Dulles International Airport). The nearby Goose Creek Rock Quarry has produced many of the salts, scrubs, and muds, and the state's dogwood tree and flower is used in the astringent for facial and body treatments. The 12,000-square-foot Spa Min-Rale opened in February 2006 as part of the resort's $55 million-dollar expansion, and Judy Stell (formerly with Ballantyne Resort & Spa in Charlotte and the Greenbrier in White Sulphur Springs) is the spa director. (877) 509–8400 or (703) 729–8400; www.lansdowneresort.com

Colvin Run Tavern is open for lunch Monday through Friday from 11:30 A.M. to 2:30 P.M., dinner Monday through Thursday from 5:30 to 9:30 P.M., Friday and Saturday from 5:30 to 10:00 P.M.; and Sunday from 5:00 to 8:30 P.M.; 8045 Leesburg Pike (near International Drive), Tysons Corner; (703) 356–9500; www.kinkead.com/colvin.

Outside Washington

It may not look pretty, but **Fran's Place** is the kind of diner you want to stop by, particularly if you've been out hiking or biking on the nearby W&OD trail, touring through horse country, working in the field, or you are just in need of some "comfortable" food. The "Fran" of Fran's Place is no longer with us, but her picture hangs over the big front table where the regulars sit. No, you shouldn't sit there, particularly during lunch. The furnishings may look a little tacky or in need of repair, but the kitchen certainly produces appetite-satisfying food.

Fran's Place is on 110 West Main Street, Purcellville; (540) 338–3200.

For breakfast or lunch only, try the **Round Hill Diner** in—you guessed it —Round Hill. This former resort for Washingtonians fleeing the summer heat has had its lifestyle heated up in the past years as the suburban sprawl—in the form of thousands of new homes— encroaches. In existence for more than three decades, this is a country kind of place where the rectangular table with the cloth is considered the "round" table and for the longtime locals only. Joan Farris's place is where you come to hear the town gossip and get great greasy

funfacts

The two-lane **Aldie Stone Bridge,** crossing Little River on Route 50, was constructed in 1824 and is one of two stone bridges still in use in Loudoun County.

trivia

On October 21, 1861, troops from the North and the South met at *Ball's Bluff,* outside of Leesburg, for one of the first Union battle disasters of the war. There are twenty-five graves holding the remains of fifty-three unknowns and one known (grave 13) soldier. Ball's Bluff Road, Leesburg; (703) 779–9372; www.nvrpa.org/balls bluff.html. The Ball's Bluff National Cemetery is the smallest national cemetery in the nation and is open from dawn to dusk. Guided tours are offered on weekends from early May through October.

food, bacon, eggs, sausages, pancakes, and biscuits.

The Round Hill Diner is at Routes 7 and 179, 2 East Loudoun Street, Round Hill; (540) 338–3663.

In May 1997 the renovated three-story brick *Aldie Mill* was opened to the public on a regular basis for the first time since 1981. Now, every Saturday from noon to 5:00 P.M. and Sunday from 1:00 to 5:00 P.M. spring through October, tours are given through the 1807 mill, showing the early machinery used to grind wheat and corn. Further work has been and continues to be done, including clearing of the head and tail races, stabilizing the archaeological sites, and creating pedestrian trails and interpretive signs. The Aldie Mill is Virginia's only known gristmill powered by twin overshot wheels (the water pours over the wheel, making the wheel turn forward, instead of "down" the wheel, which would make it turn backward). Admission is $4.00 for adults and $2.00 for seniors and children.

The Aldie Mill is located west of Aldie on Route 50; 39401 John Mosby Highway, Aldie; (703) 327–9777; www.virginiaoutdoorsfoundation.org/AldieMill /Amhistory.htm.

Within the historic district known as Leesburg is the historic *Norris House Inn,* built in 1760. Carol and Roger Healey now offer bed-and-breakfast

A Rustic Retreat

Despite the miniskyscraper and multimall population of Tysons Corner, you have only to go to Loudoun County for a taste of the rustic and a wooded view of the Potomac River. In *Algonkian Park,* just 15 miles west of Tysons Corner, are a dozen furnished, air-conditioned cabins accommodating four to ten people. There are decks for watching the scenery and fully equipped kitchens. Relax in a unit with a fireplace or one of the more elegant models, complete with hot tub. Can't unwind quite that much? There's an eighteen-hole golf course, boat landing, large swimming pool, and miniature golf within walking distance. Rentals start at $135, Monday through Thursday, and from $140 on weekends; 47001 Fairway Drive, Sterling; (703) 450–4655; www.nvrpa.org/algonkian.

Mark This Land

The village of **Waterford** was designated a National Historic Landmark in 1970, one of only three such landmarks in the United States. Waterford Foundation, P.O. Box 142, Waterford 20197; (540) 882–3018; www.waterfordva.org.

accommodations, with full use of the dining room, parlor, library, sunroom, and a rambling veranda overlooking the gardens. The bedrooms are appointed with antiques and brass and feather four-poster beds, and three guest rooms have working fireplaces. Tea service is available on weekend afternoons in the inn's compound in the Old Stone House Tea Room. Guests may use the fitness facilities (indoor pool, fitness room, gym, etc.) at the nearby Ida Lee Park Recreation Center for free. Room rates run from $115 to $150 a night on weekends, including a full country breakfast. Special weekday and weekly rates are available. The inn is located at 108 Loudoun Street SW, Leesburg; (703) 777–1806 or (800) 644–1806; www.norrishouse.com.

Since 1833, ferryboats have been moving travelers across the Potomac River between **White's Ferry** (on the Maryland side) and the Leesburg, Virginia, area. There used to be one hundred ferries crossing the Potomac; this is the only one left. It used to be known as Conrad's ferry, but after the Civil War a Confederate officer, Colonel Elija V. White, bought and renamed it. It's the only car ferry across the Potomac. For three decades the *Jubal Early* (named for a Confederate general) carried about six cars a trip, but the demand became so heavy that owner Malcolm Brown installed a new thirty-ton vessel in mid-1988 that can carry as many as twenty-four cars.

The ferry is propelled by a small diesel boat on the upriver side. When the ferry reaches the far side, the ferry pilot casts off a line, and the current carries the small boat around to point it in the right direction for the return trip. There is a general store on the Maryland side, open only in summer.

The ferry charge is $3.00 for cars one-way or $5.00 round-trip (50 cents for pedestrians and bicyclists), and the ferry operates on call from 5:00 A.M. to 11:00 P.M. daily as water levels permit. Call (301) 349–5200 to be sure the ferry is in service, unless you're planning just to take a pretty ride and you're not dependent upon the ferry taking you across the river. Take Route 15 north out of Leesburg to the signs; 24801 White's Ferry Road, Dickerson, Maryland; www.mcmullans.org/canal/whites_ferry.

Woodbridge

Now head south on Interstate 95, where in addition to **Potomac Mills,** an out-let and off-price shopping mall with more than 200 stores and more visitors than any other place in all of Virginia, you can stop by the **Veterans Memorial Park.** It has a picnic area, lighted tennis and volleyball courts, ball fields, soccer fields, horseshoe pits, a playground area, a 50-meter outdoor pool and a water slide, hiking, and a community center where classes are offered. A roller hockey league is scheduled for practice and competition. And it's accessible to people in wheelchairs. You'll see lots of four-wheeling here, but it's of the skateboard variety. At the Scott D. Eagles skateboard facility, dedicated to a man who died young but immensely enjoyed his skateboarding while he was here (no, he didn't die of a skateboard accident), there are 7,200 square feet of bowls, bumps, moguls, a half-pipe, and smooth surfaces with sidewalk and street features for urban skaters. For those who've always wanted to try skateboarding but were reluctant to invest, skateboards can be rented at the park.

Located at 14300 Featherstone Road, Woodbridge, the park is open daily year-round during daylight hours, except in bad weather. The ranger office is closed on federal holidays; (703) 491–2183; www.pwcparks.org/vetspark.

For a very long time, the Washington area was known as the dinner theater capital of the world, well, maybe the country. The area had more dinner theaters per capita than any other region. Most of them have gone now, but luckily the **Lazy Susan Dinner Theater** (10712 Richmond Highway, Wood-bridge) remains. It offers pleasant family entertainment—mostly musicals—and a real lazy Susan stage section that allows frequent scene changes. This has been a restaurant since the mid-1950s, when each table had a lazy Susan with homemade bread and other goodies. When Harold Gates and his son Glenn decided to go into the dinner theater business, they kept the name.

The menu includes some Pennsylvania Dutch selections from the buffet table, and the decor is in wood paneling and Tiffany-style hanging lamps.

The Lazy Susan is just off I–95 at the Woodbridge exit; call (703) 550–7384; www.lazysusan.com.

Fairfax County

The **Fairfax Station Railroad Museum** includes, naturally enough, a museum of railroad memorabilia, complete with a Norfolk & Western railroad line caboose. Clara Barton, founder of the Red Cross, nursed many Civil War wounded on a neighboring hill, and there's an exhibit area dedicated to her pioneering work. One of the most enjoyable parts of the museum is when a group of "N" gauge railroaders from the Northern Virginia NTRAK club come in every Sunday to display their trains from 1:00 to 4:00 P.M.

Constructed in the 1850s, the museum opened in 1989 and is open regularly on the third Sunday of the month from 1:00 to 4:00 P.M.

Admission is $2.00 for adults and $1.00 for children (four to ten). The museum, which is accessible to people in wheelchairs, is located at 11200 Fairfax Station Road, Fairfax Station (look for the caboose in the front yard); (703) 425–9225; www.fairfax-station.org.

The *Fairfax Museum and Visitor Center* is housed in the former Fairfax Elementary School, built in 1873. It was the first two-story school in Fairfax County and is listed on the National Register of Historic Places. This is where you can see fascinating exhibits on the area's history, sign up for walking tours of the historic district (spring and fall), and obtain information about places to visit and shop and where to eat and stay. The center is at 10209 Main Street, Fairfax, and is open daily from 9:00 A.M. to 5:00 P.M.; (703) 385–8414; www.fairfaxva.gov/museumvc/mvc.asp.

Prince William County

From Occoquan on the east to Manassas on the west, from the storyteller of George Washington's life to the largest tourist attraction in the state (yes, Potomac Mills Outlet Mall attracts as many as a quarter of a million shoppers in a weekend) to Civil War battlefields, Prince William County has just about everything a traveler could want. Call Historic Manassas Visitor Center, Manassas (703–361–6599), or Prince William County/Manassas Convention and Visitors Bureau, Manassas (703–396–7130 or 800–432–1792); www.visitpwc.com.

Order in the Court

The old **Prince William County Courthouse** in Brentsville started service in 1822 when there were nineteen homes, three stores, two taverns, one house of entertainment, a church, and the clerk's office and jail located in this town, the geographic center of the county. At the time there were 130 people, including three attorneys and three physicians, residing in the area. The town served as the county seat from 1820 to 1894. During the Civil War the courthouse roof was destroyed and court records were burned for fuel. By 1894 the county seat had been moved to Manassas. Restoration of the courthouse has been under way for a few years, and the restored cupola was placed on top on December 17, 2001. The Brentsville Historic Trust estimated the exterior repairs will run about $1 million; 12239 Bristow Road, P.O. Box 732, Bristow 20136; (703) 792–6600; www.brentsville.org.

Getting Stoned

The trim on the **Aquia Episcopal Church,** which celebrated its semiquincentennial anniversary in 2001, is made of Aquia sandstone, or Aquia stone, also called free-stone because it could be freely carved in any direction. Aquia sandstone was also used for the original U.S. Capitol—the center section with the dome—Mount Vernon, Gunston Hall, and some Philadelphia bridges. The church is on the National Historic Landmark register. 2938 Jefferson Davis Highway; Route 1, Stafford; (540) 659–4007; www.aquiachurch.com.

Occoquan is an Indian word meaning "at the end of the water," which is obvious once you visit the town. There are oodles of antiques and specialty stores, craft shops, and restaurants in the historic 4 blocks of town.

Start your visit at the Prince William County Visitor Center, 200 Mill Street (703–491–4045), to pick up some information about Occoquan and Prince William County. It's open daily from 9:00 A.M. to 5:00 P.M.; www.occoquan.org.

Craft lovers should be sure to visit during the spring craft show, usually the first weekend of June, and the fall show, usually the last weekend of September.

During your explorations, you'll pass the *Town Hall,* 314 Mill Street, Occoquan; (703) 491–1918. At the end of Mill Street, the main drag of Occoquan, is the *Merchants Mill Museum.* This was the site of the first automated gristmill in the nation. Ships and barges came to this mill along the Occoquan River with holds filled with grain, which was processed and then returned to the boats to be taken to Alexandria and the West Indies. The mill operated for 175 years, until fire destroyed it in 1924. The miller's office is now a museum operated by Historic Occoquan, with artifacts and displays about the town, including photographs of the damage done by Hurricane Agnes in 1972. Open 11:00 A.M. to 4:00 P.M. daily, there's no admission charge. It is located at 413 Mill Street, Occoquan; (703) 491–7525.

After your stroll and shopping, you might want to stop by the *Garden Kitchen* (404 Mill Street, Occoquan; 703–494–2848; www.gardenkitchen.com), "home of Marie-Claire's Pies," which are truly awesome. Sharadindu and Marie-Claire Kundu also offer sandwiches and salads and a lovely patio for outdoor dining. But you're going to want to try the pies.

If you love ghosts or hearing about them, then you should schedule a visit in October for the annual Haunted Ghost Tours of Historic Occoquan (703–491–0635 or 800–SHOPS–TOO). Here you meet the past and present occupants, including the 400 souls who live there now as well as a few who *once* did.

Perhaps the easiest way to see the significance of Occoquan's geographic setting is to take a forty-minute **Harbor River Cruise** (703–385–9433). While on the water you may also spot catfish, bass, beavers, birds, otters, and blue herons, so bring your camera. Boats depart from 201 Mill Street, Occoquan, Dock A from 9:00 A.M. to 8:30 P.M. from May to December.

History and beauty and recreation combine at 500-acre **Leesylvania State Park.** It has a half-mile of sandy beach; a state-of-the-art boat launch into the Potomac that is one of the largest in the state; and fishing for bass, perch, catfish, and more. For landlubbers, there's hiking through miles of scenic trails through hardwood forests, wetlands, and coastal bluffs. It's also a residence for bald eagles, beaver, deer, and other birds and waterfowl.

History buffs will appreciate the remains of a Civil War Confederate artillery battery built here to protect the Potomac River.

The Lee family plantation was built on this site in the mid-eighteenth century, and it was home to Henry Lee II and his wife Lucy Grymes Lee. Eight Lee children were born and raised here, including General Robert E. Lee's father, Revolutionary War hero Henry "Light Horse Harry" Lee.

Stop by the visitor center that interprets the Potomac River environment and the history of the land that was the estate of Light Horse Harry and Robert E. Lee. There's a discovery room with touch tables, a weather station, children's activities, and a "legacy" room with historical and archaeological displays, area maps, and historical information.

There's also a 288-foot fishing pier; in addition to daytime fishing, the pier is available for night fishing Friday and Saturday and holidays from mid-May to mid-September. Admission and some other fees are charged.

The park is at 2001 Daniel K. Ludwig Drive, Woodbridge; (703) 730–6552; www.dcr.state.va.us/parks/leesylva.htm.

Dumfries, the oldest chartered town in Virginia, is another Scot-settled town that was a major seaport until the late eighteenth century. Now, pure-white whistling swans (perhaps as many as 200) return from Canada to Quantico Creek each year as early as mid-October and leave within twenty-four hours of March 19 (the same date as the Capistrano swallows out west). You can tell when they're getting ready to leave, for they gather in from the various creeks and very noisily talk things over, and then they all take off at the same time.

Just west of Quantico Creek is the **Weems-Botts Museum,** a four-room Colonial restoration. One half of the house was once the bookstore of Parson Mason Locke Weems, the biographer of George Washington, who created the legend of the cherry tree. Jeanne Hochmuth is the curator, and her husband, Al, is president of Historic Dumfries, Inc. The museum docent tells many little-

It's the Truth, by George!

Did you know:

- George Washington's real birthday was February 21, not 22.

- The Father of Our Country had no children of his own, but when he married widow Martha Custis, he adopted her children, John, four, and Martha, two.

- Washington never wore a wig, and his light auburn (not red) hair had started turning gray by the end of the Revolutionary War, when he was in his early fifties. He was also losing his vision.

- He never chopped down a cherry tree or said, "I cannot tell a lie." That story was the fabrication of Parson Mason Locke Weems, a minister and Washington biographer. You can buy a copy of his book, *Life of Washington*, at the Weems-Botts Museum in Dumfries; (703) 221-3346 or 221-2218.

- George Washington "Washy" Parke Custis, Washington's grandson, was demonstrating Washington's strength by saying that his grandfather could throw a piece of slate across the Rappahannock River, which is not now and never has been as wide as the Potomac.

- Washington didn't sleep everywhere.

- He didn't design the layout for the city of Alexandria, but he did assist on an early (1749) survey of the town when he was seventeen.

- Washington's signature is not on the Declaration of Independence; he was busy fighting the war.

- It's said that Washington stood 6' 2½", quite tall for that time, although it's also reported that when he was measured for a coffin, that figure was 6' 3½". Washington was sixty-seven when he died in 1799, quite a long life for those days.

known facts about George. Benjamin Botts, who lived from 1776 to 1811, bought the home from Weems in 1802. He became a prominent lawyer in Prince William County and was on the defense team for Aaron Burr at his treason trial.

Copies of Weems's *Life of Washington* are sold for $16, along with other books on the history of the area from Colonial days to Civil War times. A resource library is available for genealogical research.

Of course, all is not studious and stuffy here, and probably the best way to show that is to mention that in 1998 a new annual event was started, a cherry pie contest. There's judging by a distinguished panel of community notables, followed by a pie-eating contest.

Located at 300 Duke Street, Dumfries, the museum is open February through September, Tuesday through Saturday 10:00 A.M. to 5:00 P.M.; from

October through January, Tuesday through Saturday 10:00 A.M. to 4:00 P.M. and 1:00 to 4:00 P.M. on Sunday. The museum is open on Monday if it's a legal holiday. It is closed on Easter, Thanksgiving, Christmas, and New Year's Days. Admission is $3.00 for adults, $2.00 for seniors fifty-five and over and for children ages six through twelve. For more information call (703) 221–2218 or (703) 221–3346; www.dumfriesvirgina.org.

The *Globe and Laurel Restaurant* was opened in old-town Quantico in 1968 by Richard (Major, U.S. Marine Corps, Ret.) and Gloria Spooner, but it burned, and the restaurant was reopened in its new location on Jefferson Davis Highway in 1975. Major Spooner was in the Marines for twenty-nine years and seven months and wanted a place with a pub atmosphere. You can read about some of the Major's battle experiences in his book, *The Spirit of Semper Fidelis: Reflections from the Bottom of an Old Canteen*, published in November 2004. Oh, the protagonist in the nearly 400-page book is named Pvt. Chic Yancey, but you can figure out that this is an historical novel. Music of swing bands or bagpipes fills the air as you dine. Of historic note are Spooner's Purple Heart medals and the hundreds, maybe thousands, of police department badges on the ceiling from police forces across the United States and from about thirty other countries. Also of interest is the collection of former military insignia, many of which aren't in the possession of military historians, for apparently no one thought to save them; many date from the Civil War. If you have military buttons or other memorabilia, check with Spooner before you throw them away.

While you're at the restaurant, try the prime rib. It's quite tasty. The Globe and Laurel, closed on Sunday and national holidays, is at 18418 Jefferson Davis Highway, Triangle; (703) 221–5763.

All 7 blocks of Quantico constitute the only town in the United States completely surrounded by the U.S. Marine Corps; the only land access is through the Quantico Marine Base. For years the town has been totally landlocked, but a few years ago the government deeded four and a half acres of

Wolf Trap

One of the delights of attending a Wolf Trap performance in Vienna is spreading a blanket on the lawn and enjoying a picnic. Perhaps the **Wolf Trap Foundation for Performing Arts** can help you with that with their *Four Seasons of Wolf Trap* cookbook. Co-sponsored with Reico Kitchen and Bath, the 200-page book features 150 recipes including appetizers, salads, and soups; main dishes and sides; desserts and breads; and beverages, dressings, and sauces. The book can be purchased at the Wolf Trap gift shop or through their Web site, www.wolftrap.org, where you can also find information about upcoming shows.

Snap This

Louis Lowery, World War II Marine combat photographer, took the famous picture of the first U.S. flag-raising atop Iwo Jima's Mt. Suribachi in 1945 (from which the monument was designed). He is among the 8,600 individuals buried at the **Quantico National Cemetery** on Joplin Road in Triangle. The cemetery was dedicated in 1983 and consists of 725 rolling, wooded acres. Hundreds of flags adorn the Memorial Pathway on national holidays. 18424 Joplin Road, Route 619, Triangle; (703) 221–2183 or (703) 690–2217.

waterfront property to Quantico to build a park, so now it can be reached by the Potomac River as well. The town has its own mayor, five council members, and its own police department. As an indication of the cooperation between the base and the town, Quantico is the only place in the world where Marines are allowed to wear their "utilities" (work uniforms) off base.

Heading west in Prince William County, traveling from the I–95 corridor to the I–66 corridor, you'll find the *Manassas Museum* in a Victorian Romanesque 1896 building (the community's first national bank). It has a museum and a classroom for children to experience some natural and American history.

In the exhibit area you can see why this area, halfway between Washington, D.C., and the Shenandoah Valley and the core of train transportation, spurred the region's development and why two of the Civil War's most famous battles were fought nearby. Collections include period photographs from the Civil War, children's toys of a century ago, and a major exhibit about the 1911 Peace Jubilee, which celebrated the fiftieth anniversary of the battle at Manassas. There's a gift shop with history books and souvenirs. It's open Tuesday through Sunday and federal holidays, 10:00 A.M. to 5:00 P.M., and is at 9101

Eyes Down

When you stop by the $1.9 million **Center for the Arts** in Manassas, on the site of the former Hopkins Candy Factory, take a look at the open floor area to see an exposed French drain and an adjacent trench that gave up some souvenirs of a massive fire that consumed the town in 1905. An archaeological dig was conducted during the summer of 2001 in hopes of finding Civil War relics, but the railroad tracks used for the drain were as far as they could research. There were thoughts that this might have been a bakery for Union troops, established by General John Pope. 9001 Center Street, Manassas; (703) 333–ARTS.

Prince William Street, Manassas; (703) 368–1873. Admission is $3.00 for adults and $2.00 for seniors older than sixty and students from six to seventeen.

Be sure to pick up a free all-day parking pass at the Visitor Center, 9431 West Street. It's open 9:00 A.M. to 5:00 P.M. daily except New Year's, Thanksgiving, and Christmas Days; (703) 361–6599; www.manassasmuseum.org.

The *Manassas Walking Tour,* which you can take at your leisure, covers the museum, the 1875 Presbyterian Church, the world's first military railroad, the defenses of Manassas and the Railroad Depot, the Candy Factory, Conner Opera House, and the Old City Hall. A brochure is available from the museum for this tour and the driving tour, which warns about the possible lack of parking at the historical markers and the heavy traffic. Take Route 234 south of I–66.

Manassas was the site of the first and second battles of Manassas, and many of the events are marked in the *Manassas National Battlefield Park.* To assist your historical tour, pick up a *Prince William County Historical Marker Guide* at the welcome center or one of the museums. This will be a nice companion to John S. Salmon's *Guidebook to Virginia's Historical Markers,* published for the Virginia Landmarks Commission by the University Press of Virginia, Charlottesville.

The *Battle of Manassas,* also known as the Battle of Bull Run (you don't want souvenirs marked "the first Battle of Bull Run"), was the first major battle of the Civil War. It's commemorated at the Manassas National Battlefield Park with electronic battle maps, equipment displays, battle memorabilia, and interpretative presentations of the battlefield's history. 6511 Sudley Road, Route 234, Manassas; (703) 361–1339; www.nps.gov/mana.

The Henry Hill Visitor Center has a museum, slide program, and a 3-D map charting the strategies of the two battles. The grounds are open daily from 8:30 A.M. to dusk. The center is open daily 8:30 A.M. to 5:00 P.M. It's closed Thanksgiving and Christmas Days. The Stone House, which served as a field hospital during the battles, is open from 1:00 to 4:00 P.M. Monday through Friday and 10:00 A.M. to 4:00 P.M. on weekends from mid-June through Labor

If These Walls (Bars) Could Talk

The *Old Jail* in Warrenton in Fauquier County, now a museum, is one of the few perfectly preserved old jails in the state. The two buildings date from 1808 and 1823 and now house exhibits about the Civil War, Revolutionary era, Native Americans, and Colonel John Mosby; P.O. Box 675, Warrenton 20188; (540) 347–5525; www.historic warrenton.org.

Day. Admission is $3.00. The park is located north of I–66 in Manassas; call (703) 361–1339.

The *Freedom Museum,* located in the Manassas Regional Airport terminal building at 14420 Bristow Road, Manassas, honors the military maneuvers of the twentieth century with photographs, posters, and colorful vignettes, and was spearheaded by Chuck E. Colgan Jr., an Army photographer during the Vietnam War. A second facility is being planned for a piece of property near the airport. It will house some photos, the current Museum of Military Vehicles, and additional acquired collections. Called the *National Museum of Americans at War,* it's scheduled to open in 2009 and will chronicle all of the major U.S. battles, and warfare techniques and tactics utilized by various branches of the military. It will incorporate aircraft and armored vehicle demonstrations. The museum is open daily from 10:00 A.M. to 4:00 P.M.; (703) 393–0660; www.freedommuseum.org.

Fredericksburg

We're back along I–95 when we stop in the Fredericksburg area, which boasts that "George Washington slept in a lot of places, but he lived here." With 350 original buildings built before 1870, the area is steeped in history from colonial times and the Revolutionary and Civil Wars. It's possible to stay here several days without seeing everything. Be sure to get your free all-day parking pass at the *Fredericksburg Visitors Center,* see the audiovisual display, and obtain directions and operating hours for museums, the national parks, and other attractions.

A Passport tour ticket, at $29.00 for adults and $9.50 for students ages six through eighteen, provides a 40 percent discount for admissions to the Fredericksburg Area Museum, Kenmore, Mary Washington House, Rising Sun Tavern, Hugh Mercer Apothecary Shop, Belmont, the James Monroe Museum and Memorial Library, and Ferry Farm. These passes are undated and may be used for any future visits. They're available at the visitor center or at any of these homes. The visitor center is at 706 Caroline Street (Fredericksburg) and can be reached by calling (540) 373–1776 or (800) 678–4748; www.visitfred.com.

The Apocryphal Stone's Throw

George Washington inherited **Ferry Farm** when he was eleven and spent his boy-hood years on this property, 1 mile east of Fredericksburg and 38 miles south of Mount Vernon, on the banks of the Rappahannock River. Legend claims the cherry tree story ("I cannot tell a lie") and his powerful toss of a "silver dollar" across the Rappahannock took place here. George Washington's Ferry Farm, now a National Historic Landmark, is located on Route 3, Kings Highway, Fredericksburg; (540) 370–0732; www.kenmore.org.

The tobacco-leaf–topped lamps in the historic area are not relics of the 1780s or an 1880s event. They've been erected since 1980 and reflect Fredericksburg's part in the tobacco industry as the central licensing point for tobacco inspection for some years. Fredericksburg is home to Mary Washington College, so you can feel a historic or a more modern atmosphere depending on where you travel. In addition to the dozens of historic and interesting sights to see, particularly in the city's 40-block National Historic District, you can participate in an annual rubber duck race at Old Mill Park (540–37–DUCKS), take a "ghost" walk, and ride a trolley for about an hour's tour of the city ($15.00 for adults and $5.00 for children for the trolley tour; buy your tickets at the welcome center). For great souvenirs and items to ship to your friends, stop by John Mitchell's Made in Virginia store at 807 Caroline Street (Fredericksburg), which offers wonderful edibles ranging from Brunswick stew to Graves' Mountain red raspberry preserves to Barboursville Cabernet Blanc wine. For more information call (540) 371–2030 or (800) 635–3149; www.madeinva.com.

While in the historic area, you'll notice about forty antiques stores and a few "malls" of antiques within about a 4-block area. Pick up a brochure at the visitor center for specialty listings.

As long as we're discussing written material, stop by the **Wallace Library** of the Central Rappahannock Regional Library system. There's a great Virginiana room with lots of historical books about the area, and as of this writing, Barbara Willis will be delighted to help you. She's usually there between 9:00 A.M. and 1:00 P.M. on Monday and Wednesday, but call to set an appointment. There's also a law library and a really pleasant, quiet reading room.

Surrounding the library are some wonderful plants donated by the Rappahannock Valley Garden Club. From crab apple to creeping lilyturf, from fringe tree to highbush blueberry, you can pick up a brochure in the library that shows where the plants are and details some interesting information about them.

By Women for a Woman

President Grover Cleveland unveiled the Mary Washington monument, at Washington Avenue and Pitt Street in Fredericksburg, in 1894. Washington (George Washington's mother), who died in 1789 at the age of 81, was buried at her favorite spot near her daughter's home. President Andrew Jackson laid a cornerstone for the monument in 1883, but it was never finished. A new monument was commissioned in 1893 thanks to the efforts of a group of women called the Mary Washington Monument Association. The new monument was dedicated in 1894. It is the first monument ever erected to a woman by women; (800) 678–4748.

Located at 1201 Caroline Street (Fredericksburg), the library is open 9:00 A.M. to 9:00 P.M. Monday through Thursday, 9:00 A.M. to 5:30 P.M. on Friday and Saturday, and 1:00 to 5:00 P.M. Sunday from October to May; (540) 372–1144.

A relatively new institution of Fredericksburg (in historic terms), but an ice cream institution nonetheless, is **Carl's,** at the intersection of Princess Anne and Hunter Streets. Carl's is open from Valentine's Day to Thanksgiving Day, and if you've never had a hot fudge milkshake, you're in for a treat. (Well, you're in for a treat whatever you order, but that's one of their best-selling items.) 2200 Princess Anne Street, Fredericksburg.

Kenmore, a mid-Georgian structure, was built in 1752 by Colonel Fielding Lewis for his second wife, Betty, only sister of George Washington. Kenmore contains the finest ornamental plasterwork in America and authentic (but not original) furnishings of the period. (Lewis was providing munitions for the war and, not receiving payment, eventually was forced to auction the furnishings.)

You'll love the hot, fresh gingerbread and spiced tea at the end of the tour (from Mary Washington's original recipe, which you can purchase in the gift shop), and you can have tea in the kitchen or on the lawn. Stroll through the boxwood gardens, restored by the **Garden Club of Virginia.** There's a marvelous 9½-foot Daniel Hadley diorama of Colonial Fredericksburg, done in cooperation with the Hagley Museum in Delaware. If you've been taking your walking tour, been to the Stone House, and paid attention to all the details, you'll realize that there are some errors in the depiction, such as the height of Sophia Street compared to the river, and that the Baptist Church is the newer one, not the older one, but this is such a magnificent diorama that it shouldn't be missed. The Lewis family tree is on display, filling a matrix that is twenty-nine 1-inch squares across and forty-nine 1-inch squares down.

Besides being known for some of the most beautiful rooms in the country, Kenmore is cited as one of the first victories in the fight against suburban development; in 1922 a developer bought Kenmore and planned to demolish the house or convert it into apartments and subdivide the remaining two acres of land. His plans were thwarted by local historical preservationists. Kenmore is undergoing an extensive multi-year renovation so there is no furniture in the rooms; however, admission prices have been lowered because of this.

Located at 1201 Washington Street, Fredericksburg, Kenmore is open seven days a week, 9:00 A.M. to 5:00 P.M. March through December and from 11:00 A.M. to 5:00 P.M. on Saturday, January through February. It's closed December 24, 25, and 31 and January 1. Admission is $8.00 for adults and $4.00 for students ages six through eighteen. Call (540) 373–3381 for more information; www.kenmore.org.

Fredericksburg is surrounded by battlefields and cemeteries, including Fredericksburg, Chancellorsville, Wilderness, and Spotsylvania Courthouse, each with programs run by the National Park Service. Descriptive audiotapes for driving tours are usually available at each headquarters building. Get directions from the Fredericksburg Visitors Center.

The **National Park Service Visitors Center,** the starting place for a self-guided tour through Fredericksburg and Spotsylvania Civil War battlefields, is open daily from 9:00 A.M. to 5:00 P.M. with extended hours during summer months. A small museum includes an orientation program and some exhibits. There is no admission charge. Guided tours of the Sunken Road are given three times daily in summer. You need permission from the National Park Service, but you can visit the place where Confederate general Thomas Jonathan "Stonewall" Jackson's arm was buried after it was amputated on May 3, 1863.

> ## funfacts
>
> **Goolrick's,** a great place for a refreshing drink, claims to be the oldest continuously operating soda fountain (since 1867) in the nation. It's located at 901 Caroline Street, Fredericksburg; (540) 373–3411; http://goolricks.com.

And they swam and they swam . . .

On the chilly morning of February 23, 2004, thousands of spectators watched as the Embrey Dam on the Rappahannock River at Fredericksburg was destroyed. The 770-foot-wide dam was constructed in 1854 to provide power and a drinking water reservoir to the growing community. By the 1960s, the power plant was no longer in service and the movement was afoot to undo this insult to nature. Now the 184-mile Rappahannock is the longest free-flowing river leading into the Chesapeake Bay watershed and the shad can swim upstream to spawn.

During the Battle of Chancellorsville, Jackson was shot by friendly fire, and his left arm was amputated in a field hospital. It was taken to the family home, Ellwood Plantation, and a marker notes the spot. Jackson died a few days later and was buried in Lexington, Virginia. Stop by the visitor center for a map and a pass. For permission call (540) 371–0802. The visitor center is located at Lafayette Boulevard and Sunken Road. The Chancellorsville Battlefield Visitors Center is located off Route 3 West and is open from 9:00 A.M. to 5:00 P.M. daily. Write Fredericksburg and Spotsylvania National Military Park/Chatham Manor (headquarters for Civil War battlefields), 120 Chatham Lane, Fredericksburg 22405, or call (540) 654–5121; www.nps.gov/frsp.

Gari Melchers, one of America's finest impressionist painters, lived at **Belmont** from 1916 until his death in 1932. His former home now houses the Memorial Gallery, where spacious rooms are filled with antiques and paintings by Melchers and others, such as Jan Brueghel, Frans Snyders, Auguste Rodin, and Berthe Morisot.

funfacts

Gari Melchers painted the murals that adorn the walls of the Library of Congress, in Washington, D.C.

Belmont is open Monday through Saturday 10:00 A.M. to 5:00 P.M. and Sunday from 1:00 to 5:00 P.M. March 1 through November 30. At other times it's open Monday through Saturday 10:00 A.M. to 4:00 P.M. and Sunday from 1:00 to 4:00 P.M. It's closed New Year's and Thanksgiving Days and December 24, 25, and 31. Admission fees are $7.00 for adults, $5.00 for AAA members and seniors, and $1.00 for children six through eighteen. Belmont is located at 224 Washington Street, Falmouth. For more information call (540) 654–1015; www.umw.edu/belmont.

Falmouth, about a mile outside Fredericksburg, offers a popular Falmouth Historic Walking Tour in late October that includes private homes and historic spots, crafts demonstrations, an introduction to the village witch, and usually music and street dancing.

A few miles west of Fredericksburg is the town of **Culpeper,** originally called Fairfax, founded in 1759 when George Washington (who was seventeen at the time) was commissioned to survey and plot the town and county of Culpeper. Over the years it thrived and suffered. During the Civil War, there were more than one hundred battles and skirmishes in the area, primarily because its central railroad was vital to the North and the South. Homes became military lodging and hospitals, and over the years many farms, houses, historical artifacts, and, of course, lives were lost. About one hundred years later, in the 1960s, the town was nearly devastated financially when a highway

They Went Westward

The **Germanna Historic Site** honors this community that was established by Alexander Spotswood in 1714 and, for a while, was the most western English settlement in the New World. The beginning of the **Lee vs. Grant Civil War Trail** is located here. The Memorial Foundation of Germanna Colonies, P. O. Box 279, Locust Grove 22508-0279; (540) 423–1700; www.germanna.org.

bypass was constructed, taking residential, commercial, and industrial growth away from the town center. A major Main Street project has strengthened and revitalized the historic core.

Stop by the old railroad depot, now the *Visitor Information Center,* 109 South Commerce Street, for information about area activities and attractions. You can call (540) 727–0611 or (888) CULPEPER or visit the town's Web site at www.visitculpeperva.com.

More than 200,000 people visit the *Culpeper National Cemetery* every year as they follow Civil War events. Established on April 13, 1867, as a burial site for Union soldiers, the cemetery now is home to soldiers from all American wars and is listed on the National Register of Historic Places. Note the stone lodge/gatehouse near the entrance. Its mansard roof is unique in the Culpeper area but typical of cemetery architecture. Originally, the building was

OTHER PLACES TO SEE

Alexandria
Lee-Fendall House
Museum & Gardens (703) 548–1789
Pope-Leighey House
(Frank Lloyd Wright) (540) 780–4000

Arlington
Arlington National Cemetery
(703) 607–8052
www.arlingtoncemetery.org
U.S. Marine Corps War Memorial
(Iwo Jima Memorial)
(202) 289–2500

Great Falls
Great Falls National Park
(703) 285–2966

Manassas
Manassas Industrial School/
Jennie Dean Memorial
(703) 368–1873

Mount Vernon
Woodlawn Plantation
(703) 780–4000

Vienna
Wolf Trap Farm Park
for the Performing Arts
(703) 255–1900
www.wolf-trap.org

the residence and office of the cemetery's superintendent. The office is open weekdays from 8:00 A.M. to 4:30 P.M., and the grounds are open daily from dawn to dusk. (540) 825–0027.

Many people think "old" when they think of Virginia, particularly those coming from the West Coast. At the *Museum of Culpeper History,* they're showing really old with exhibits from dinosaur activity, including tracks from a theropod, aetosaur, and pytosaur, discovered and removed from the Culpeper Stone Company Quarry. Also on display are artifacts from Native American life and the Civil War.

The museum is open Monday through Saturday from 10:00 A.M. to 5:00 P.M. and on Sunday from 12:30 to 4:00 P.M. between May and October. The suggested admission is $3.00 for adults; 803 South Main Street, Culpeper; (540) 829–1749; www.culpepermuseum.com.

From spring through fall, you can see a variety of equestrian events at *Commonwealth Park,* including Grand Prix, Hunter, and Jumper events. This

TOP ANNUAL EVENTS

February
Breakfast with George Washington,
Mount Vernon
(703) 780–2000 or (800) 388–9119
www.mountvernon.org

March-April
Easter Sunrise Service,
Arlington
(202) 685–2851
www.arlingtoncemetery.org

April
Annual Historic Garden Week,
Statewide
(804) 644–7776 or
(804) 643–7141
www.vagardenweek.org

June-August
City of Fairfax Band Outdoor
Concert Series
Veteran's Amphitheater at Fairfax City
Hall; Thursday nights
Fairfax
(703) 757–0220
www.fairfaxband.org

July
World Championship
Scottish Highland Games,
Alexandria
(800) 388–9119 or (703) 912–1943
www.vascottishgames.org

August
Hot Air Balloon Festival,
Bealeton
(540) 439–8661
www.flyingcircusairshow.com/balloon

September
International Children's
Festival, Wolf Trap Farm
Park for the Performing Arts
(703) 642–0862
www.wolf-trap.org

December
First Night, Alexandria
(703) 838–4200 or
(800) 388–9119
www.funside.com

continues an equestrian history that started in 1897 and continued for the next fifty-four years. Show jumping returned to Culpeper in the 1980s, and some of the country's richest show jumping competitions have been held here. Children twelve and under get in free; 13256 Commonwealth Parkway, Culpeper; (540) 825–7469; www.hitsshows.com.

When it's time to eat, stop by **Baby Jim's Snack Bar,** a diner known for its burgers and shakes. For a "local" experience, go to the window and order "two dogs with the works, an order o' fries, and an RC." Established in the 1950s, Baby Jim's remains in the ownership of its founder's family; 701 North Main Street, Culpeper; (540) 825–9212.

For doughnuts, éclairs, and other pastries, it's **Knakal's Bakery.** Founded by Joseph Knakal in 1935, the bakery is now run by Ken Whitt and family, who prepare at least a hundred dozen doughnuts every day, dozens of biscuits, and as many as a dozen wedding cakes every weekend. The aromas are enough to start the taste buds salivating for the cakes, pies, and cookies. Open Monday through Friday from 7:00 A.M. to 5:30 P.M. and Saturday from 7:00 A.M. until 4:00 P.M.; 146 East Davis Street, Culpeper; (540) 829–6445.

Where to Stay in Northern Virginia

ALEXANDRIA

Morrison House
116 South Alfred Street
(703) 838–8000 or (800) 367–0800

ARLINGTON

Westin Arlington Gateway
801 North Glebe Road
(703) 717–6200 or (703) 717–6204.

FREDERICKSBURG

Kenmore Inn
1200 Princess Anne Street
(540) 371–7622

Richard Johnston Inn
711 Caroline Street
(540) 899–7606 or (877) 557–0770

LEESBURG

Lansdowne Resort
44050 Woodridge Parkway
(703) 729–8400 or (800) 541–4801

MANASSAS

Bennett House Bed and Breakfast
9252 Bennett Drive
(703) 368–6121 or (800) 354–7060

MINERAL

Littlepage Inn
15701 Monrovia Road
(540) 854–9861 or (800) 248–1803

UPPERVILLE

1763 Inn
10087 John S. Mosby Highway
(540) 592–3848 or (800) 669–1763

Where to Eat in Northern Virginia

ALEXANDRIA

Cafe Marianna
1201 North Royal Street
(703) 519–3776

Dandy Restaurant Cruise Ships
Zero Prince Street
(703) 683–6076 or (800) 40–DANDY

Potowmack Landing
1 Marina Drive
(703) 548–0001
or (800) 298–2532

Rocklands Barbeque and Grilling
25 South Quaker Lane
(703) 778–9663

Tom Sarris Orleans House
1213 Wilson Boulevard
(703) 524–2929

ARLINGTON

Athena Pallas
556 22nd Street South
(703) 521–3870

Jaleo
2250 Crystal Drive
(703) 413–8181

Tandoori Nights
2800 Clarendon Boulevard
(703) 248–8333

FAIRFAX

Artie's
3260 Old Lee Highway
(703) 273–7600

Connaught Place
10425 North Street
(703) 352–5959

Coyote Grille and Cantina
10266 Main Street
(703) 591–0006

Dolce Vita
10824 Lee Highway
(703) 385–1530

Mama's Italian Restaurant
9715 Fairfax Boulevard
(703) 385–9775 or (703) 385–2646

FALLS CHURCH

Flavors Soul Food
3420 Carlyn Hill Drive
(703) 379–4411

Old Hickory Grille
7263 Arlington Boulevard
(703) 207–8650

LEESBURG

Knossos
341 East Market Street
(703) 771–9231

MANASSAS

Carmello's
9108 Center Street
(703) 368–5522

RESTON

Bread and Chocolate
11920 Market Street
(703) 467–0460

TYSONS CORNER

Clyde's of Tysons Corner
8332 Leesburg Pike
(703) 734–1901

VIENNA

Amphora Diner
377 Maple Avenue West
(703) 938–7877

Eastern Virginia

The eastern section of Virginia includes the northern neck (along the southern reaches of the Potomac River), the area called Hampton Roads where the James River meets the Chesapeake Bay, and the southern part of what is known as the DelMarVa (Delaware, Maryland, Virginia) Peninsula, which is across Chesapeake Bay from the rest of the state.

Habitation in the area dates from prehistoric times, when Native Americans settled here. The European presence in America was born with the 1607 settlement of Jamestown. Shipping, vital to our continuance, came through these ports. Our reliance on the Virginia waterfront—for recreation and commerce—is just as strong today. Goods have to be shipped in and out, and they need harbors to do that. Foods are harvested from the waters.

Much has changed throughout Virginia, but the biggest changes seem to be happening or getting ready to happen on the Eastern Shore. Cape Charles was a bustling place until the Chesapeake Bay Bridge Tunnel opened. Then it became the place where they "have all those Sears Catalog mail-order houses." Maybe there was one traffic light.

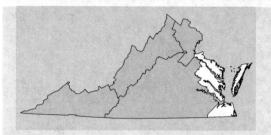

King George

3

301

MARYLAND

VIRGINIA

Rappahannock R.

Potomac R.

17

360

Tappahannock

360

Saluda

New Kent

33

17

Gloucester

York R.

64

Williamsburg

James R.

Hampton

Newport News

Portsmouth

Norfolk

64

Chesapeake

58

Suffolk

17

168

VIRGINIA

NORTH CAROLINA

MARYLAND

VIRGINIA

Chincoteague

Accomac

13

Eastville

Cape Charles

CHESAPEAKE BAY BRIDGE-TUNNEL

Virginia Beach

CHESAPEAKE BAY

N

0   20 mi
0   20 km

Boy, is that changing. Cape Charles and the other "sleepy" towns have become a mecca of ecotourism, artistic and creative ventures, and high-price gated communities with golf course and marina and tony boutiques. It's a nice mix.

You can experience it all—from Native American settlements, to Colonial life, to modern technology.

Middlesex County

We'll start our tour by leaving Washington, D.C., and heading down the **Northern Neck.** Here you'll find miles of shoreline, forests lands, historic explorations from Colonial days forward, quaint towns, good eats, and friendly people.

In looking for a base of operations, you need look no farther than **Bethpage Camp-Resort** in Urbanna. In fact, you may enjoy Connie McGuire's hospitality so much that you decide to spend all your days there. Rating five stars from *Woodall's* and top ratings from *Trailer Life* let you know their amenities and recreational opportunities are exceptional. Set along the southern reach of the Rappahannock River, there are plenty of water activities, including a swimming lake with sandy beach, boat ramp, fresh- and saltwater fishing, crabbing, charter boat fishing, and swimming pools with lifeguards. Once you've caught your day's limit, you can take it in to one of the fish cleaning stations so you don't have to do the "messy stuff."

There's a lake pier with a band gazebo, two recreation centers (2,000 square feet and 12,000 square feet), catering facilities, camp store, laundry rooms, basketball and tennis courts, horseshoe pits, children's playground, activities, and game room. The 700-plus sites are level and either in the open or in the naturally wooded and beautifully landscaped setting with water, electric (30 and 50 amp service), and sewage hookup.

The season, from April 1 through mid-November, offers plenty of organized activities, from a Cinco de Mayo weekend with Mexican crafts and piñatas through Halloween and the expected costume contest.

Daily, weekly, and monthly rates are available, starting at $29.95 a night (for calendar year 2005 for four people. For more information contact Bethpage Camp-Resort at P.O. Box 178, Urbanna 23175; (804) 758–4349. www.bethpagecamp.com

The **Middlesex County Museum** in Saluda, in the old clerk's office adjacent to the courthouse, is the oldest county museum in the state. It was started in the days of the Depression, closed during World War II, and reopened in 1976 for the country's bicentennial. It is open from 10:00 A.M. to 3:00 P.M.

Annual Pony Swim and Auction, July, Chincoteague, (757) 336–6161; www.chincoteaguechamber.com/pony

Arts Enter Cape Charles (757) 331–2787; www.artsentercapecharles.org**Chrysler Museum,** Norfolk, (757) 664–6200; www.chrysler.org

Hampton University Museum, Hampton, (757) 727–5308; www.hamptonu.edu/museum

Mariners' Museum, Newport News, (757) 596–2222 or (800) 581–7245; www.mariner.org

Nauticus the National Maritime Center, Norfolk, (757) 664–1000 or (800) 644–1080; www.thenmc.org

Norfolk Botanical Gardens, Norfolk, (757) 441–5830; www.nbgs.org

Refuge Waterfowl Museum, Chincoteague, (757) 336–5800; www.chincoteaguechamber.com

Virginia Air and Space Center, Hampton, (757) 727–0900 or (800) 296–0800; www.vasc.org

Virginia Marine Science Museum, Virginia Beach, (757) 425–FISH; www.vmsm.com

Monday through Friday. Court House Square, Saluda; (804) 758–3663; www. museums.org/museums/info/1162588.

Down the road is Deltaville, "the Boatbuilding Capital of the Chesapeake." At one time there were more than twenty boatbuilders in this area, many of them second and third generation, creating craft that still are used today. Some of the finest houses along the Northern Neck can be found in this area, and a maritime museum is in the developmental stages.

King George County

The ***King George County Museum and Research Center*** is located on Route 3 in King George. It opened in September 1997 and is located in the old jail on the east end of the courthouse. Although the county dates from 1721, the Historical Society formed only in the late 1980s. Such items as a pocket pistol from 1863, Civil War relics, Indian projectile points that are about 10,000 years old, photographs, letters, and other articles have been assembled chronologically. Check out the area recipe book (including instructions on how to cook rabbit and squirrel) and the new *Cemeteries of King George County* with listings through 1999. The center is open Thursday and Saturday from 10:00 A.M. to 2:00 P.M. March through October and Saturday from November through February;

9483 King's Highway, King George; (540) 775–9477; www.kghistory.orb/
HistoricalSociety/index.html.

Westmoreland County

Wandering through the rest of the Northern Neck is more or less whether you
feel like turning right or left. There are plenty of historic museums, beaches,
famous birthplaces, Westmoreland State Park, great restaurants, and interesting
shops, mostly featuring antiques.

Kinsale, a quaint maritime village
founded in 1706 on the Yeocomico
River, is still considered one of the best
deepwater ports in the lower Potomac.
It thrived until the early twentieth century when steamboat traffic died. The
Kinsale Museum, in a restored eigh-

funfacts

George Washington and Robert E.
Lee were both born in Westmoreland County.

teenth-century pub, chronicles this period with changing exhibits and artifacts
of those times. The museum is located on the green in what was a meat market at the turn of the century. A walking tour of the historic village is available
at the museum. It's open Thursday through Saturday 10:00 A.M. to 5:00 P.M. May
through September; (804) 472–3001; www.westmoreland-county.org.

Lancaster County

The ***Mary Ball Washington Museum*** in Lancaster has a marvelous collection
of local memorabilia, Civil War artifacts (including two battle flags used by

Water Sports and Fossils

Westmoreland State Park (camping, boating, fishing, swimming) was built in 1936
by the Civilian Conservation Corps, one of the original six in the state system. At the
edge of the Potomac River, the soft shale and sandstone Horsehead Cliffs rise about
200 feet above the water and stretch 300 to 400 feet along the shore. The formations occurred five million to fifteen million years ago, when a shallow subtropical sea
stretched all the way to the fall line. Thousands of fossils of Miocene-era sharks,
whales, porpoises, clams, shells, coral, and plants are contained in these rocks, but
check with the ranger about where you're allowed, and not allowed, to look for them.
A ranger-guided fossil walk is available (804–493–8821). Call (800) 933–PARK for
camping or cabin reservations.

troops from Lancaster County), and displays on Northern Neck Indians and life on the water. The genealogical library, said to be one of the best on the East Coast, includes Southern Maryland and Virginia and the migratory paths taken through Virginia into Kentucky. There's also a historical lending library, programs, workshops, and films. Organized to honor the Lancaster County–born mother of George Washington, it's located in the Lancaster House (ca. 1800), which was lovingly restored by the Lancaster Women's Club. The museum is open from 10:00 A.M. to 4:00 P.M. Tuesday through Friday and by appointment. Admission is $2.00 for the museum house and grounds; $5.00 to work at the library; 8346 Mary Ball Road, Lancaster. Call (804) 462–7280 for more information, or visit www.mbwm.org.

Next to the museum are the Old Jail (ca. 1819) and the Clerk of Courts (1797) building on exhibit as it was, in a first-person living-history museum. It's as though the clerk of courts himself had just stepped out of the building. He will not know what your camera is or any of your other modern contraptions.

There is an architectural walking tour of the historic district, and for 25 cents you can buy the self-guided tour pamphlet.

Merry Point Ferry, one of four remaining historic river ferries in Virginia (in operation since 1668), crosses the western branch of the Corrotoman River. For years the *Arminta* had plied these waters, carrying three small cars or two regular-size cars and taking about ten or fifteen minutes to cross, but the *Lancaster,* a new, all-in-one steel boat and scow, is now in service. The *Lancaster* carried 16,378 vehicles and 26,097 passengers in the hurricane-shortened summer of 2003. Taking the ferry from Corrotoman to Ottoman will land you in the town of Lively.

Merry Point Ferry

The ferry runs from 7:00 A.M. to 7:00 P.M. (if daylight) daily except Sunday and major holidays (it may not operate at times of extreme tides or adverse weather). There's no charge to the passengers. Take Route 604 off either Route 3 or Route 354 to Ottoman Ferry and Merry Point Roads, Merry Point; (800) 453–6167 or (804) 333–3696; www.virginiadot.org/comtravel/ferry.asp.

Irvington is the home of **The Tides Inn,** one of the Chesapeake's favorite resorts for almost sixty years. Managed by Sedona Resorts of Sedona, Arizona (which also operates the Enchantment Resort and Mii amo Spa in Sedona), the resort is situated on a bluff overlooking Carters Creek and on to the Rappahannock River. Over the winter of 2001–2002, it enjoyed a major renovation, with a reopening in the spring of 2002. Enjoy boating, golfing, spa treatments, fine dining, and the services of an extremely dedicated staff.

Whether you're a first-time visitor or have been coming back for generations, Tides Inn has some delightful "welcome home" and local touches. The food is superb, with an emphasis on fresh seafood and shellfish (I can't begin to get enough of the fresh fried oysters, and even the crab cakes are lip-smacking delicious.) The daily "rum-runner" trip aboard the teak-decked and -furnished *Miss Ann* still goes up to Urbanna so guests can enjoy an hour-or-so stroll around town (there's still a drug/general store with a soda fountain

antebellumtime

The antebellum manor house that's now the *Inn at Levelfields* was built for Thomas Sandford Dunaway in 1857–1858 and is one of the last antebellum mansions constructed in the commonwealth. John Dunn and Charlotte Hollings are the innkeepers; 10155 Mary Ball Road, Lancaster 22503; (800) 238–5578 or (804) 435–6887; www.innatlevelfields.com.

and a church with oyster shells in a wreath on the door). In your room are bottles of Northern Neck ginger ale (Carver's Original Ginger Ale), bottled by Coca Cola, just up the road in Montrose, made with real ginger extract.

For reservations and information call (804) 438–5000 or (800) 843–3746; 480 King Carter Drive, Irvington; www.the-tides.com.

Urbanna, one of America's original harbor towns (established in 1673), enjoys a marvelously picturesque setting and is the home of the **Urbanna Oyster Festival.** Thousands (perhaps 75,000) come to the little harbor on Urbanna Creek every first weekend in November to enjoy the harvest of the famous oyster beds on the Rappahannock River. From here oysters are sold by the bushel, processed, packed, frozen, and shipped all over. During the festival there are 125 craft and food booths (where you can find oysters fried, stewed, on the half shell, roasted, ready to shuck yourself, or in chowder). For more information call (804) 758–0368; www.urbannaoysterfestival.com.

funfacts

The site of James Monroe's birthplace, Monrovia, has been swallowed up by the modern but old-time resort town of Colonial Beach. This land was first settled by James Monroe's great-great grandfather, Andrew, a Scot, in 1647.

A few years before Urbanna was established, Christopher Robinson, a member of the House of Burgesses, lived in a manor home in the area. **Hewick Plantation** (Routes 602/615, Urbanna) is now a bed-and-breakfast inn, with two guest bedrooms (each with private bath). The 1678 manor home is set on sixty-six acres, with lush old pecan, walnut, and oak trees and old English boxwoods. Your pets aren't allowed, but they have outdoor pets, including three quarter horses. If you can't spend the night, give innkeeper Helen Nichols Murphy a call for a tour at (804) 758–4214 or (800) 484–7514; www.hewick.com.

For those who like old churches, there's a dandy one in Irvington. The **Historic Christ Church** was finished about 1735 and is an excellent example of a Colonial American church that has been virtually unchanged since that time. Built in cruciform design, the church has 3-foot-deep walls. A marvelous three-decker pulpit lets you know immediately where your attention should be focused (whether you were there for services or serenity). The individually enclosed high-backed pews seem to offer privacy for your spiritual thoughts. Stop at the reception center for a slide presentation about the church and then browse through the museum.

The church is open 10:00 A.M. to 4:00 P.M. Monday through Saturday, and 2:00 to 5:00 P.M. Sunday (both April through November); 420 Christ Church Road, Irvington; (804) 438–6855; www.christchurch1735.org.

Essex County

The small town of **Tappahannock** on the Rappahannock River was founded in 1680, the same year as the founding of Philadelphia, and had seen several name changes before settling on this Indian name meaning "rise and fall of water." Thirteen buildings are on the National Register of Historic Places, and you can walk the streets (which still carry their original names) to view the buildings, including the Old Debtors' Prison on Prince Street between Church and Cross Streets. The Confederate soldier statue on Prince Street in Tappahannock, a common memorial in many Virginia cities, lists all the local men who fought in the war. Look for a booklet entitled *Essex County Virginia— Its Historic Homes, Landmarks and Traditions* at the Essex County Museum (218 Water Lane; 804–443–4690), or check with the Tappahannock–Essex

County Chamber of Commerce (757–443–2717) about the buildings and other attractions in the area; www.essex-virginia.org.

Gloucester County

Gloucester County is the home of the annual ***Daffodil Festival,*** held the first Saturday in April. Enjoy the parade, entertainment, 5-K race, and a pet show (bring your own) when the fields are abloom with these gorgeous messengers of spring; call (804) 693–2355 for information. www.gloucesterva.info/pr/tourism.

Gloucester County is also the home of two of America's oldest churches: ***Ware Episcopal Church*** (ca. 1690), with an interesting graveyard and beautiful paintings, open for Sunday and Wednesday services; and ***Abingdon Episcopal Church*** (ca. 1755), with beautiful brickwork, open grounds, and services on Sunday. There are also some marvelous homes that are privately owned but open to the public during Garden Week, one of a series of events scheduled throughout the state during the fourth week of April. Call the Garden Club of Virginia at (804) 643–7141 for additional information. The Ware Episcopal Church is located at 7825 John Clayton Memorial Highway, Gloucester; (804) 693–3821; www.warechurch.org. The Abingdon Episcopal Church is located at 4625 George Washington Memorial Highway, almost midway between Gloucester Courthouse and Gloucester Point, in White Marsh; (804) 693–3035; www.abingdonchurch.org.

Gloucester is the birthplace of ***Dr. Walter Reed,*** and his home at the intersection of Routes 616 and 614 is one of the buildings maintained by the Association for the Preservation of Virginia Antiquities. The grounds are open to visitors daily, and the building is open on special occasions or by appointment. Call (804) 693–3992 for more information.

Mathews County

For a delightful escape, head over to ***Gwynn's Island,*** a 2-by-1½-mile piece of land off the coast of Mathews County where the Piankatank River flows into the Chesapeake Bay, named after Hugh Gwynn. The island was given to him by Chief Powhatan as a reward for saving Pocahontas's life. Gwynn's Island was the site of one of the first Revolutionary War battles, when in 1776 Lord Dunmore, the last Colonial governor of Virginia, was bombarded by Continental forces at Cricket Hill.

Stop by the local museum that's dedicated to preserving the history of Gwynn's Island and Mathews County and to honoring men lost at sea and all who served their country. Housed in a one-hundred-year-old building that was an Odd Fellows Lodge and then the island's first public school, a general store, and a barber shop, it contains school memorabilia, prehistoric fossils, a humpback whale skull, Indian and Colonial artifacts, and other displays from the Civil War to the present in its two floors of exhibits.

It's open from 1:00 to 5:00 P.M. Friday, Saturday, and Sunday from May 1 through November 1 or by appointment; P.O. Box 109, Gwynn's Island 23066; (804) 725–7949; www.qsl.net/w4rzb/gimuse.html.

The cultural center, the former Methodist Church built in 1890, is home to the annual island festival, celebrations, historical seminars, and civic league meetings; P.O. Box 311, Gwynn's Island 23066; (804) 725–7941.

King William County

Back toward Richmond is the ***Pamunkey Indian Museum*** (King William), which has several nice displays and a videotape about the Pamunkey people and their way of life, from the Ice Age to the present. These people were members of the tribe under the leadership of Chief Powhatan (the name he told the settlers), who was the father of Pocahontas. Some of the items in the fifteen display windows are original; some are as it's assumed they were. Of special interest is Pamunkey pottery: a new form, which is glazed and burned, as well as the older coil method. If you time your visit right, you might see a demonstration.

The museum is open Tuesday through Saturday 10:00 A.M. to 4:00 P.M. and Sunday 1:00 to 5:00 P.M. (closed on major holidays). The museum may not open exactly on time, but stay around a few minutes and someone will come by. Admission is $2.50 for adults, $1.25 for children six to thirteen, and $1.75 for seniors. Picnic tables are available. It's located about 10 miles off Route 30 (off I–95) on Route 633 and then Route 673, past the Lanesville cemetery and over the railroad tracks. The road turns, but the signs are easy to follow. For more information call (804) 843–4792; www.baylink.org/Pamunkey.

Not far away, in West Point, is the ***Mattaponi Museum,*** with historical presentations, a fish hatchery, a church, a museum, and a nature trail. Webster "Little Eagle" Custalow is the chief, and Carl "Lone Eagle" Custalow is the assistant chief of this tribe that has had this reservation since 1658. The reservation is approximately 150 acres, with much of it being dedicated to wetlands and approximately 60 of the 450 Mattaponi Indians living on this property.

When you visit both reservations, you'll notice that the Pamunkey property is mostly agricultural, with lots of cornfields and homes scattered throughout the land. The Mattaponi have houses in clusters, with most of their efforts spent on shad fishing.

Mattaponi Museum, Route 2, P.O. Box 225, West Point 23181; (804) 769–2229; www.baylink.org/Mattaponi.

Northumberland County

According to the Northern Neck Visitor Information bureau, Reedville is a small town of 400, with "no restaurants, bars, alcohol, traffic lights, or police," but they do have a "post office the size of your thumb . . . four churches, Victorian-style homes, and the **Reedville Fishermen's Museum.**" Reedville prospered from the menhaden fishing industry, and the plethora of Victorian mansions lining Main Street indicates that it may well have been the richest town per capita in the United States at the turn of the twentieth century. The oldest house now standing is part of the Reedville Fishermen's Museum, located on the banks of Cockrell's Creek (504 Main Street, Reedville). Still one of the most active fishing ports in the country, the town was established by Captain Elijah Reed in 1867. The museum contains artifacts and historical items relating to the

funfacts

The American social novelist, and a major figure in post–World War I literature, John Dos Passos (b. Chicago, Jan. 14, 1896, d. Sept. 28, 1970) is buried in the Yeocomico Church graveyard, near Hague. He and his wife, Elizabeth Dos Passos, retired to Westmoreland County.

menhaden fishing industry. Here you'll see unique models of boats and tools used in constructing and maintaining the fleet, and information about oystering, crabbers, and pound fishermen. Rotating exhibits and educational programs are scheduled regularly. From May through December the boats still head out for menhaden, and you can view Cockrell's Creek and the boats from a deck at the museum.

Part of the museum is the William Walker House, built in 1875. It has been refurbished and refurnished and represents a waterman's home at the turn of the twentieth century.

The museum is open daily 10:30 A.M. to 4:30 P.M. May through October, and Friday through Sunday from 10:30 A.M. to 4:30 P.M., November through mid-January and Saturday and Sunday mid-March through April. It is open by appointment at other times. Call (804) 453–6529 for additional information or visit www.rfmuseum.org. Admission is $5.00 for adults and $3.00 for seniors; for children under twelve it's free.

Drive off Route 17, following the signs for the **Virginia Institute of Marine Science** (VIMS), but for just a moment keep on driving down to the water. Gloucester Point is a great place for a view of the Yorktown River Bridge (have your camera ready). At VIMS, part of the College of William and Mary, is a free aquarium with more than fifty species of marine organisms from throughout Virginia's waters. There are eight tanks, containing from 50 to 3,000 gallons of water, and a special 200-gallon touch tank, so you may, as they say, get up close and personal.

VIMS is open Monday through Friday from 9:00 A.M. to 4:30 P.M. Be sure to ask for a complete set of some great seafood recipe brochures, at no charge. A one-acre **Teaching Marsh,** an area restored both for practical and educational purposes, provides a demonstration area for regulated wetland plant species (the educational side) and to naturally remove contaminants from the Coleman Bridge storm water runoff, thus improving the water quality in the York River (the practical side). Ninety-minute public walking tours (best suited for adults and older children) are available and can include the Teaching Marsh. They are offered on Friday from late May through August (call 804–684–7846 for tour times). Tours start in the Watermen's Hall. There's a gift shop on the premises, too. Write to VIMS, P.O. Box 1346, Gloucester Point, VA 23062, or call (804) 684–7000; www.vims.edu.

Newport News

Now, it's across the York River and into Hampton Roads. We'll head east and south and then come back to tour the historical triangle area of Williamsburg, Jamestown, and Yorktown.

Maybe it's time to write a few postcards back home, so stop at the old Newport News Post Office (101 Twenty-fifth Street, Newport News) to see the five **WPA sculptures** Mary B. Fowler was commissioned to do in 1943. They were part of the Works Projects Administration, Roosevelt's New Deal program to keep unemployed artists working. The sculptures collectively are called *Captain Newport Bringing News and Aid to the Starting Colonists* and portray progress in agriculture, medicine, and other areas of early life in the colonies.

Set on the grounds of Christopher Newport University, the **Ferguson Center for the Arts** is a new 1,700-seat concert hall where the Russian National Ballet, Sir James Galway, Ralph Stanley and the Clinch Mountain Boys, and Bill Cosby were among the performers during its 2006 inaugural season. The concert hall joins a 440-seat music and theater hall, a 200-seat studio

When Is a Mall Not Just a Mall?

Jefferson Commons, on Jefferson Avenue at Bland Boulevard in Newport News, may be just the thing natives need. Its 385,000 square feet has department stores, restaurants, boutiques, and whatever one would expect. But for travelers and come-heres (particularly those from California), the real news is there's a Trader Joe's grocery store. Now that's making progress. (757) 951–1017.

OTHER PLACES TO SEE

Fort Eustis
U.S. Army Transportation Museum
(757) 878–1115
www.transchool.eustis.army.mil
/museum/museum

Hampton
African-American Heritage Tour
(757) 727–1102 or
(800) 800–2202

Norfolk
Norfolk Tides Baseball Club
(757) 622–2222
www.norfolktides.com
Waterside Festival Marketplace
(757) 627–3300
www.watersidemarketplace.com

Oak Grove
Ingleside Plantation Vineyards and
Winery (804) 224–8687
www.ipwine.com

Virginia Beach
Ocean Breeze Fun Park
(757) 422–0718 or (800) 678–WILD
www.oceanbreezewaterpark.com

Williamsburg
Busch Gardens Williamsburg
(757) 253–3350
www.buschgardens.com
Water Country USA
(757) 253–3350 or (800) 343–7946
www.watercountryusa.com

theater, and rehearsal space. The firm of Pei Cobb Freed and Partners (of I. M. Pei fame) designed the $54 million complex (incorporating part of the old Ferguson High School) with perfect acoustics and sight lines. William R. Biddle serves as executive director. One University Place, Newport News; (757) 594–7000; www.cnu.edu/fergusoncenter.

When people say you can discover some of the best craftsmanship on Earth at the *Mariners' Museum,* believe them. Founded in 1930 by Archer M. Huntington, the museum contains one of the world's finest collections of figureheads and perhaps the largest figurehead of all time: the Lancaster Eagle.

August F. Crabtree's collection of sixteen miniature ships (at a scale of about a quarter-inch to the foot) follows the evolution of the sailing ship. Born in 1905 in Oregon, Crabtree was the grandson of a Glasgow shipbuilder. It took Crabtree and his wife, Winnifred (they met when he was building model ships for Hollywood movies and she was painting them), more than twenty-seven years to complete this world-famous collection. The ships are enclosed in glass cases with mirrors underneath so that you can see completely around them. Some boards are not in place so that you can see inside, and there's a magnifying glass on some so that you can appreciate the exacting detail work. This display is worth the visit, all by itself.

Guided tours are available, during which you might hear how Admiral Lord Nelson was shipped home in a wine casket or learn some other interesting military information.

Raising the *Monitor*

During the summer of 2001, the thirty-ton steam engine of the shipwrecked Civil War ironclad **Monitor** was raised and taken to the Newport News Shipbuilding yard on July 18. The Mariners' Museum in Newport News will take it through a ten-year conservation process. It took twenty-eight days of around-the-clock work to lift the engine from some 240 feet below the surface of the Atlantic Ocean, off the shore of Cape Hatteras, North Carolina. This project took years of planning and a coordinated recovery effort involving 148 divers from twenty-four diving commands, including 20 diving officers, 4 diving warrant officers, and 10 master divers. Some had just completed diving school, while others had more than two dozen years of diving experience.

There are twelve galleries featuring decorative arts, ship models, small crafts from workboats to pleasure craft, with one hundred fascinating full-sized boats from around the world, ships' carvings and seapower, as well as a gallery for changing exhibits.

The joy of the Tidewater-related museums probably cannot be emphasized enough, and the Mariners' Museum is no exception. Always one of my favorites, its miniature and handcrafted ship models, detailed scrimshaw, intricately carved figureheads, maritime paintings, and fine and decorative arts have left thousands speechless.

To ice that wonderful cake is the Age of Exploration Gallery, which opened in March 1992. Guarded by the 10-foot-4-inch statue (and it seems much taller) of Leif Eriksson, this display shows how scientific and technological developments in shipbuilding, ocean navigation, and cartography led to the explorations of the fifteenth and early sixteenth centuries. Exhibited in the gallery, which opened in conjunction with the quincentenary celebration of Columbus's voyage to the New World, are ship models, rare books, illustrations, maps, navigational instruments, shipbuilding tools, and other maritime artifacts. Fifteen short videos that bring the Age of Exploration to life feature footage filmed in Spain, India, and other countries. The hands-on Discovery Library features reproductions of navigational instruments and facsimiles of charts and books used by early mariners. Do you have an explorer growing up in your family? It's all sensational and can be found here.

funfacts

The Lancaster Eagle at the Mariners' Museum is a hand-carved 3,000-pound gilt eagle figurehead from the frigate USS *Lancaster,* 1881 to 1921. It has an 18½-foot wingspan.

Be sure to stop by the museum shop, which contains a large selection of maritime books, educational toys, gifts, and prints. The shop is open 10:00 A.M. to 5:30 P.M. Monday through Saturday and noon to 5:30 P.M. Sunday.

The Mariners' Museum, located at 100 Museum Drive, Newport News, is open 10:00 A.M. to 5:00 P.M. Monday through Saturday and noon to 5:00 P.M. on Sunday. It is closed on Thanksgiving Day and December 25. Admission is $8.00 for adults and $6.00 for students (757–596–2222 or 800–581–7245); www.mariner.org.

funfacts

A Fresnel lens, used at the Cape Charles, Virginia, lighthouse from 1895 until 1963, produced a concentrated beam of light that was visible up to 20 miles at sea. It now greets visitors to the Mariners' Museum's Chesapeake Bay Gallery.

The *Virginia Living Museum* combines the best and most enjoyable elements of a native wildlife park, science museum, botanical garden, aquarium, and planetarium. They are all in one inspiring, beautiful setting. Hundreds of native American eastern coastal creatures—including mammals, birds, marine life, reptiles, and insects—go about their daily routines as you discover the secrets of life in the wild. Indoors, you will find a 60-foot living panorama of the James River, beginning with life in a mountain stream and ending in the amazing depths of the Atlantic.

There's an ever-popular touch tank for a safe approach to the up-close feel. Outdoors you can stroll amid the natural beauty of the lakeside forest as a picturesque boardwalk leads you on an up-close safari into the lives of native water animals. The walk is less than $^6/_{10}$ of a mile, and there are benches along the way. You are asked to stay on the paths and not to touch the animals, enclosures, or electric fences.

If you've ever wondered how things work—say, you have a family of four with two parents working, two children in school, car pools for extracurricular activities, civic responsibilities—then take the museum's Behind the Scenes Tours. You'll learn how the animals and fish are acquired, how their diets are prepared and how the water matches the oceans and rivers, what happens when critters get sick or injured, and then learn what a herpetologist and an aquarist do. You can even watch trout being fed and see where coyotes sleep at night. The list could be endless—even longer than your to-do list.

The museum is open 9:00 A.M. to 6:00 P.M. daily from Memorial Day to Labor Day. Winter hours are 9:00 A.M. to 5:00 P.M. Monday through Saturday and noon to 5:00 P.M. Sunday. It is closed Thanksgiving, Christmas Eve, Christmas Day, and New Year's Day. Combination tickets (for museum/observatory and planetarium) are $13.00 for adults and $10.00 for children from three to twelve.

Children under three are admitted free. Children under four are not permitted in the planetarium. The museum is located at 524 J. Clyde Morris Boulevard, Newport News; (757) 595–1900; www.valiving museum.org.

For additional information about Newport News, stop by the **Newport News Visitor Center,** 13560 Jefferson Avenue (I–64, exit 250B); (888) 4WE–RFUN or (757) 886–7777; www.newport-news.org.

Hampton

The **Hampton Visitors Center** staff are available to answer your questions about area attractions and accommodations. Brochures and maps are available. Cruises of Hampton Roads Harbor, Fort Wool, and the Norfolk Naval Station also are available. The center, at 120 Old Hampton Lane, is open daily from 9:00 A.M. to 5:00 P.M. except major holidays; call (757) 727–1102 or (800) 800–2202 or visit www.hamptoncvb.com for more information.

When most Americans think of our space program, they think of the centers at Houston and Cape Canaveral. The original seven Mercury astronauts, however, trained right here, thus the street name Mercury Boulevard—thus, also, the Space Center, but back to that in a minute.

In addition to Mercury Boulevard and Commander Shepard Boulevard (named for Alan B. Shepard), there are bridges named for M. Scott Carpenter, L. Gordon Cooper, John H. Glenn, Virgil I. Grissom, Walter M. Schirra, and Donald K. Slayton. One of these days when you have nothing better to do, spend some time wandering around Hampton or poring over a map to find these historic spots. When you give up, try the Hampton Visitors Center, at 710 Settler's Landing Road. They compiled a list for me and promised to keep it handy for you.

The **Virginia Air and Space Center/Hampton Roads History Center** (600 Settlers Landing Road, Hampton) is a blast (off?). It isn't as large as the Air and Space Museum in Washington, D.C., but it isn't nearly as crowded either. Shaped like a huge wing ready for takeoff, it features walls of windows and light and space that set your creative mind in motion and your quest for adventure throbbing. Taking the Hampton city theme "from the sea to the stars," the displays are informative, interactive, touch-me, and unusual.

Imagine standing face-to-face with aviators from the past. There are thirty life-size mannequins of such people as Christopher Newport (as in Newport News), Samuel P. Langley, Orville Wright, Alan Shepard, and a generic female pilot. It's fun to check your size and stature against these giants of aviation. You can pretend you're an astronaut for a moment by projecting your face into a replica of an official NASA space suit. It makes you feel as though you're floating above it all. Little ones can pop their heads through a moon landscape like lunar gophers. For a moon relic take a look at the three-billion-year-old moon rock. Check out the ten air- and spacecraft suspended from the center's 94-foot ceiling, and take a serious gander at the *Apollo 12* command capsule, which journeyed to the moon and back, in the middle of the gallery's floor. Take your time as you walk the gantry and pretend you're going on the next shuttle launch.

At nine stories tall, the center covers 110,000 square feet, sitting on two and one-fifth acres. Within this area there are more than a hundred history, aeronautic, and space exhibits. Each end of the building is a glass wall that lets light cascade in and through the structure. The solid walls are painted a neutral color that seems to make them disappear into the horizon, so you feel as though you're standing in and among all the planes that are suspended above and around you.

You'll also want to save some time for the IMAX movie, which has included such features as *The Old Man and the Sea, Bears, Harry Potter and the Goblet of Fire,* and *Extreme.*

The Air and Space Center is open Monday through Wednesday 10:00 A.M. to 5:00 P.M. and Thursday through Sunday 10:00 A.M. to 7:00 P.M. from Memorial Day through Labor Day. The rest of the year it's open from 10:00 A.M. to 5:00 P.M. Monday through Saturday and noon to 5:00 P.M. on Sunday. The IMAX films are shown every hour on the half-hour. Admission prices for the museum only are $8.75 for adults, $7.75 for seniors, and $6.75 for students. Group discounts and combination tickets are available. For more information call (757) 727–0900 or (800) 296–0800 or visit www.vasc.org.

The NASA Visitors Center is open Monday through Saturday 8:30 A.M. to 4:30 P.M. and Sunday from noon to 4:30 P.M.; it's closed New Year's Day, Easter, Thanksgiving, and Christmas. For more information write NASA Visitors Center, Langley Research Center, Mail Stop 480, Hampton 23665-5225, or call (757) 865–2855. There's no admission charge. NASA Langley Tour tickets and tour departures are available at the Virginia Air and Space Center, (800) 296–0800 or (757) 727–0900.

The park is open daily 9:00 A.M. to 4:30 P.M. It's closed Thanksgiving, Christmas, and New Year's Days. There's no admission charge; (757) 727–1163; www.vasc.org.

To bring yourself gently down to Earth, walk out onto the plaza to see the marvelously restored 1920 Hampton Carousel, taken from Buckroe Beach. If it's open (daylight, April through December) take time for the four-minute ride ($1.50) on jumper horses with very sad eyes. For information call (757) 727–0900; 602 Settlers Landing Road, Hampton.

Aviation buffs should also catch the ***Air Power Park,*** with its awesome outdoor exhibit of missiles, rockets, and military aircraft from the country's various service branches, including a Nike surface-to-air missile, an F-105D Thunderchief, and an F-100D Super Sabre, the first Air Force fighter with supersonic performance. There's also a model airplane collection and a wind tunnel exhibit.

The park is at 413 West Mercury Boulevard, Hampton, and is open daily 9:00 A.M. to 4:30 P.M. It is closed Thanksgiving, Christmas, and New Year's Days. There is no admission charge, and the park is wheelchair accessible; (757) 727–1163.

The *Hampton University Museum* is the oldest African-American museum in the country. The world-renowned American Indian Collection consists of more than 1,600 pieces from ninety-three tribes. The collection was established in 1878 when the U.S. government began sending young Indians from western reservations to be educated at Hampton Institute. Now located in the recently renovated Beaux Arts–style Huntington Building, the museum's galleries include the Native American Gallery, the Asian and Pacific Gallery, and the Hampton (Institute/University) Gallery.

The Hampton Museum is open 8:00 A.M. to 5:00 P.M. Monday through Friday and noon to 4:00 P.M. Saturday; closed on major and campus holidays. There is no admission fee; (757) 727–5308; www.hampton.edu/museum.

The *Casemate Museum,* set in an impressive location—a cavern of rooms built within the thick walls of Fort Monroe—relates the battles of Hampton Roads, particularly during the Civil War. The story of the *Monitor* and *Merrimac* battle is told here, and you can see the area where Confederate president Jefferson Davis was imprisoned after the war. When construction of Fort Monroe was completed in 1834, it was referred to as the "Gibraltar of the Chesapeake" because of the strength of its fortifications. You can walk through the fort, the third oldest in America, and take a look at the *Old Point Comfort Lighthouse,*

A Little Chapel

The *Little England Chapel,* built around 1879 to introduce religion to post–Civil War blacks in Virginia, is the state's only known African-American missionary chapel. It contains a permanent exhibit explaining the religious lives of post–Civil War blacks in Virginia. There are handwritten Sunday school lessons, photographs, nineteenth-century religious books, and a twelve-minute video. The chapel has been designated a State and National Historic Landmark. 4100 Kecoughtan Road, Hampton; (757) 723–6803.

Old Point Comfort Lighthouse

built in 1802 and in continuous use since then. Fort Algernoume was on this site from 1609 to 1667. Fort George was built in 1727 and destroyed by a hurricane in 1749. Weakened coastal defenses during the War of 1812 allowed the British to sack Hampton and capture Washington by sailing up Chesapeake Bay.

Fort Monroe is America's only active-duty fort that is completely surrounded by a moat and is the largest stone fort ever constructed on this continent. A walking tour is available—note Quarters Number One, stop nine on

From Little Acorns

In 1863 the members of the Virginia Peninsula's black community gathered around an oak tree on the grounds of what is now Hampton University to hear the first reading of President Lincoln's Emancipation Proclamation. Mrs. Mary Peake, daughter of a free black woman and a Frenchman, conducted the first lessons taught under that tree on the university's campus. The National Geographic Society designated the *Emancipation Oak* as one of the 10 Great Trees of the World.

TOP ANNUAL EVENTS

March
Williamsburg Film Festival, Williamsburg
(757) 482–2490
www.williamsburgfilmfestival.org

March/April
Easter Decoy and Art Festival,
Chincoteague (757) 336–6161
www.chincoteaguechamber.com
Downtown Doo Dah Parade, Norfolk
(757) 441–2345

April
Ella Fitzgerald Jazz Festival
Newport News
(757) 594–8752
www.fergusoncenter.org
Flounder Fishing Tournament,
Wachapreague
(757) 787–2105
www.wachapreague.com/tournies
/spring-application.html
Historic Garden Week, statewide
(757) 428–2285 or (800) 822–3224
www.vagardenweek.org
Norfolk International Azalea Festival,
Norfolk (757) 282–2801;
www.azaleafestival.org

June
Afrikan–American Festival, Hampton
(757) 838–4721
Harborfest, Norfolk (757) 441–2345

July
Annual Pony Penning and Auction,
Chincoteague (757) 336–6161

September
Neptune Festival Boardwalk Weekend,
Virginia Beach
(757) 498–0215 or (800) 822–3224
www.neptunefestival.com

October
Eastern Shore Birding and Wildlife
Festival, Cape Charles
(757) 787–2460
www.esvachamber.org/festivals/birding
Eastern Shore of Virginia Harvest
Festival, Kiptopeke (757) 787–2460

November
100 Miles of Lights, Hampton,
Newport News, Norfolk, Portsmouth,
Virginia Beach, and Williamsburg
(800) 800–2202
Urbanna Oyster Festival, Urbanna,
(804) 758–0368

the tour. The oldest building at the fort, it was built between 1819, shortly after the fort's construction began, and 1823 and has been in use ever since.

funfacts

The Zero Mile Post at Fort Monroe is a replica of the original post that stood at Fort Monroe on Old Point Comfort, marking the end of the track on the Chesapeake and Ohio Railway, from which point all main line distances have been measured.

Follow the signs off I–64. Write to P.O. Box 51341, Fort Monroe 23651, call (757) 788–3391, or visit www.tradoc.army .mil/museum.

In Phoebus the post office's **WPA mural** is by William Calfee (who also did one of the Petersburg murals as well as those in Tazewell and Harrisonburg). It was painted in 1941 and is entitled *Chesapeake Fishermen,* a self-explanatory title.

Virginia Beach

Okay, it's time to zip across the Hampton Roads Bridge–Tunnel and head toward *Virginia Beach,* where residents and vacationers have a lot of options for their leisure time, with Mount Trashmore, outlet shopping, catching rays, or traveling back and forth across the Chesapeake Bay Bridge-Tunnel, that 20-mile-long route connecting Cape Charles on the DelMarVa Peninsula to the western shore.

The Virginia Beach **WPA mural** in the post office on Atlantic Avenue and Twenty-fourth Street is a 1939 piece by John H.R. Pickett entitled *Old Dominion Conversation Piece,* about tobacco and settlers.

Across the street is the **Norwegian Lady Statue** (a gift to Virginia Beach from the residents of Moss, Norway, in memory of the wreck of the Norwegian bark *Dictator* off the city's shore in 1891) and the **Old Coast Guard Station,** housed in the former Life Saving Station (which became the Coast Guard), the only station in Virginia that's open to the public. It was built in 1903, when the men who risked their lives to save others worked for little more than a dollar a day. There's now a gift shop inside as well as the historical memorabilia of ship-wrecks and lives saved. A Tower Cam lets you see the ocean and beach as the old sailors did (www.oldcoastguardstation.com/towercameracontent). The **Old Coast Guard Station** museum is open from 10:00 A.M. to 5:00 P.M. Monday through Saturday and noon to 5:00 P.M. on Sunday Memorial Day through September. It is closed on Sunday and Monday the rest of the year. Admission to the station is $3.00 for adults and $2.50 for seniors, and $1.00 for children six to eighteen. The museum is at the corner of Twenty-fourth Street and Atlantic Avenue, Virginia Beach; (757) 422–1587; www.oldcoastguardstation.com.

Two-thirds of the 8,000-plus acres of the **Back Bay National Wildlife Refuge** is marshlands while the rest is beach, dunes, woodland, and farm fields. The refuge is home to waterfowl, loggerhead sea turtles, and barner beach ghost crabs. Some 10,000 snow geese and a large variety of ducks stop by the refuge during December, the peak of the fall migration. You can take a self-guided walking or biking tour, or enjoy fishing to your heart's content. Stop by the visitor center for information and a bird list. It's open from 8:00 A.M. to 4:00 P.M. on weekdays and 9:00 A.M. to 4:00 P.M. on weekends, but it's closed on Saturday from November 1 through March 31.

turnonthefootlights

After a $2.6 million renovation of the 1908 vaudeville stage, the **American Theatre** reopened in Phoebus in 2000. Among the theatrical presentations are international artists, classic movies, and children's programs; 125 East Mellen Street, Hampton; (757) 722–ARTS; www.theamerican theatre.com.

Parking is $5.00, or if you're walking or biking in, it's $2.00 a family, except on those Saturdays when the center is closed and free. Pick up a bird list at the refuge office and check the Web site for fishing regulations. 4005 Sandpiper Road, Virginia Beach; (757) 721–2412; http://backbay.fws.gov.

Virginia Beach is noted for *Mt. Trashmore,* which solved two major problems in this community. First, it provided a place for a solid-waste landfill. Instead of filling shallow holes (impossible because of the high water table), the city built a mountain. Second, it provided a large recreational facility, which includes a soapbox derby run, for which you need a hill, and hills, to say the least, aren't too plentiful in this oceanside community. Mt. Trashmore, measuring 60 feet in height and more than 800 feet long, was the first overground landfill created especially as a municipal park.

Kite flying is a trip in the spring, and on a brisk March day the air is filled with colorful boxes and other flights of fancy. The park is open from 7:30 A.M. to sunset daily. Without fear of contradiction I can say that Mt. Trashmore was an inspiration for dozens of other cities in this country and in other countries as a solution for solid waste and recreational problems. Mt. Trashmore will be on the right as you drive from I–64 to Virginia Beach on the expressway. 310 Edwin Drive; (757) 473–5237; www.vbgov.com/parks.

Lynnhaven Inlet Pier has many tales to tell, if piers could talk. It was one of the longest fishing piers in the area until 2003, when Hurricane Isabel decided to alter the pier's structure. It was repaired quickly and reopened within a week. Fortunately, it's not one of the most frequented piers in the area (head for other places along the Lynnhaven Inlet or the beach at the end of the bridge-tunnel for more company and competition). However, you can catch spot, croaker (during season), trout, flounder, puppy drum, and even red.

The pier is about 5 miles north of Virginia Beach along Shore Drive to Great Neck Road. Then turn right on Starfish Road and follow it to the bay.

Sands in an Hourglass

The Guinness Book of World Records has named Virginia Beach as the world's largest pleasure beach. During 2001 the city brought in more than three million cubic yards of sand during a "Big Beach" campaign, the equivalent of a football field stacked 1,290 feet high with sand, or taller than the Empire State Building. It extended the beach to more than 300 feet wide. If standard sand pails had been used, it would have taken a line of buckets 164,000 miles long, equal to six times around Earth's equator.

Another notable attraction is the ***Lynnhaven Fish House Restaurant.*** First, a warning from Dick, a Connecticut friend who had spent a long, hard day at the Virginia forensics lab in the Virginia Beach area before dining at the restaurant. He ordered a glass of wine and, in his words, "slugged it down and found, previously invisible in the nectar of the gods, a whole grape that tried to get in my throat."

Well, obviously, wine should be sipped, not slugged, which is why the friend remains anonymous. Apparently though, there were enough "Dick" incidents that the restaurant no longer serves a grape in each glass of wine. Now, to the food itself.

Opened in 1981, the restaurant offers indoor and outdoor dining (in season). They have fresh oysters and clams, steamed shrimp, and, as they say, the largest selection of the freshest fish in all of Hampton Roads. Included with each dinner are fresh-baked Lynnhaven Bread, hush puppies, and melted marshmallows if you order the sweet potato as a side dish. The restaurant expanded its wine selection to include key vintages from all over the world, and the fully trained staff is available to assist you in making just the right choice for your dining pleasure. Look for your favorites, or establish a favorite from the selection of blush, cabernet sauvignon, chardonnay, dessert wine, merlot, pinot noir, sauvignon blanc (and other white wine), sparkling wine, and various blends and other reds.

The support staff has been with the restaurant for years, meaning you're sure to find the service is friendly and efficient. If that's not enough, the view is "second to none."

The Lynnhaven Fish House Restaurant is at 2350 Starfish Road, Virginia Beach; (757) 481–0003; www.lynnhavenfishhouse.net.

"Is there gold in seawater?" "How do waves change our coastline?" "What is it like beneath the surface of Chesapeake Bay?" The answers to these questions and more are waiting to be discovered at the ***Virginia Aquarium and Science Museum.*** From the Journey of Water section, which features a walk through the Coastal Plains River habitat and an outside boardwalk loop to view the many creatures that live in this tidal environment, to the Chesapeake Bay Hall to the Man and Marine Environment, this museum should be able to answer any question you have ever had about this tidewater area. From a 50,000-gallon aquarium to artifacts of early Indian inhabitants of the Chesapeake Bay area, the Virginia Marine Science Museum has

mascot

The lookdown fish is the mascot of the Virginia Aquarium and Marine Science Museum. The animals you see near the main entrance to the museum are harbor seals, not sea lions.

Virginia Beach Trivia

The Virginia Beach Boardwalk (actually concrete) is 40 blocks long and open for in-line skating, jogging, or strolling. A bikes-only strip of asphalt with lane markings runs next to the boardwalk.

The *Virginia Beach Sportsplex* is the first stadium in America built specifically for soccer and is the home of the Hampton Roads Mariners professional soccer team. The stadium seats 6,000 spectators and can be expanded to accommodate 45,000. 2181 North Landstown Road, (757) 427–5117.

No, you're not suddenly transported to La-La Land, but you are seeing plaques honoring such famous Virginians as Arthur Ashe, Patsy Cline, Thomas Jefferson, Pocahontas, and Edgar Allan Poe along the Virginia Legends Walk at Virginia Beach's Thirteenth Street Park. Twenty-four such notables were honored with the first plaques, which include biographical information; others will be added. 1300 Atlantic Avenue.

tried to anticipate your every wish and interest. This is a "hands-on" educational facility where you can study the waves of the Atlantic, tong for oysters of the Chesapeake Bay, examine the hidden life of coastal rivers, or watch the feeding habits of indigenous fish in the museum's huge aquarium. And with one single button, you can cause the tidal waters to flow into Chesapeake Bay.

Think turtles are just turtles? Pick up the brochure from the VMSM about saving Virginia sea turtles and think again. Learn about their body parts, nesting, diet (and learn that leatherback turtles primarily eat jellyfish, yeah!), and much more. This is another one of those places where learning is so much fun.

This is one of the most visited museums in the state and one of the most popular science museums and aquariums in the country. It's an enjoyable, hands-on educational operation from just about the moment you walk in.

The museum has undergone a $35 million expansion that tripled the size of the facility. Its 800,000 gallons of aquaria show fish that are not necessarily indigenous to Virginia but demonstrate such things as why fish swim in schools or how they use color or poison to protect or defend themselves.

There are more than one hundred hands-on interactive exhibits and a larger-than-life movie, *Into the Deep,* which is shown on the only 3-D IMAX in the state of Virginia. They show 2-D IMAX films as well.

Dolphin (summer) and whale-watching (winter) boat cruises are offered.

The museum, at 717 General Booth Boulevard, Virginia Beach, is open daily 9:00 A.M. to 7:00 P.M. from June through Labor Day and, during the rest of the year, daily 9:00 A.M. to 5:00 P.M. Museum admission is $11.95 for adults, $10.95 for seniors (sixty-five plus), and $7.95 for children (twelve and under).

IMAX admission is adults $7.50, seniors $6.75, and children $6.50. Combination tickets are $16.95, $15.95, and $12.95. Group rates are available with prior reservations. For information call (757) 437–4949 or (757) 425–FISH (425–3474) for recorded information or visit www.vmsm.com. The boat reservation number is (757) 437–BOAT (437–2628).

The **Old Cape Henry Lighthouse,** authorized and funded by America's first Congress, was built in 1791 and was the first public building authorized by that body. This lighthouse, near the entrance to the Chesapeake Bay, was used for almost ninety years, until 1881. The stones were mined in the Aquia Quarries, which also provided stone for the U.S. Capitol, the White House, and Mount Vernon. It's open from 10:00 A.M. to 5:00 P.M. mid-March to November 1, and 10:00 A.M. to 4:00 P.M. the rest of the year. For a small admission charge you can visit inside ($4.00 for adults and $2.00 for students). Enter through the Fort Story gate, off Route 60; 583 Atlantic Avenue, Fort Story. For more information, call (757) 422–9421 or visit www.apva.org/capehenry.

It was off Cape Henry that the ships of Admiral François Joseph Paul Comte de Grasse—while the land side was blocked by the Franco-American armies of Washington, Rochambeau, and Lafayette—prevented action by General Lord Cornwallis and led to his surrender to Washington on October 19, 1781. This little-mentioned skirmish apparently had no victor, but it allowed the Americans time to bring up their heavy siege guns, which marked the beginning of the end of the Revolutionary War. A statue of Admiral de Grasse, a gift from France, is located at Fort Story in Virginia Beach, within sight of the Old Cape Henry Lighthouse.

Norfolk

Travel west from Virginia Beach and you'll run into **Norfolk,** where the appeal starts at its international airport. In other airports you're almost held captive between flights. At Norfolk you can take a fifteen-minute walk and arrive at the enchanting paradise of the **Norfolk Botanical Gardens,** with its 155 acres of azaleas, camellias, dogwoods, roses, and other flora nestled among tall pines and placid waters, where something always is in bloom. The garden was started in 1938, with 200 African-American women and 20 men planting 4,000 azaleas as a WPA project. It now boasts one of the largest azalea collections on the East Coast. Norfolk's unique climate allows the coexistence of botanical species that are usually found widely separated geographically. The presence of California redwoods in the garden's collections is a perfect example. Start in the Baker Hall visitor center with its state-of-the-art audiovisual program that will help orient you to the garden's lush landscapes. A changing educational exhibit area will have programs on plant groups and other horticultural topics. Thirty-minute narrated tours are offered; they are provided on trackless train and canal boats.

If flowers aren't your primary interest, you can spend your between-flight time joining others as they do their daily walking and jogging exercises along 12 miles of meandering pathways surrounded by more than twenty theme gardens, including the Renaissance, Japanese, camellia, and holly gardens.

When you're through with the viewing or the exercising, stop by the gift shop for garden books, tools, and gifts, or visit the teahouse for lunch, snacks, and refreshments.

The grounds are the site of more than one hundred weddings a year and the annual April International Azalea Festival. The gardens are open daily 9:00 A.M. to 7:00 P.M. mid-April through mid-October and 9:00 A.M. to 5:00 P.M. the rest of the year. Adult entry fee is $6.00; seniors and military $5.00; and youths (six to sixteen) $4.00. Canal boat tours are $3.00. Look for the sign at the airport, or follow the road signs from I–64 to 6700 Azalea Garden Road, Norfolk; (757) 441–5830; www.norfolkbotanicalgarden.org.

Beautifully landscaped MacArthur Square in downtown Norfolk is the site of the four buildings that make up the ***Douglas MacArthur Memorial,*** honoring the life of Gen. Douglas MacArthur.

Inside the memorial is a theater with a continuously running twenty-four-minute film on the life and times of the general, one of the most colorful and controversial men in American history. The Jean MacArthur Research Center (named after the general's late wife) houses the library and archives, an education wing, and the administrative offices for the MacArthur Memorial and the General Douglas MacArthur Foundation. The gift shop displays General MacArthur's 1950 Chrysler Imperial limousine, which he used from 1950 to the end of his life. Nine galleries on two floors circle the rotunda where the general and his wife are buried.

Get on the NET

Getting around downtown Norfolk is easier than ever with the free *Norfolk Electric Transit (NET).* These bright blue electric buses run from the Tides baseball home at Harbor Park through the middle of town and connect to the renovated shopping and restaurant district. *MacArthur Center,* the 100,000-square-foot shopping mall of Norfolk, has Nordstrom, Dillard's, and 150 other shops, restaurants, services, and entertainment venues. The center is at 300 Monticello Avenue, Norfolk; (757) 627–6000; www.shopmacarthur.com.

There is no admission fee to the memorial, which is open 10:00 A.M. to 5:00 P.M. Monday through Saturday and 11:00 A.M. to 5:00 P.M. Sunday. It is closed New Year's, Thanksgiving, and Christmas Days. For additional information, call (757) 441–2965 or visit www.macarthurmemorial.org.

Early Jewish immigrants played an important part in Norfolk history, and their traditions are interpreted at the **Moses Myers House.** The original part of the house was constructed in 1792, then expanded in 1797 to house a commodious dining room for entertaining and two bedrooms to house the nine children Moses and Eliza Myers had. Five generations of descendants of the Myers family lived in this home until it was sold to a preservation group in 1931. In the early 1950s the City of Norfolk bought the residence, and the property is administered by the Chrysler Museum. Nearly 70 percent of the furnishings are original.

As you tour the house, you may see some renovation taking place. The interior is being redone to its 1820 appearance. The first phase, now completed, included the main rooms on the first floor and the stair hall. The color schemes and neoclassical architectural ornaments are back to where they were.

You know the famed Gilbert Stuart painting of George Washington; well, there's a matched set of portraits of the senior Myers hanging in the drawing room. Other noted American artists are also represented.

The house is at 331 East Freemason Street, Norfolk; (757) 441–1526; www .chrysler.org. It's open Wednesday through Saturday, 10:00 A.M. to 4:00 P.M., Sunday 1:00 to 4:00 P.M. Admission is $5.00 for adults and $3.00 for children. www.chrysler.org/Myers_house.asp.

The **Chrysler Museum** was named for Walter Chrysler Jr. in 1970, when Norfolk offered to add a wing and rename its museum for him if he would move his art collection from Provincetown, Massachusetts, to Norfolk. The city also named a concert hall at Scope Arena for him.

Long considered one of the finest galleries in the country, the Chrysler suffered a potentially severe setback when Chrysler, the museum's chief benefactor, died and left 751 of his works to a nephew. They had been on loan to the museum, and the blow could have been devastating. The museum, however, retains more than 15,000 works (all gifts of Chrysler) in the permanent collection, valued at more than $100 million. After a $13.5 million renovation and new wing project that increased the museum's space by half, the gallery had a reopening. Also unveiled at this time was the James H. Ricau collection of American neoclassical sculpture, considered the most splendid of its kind. The museum is open Thursday through Saturday, 10:00 A.M. to 5:00 P.M., Wednesday from 10:00 A.M. to 9:00 P.M. (voluntary donation), and Sunday 1:00 to 5:00 P.M. It is closed Monday, Tuesday, and major holidays. Admission fees are $7.00 for adults and $5.00 for students, seniors, and military. Children twelve and under are admitted free. The museum is located at 245 West Olney Road, Norfolk; (757) 664–6200; www.chrysler.org.

For family research the **Kirn Memorial Library** is the location of the Sargeant Memorial Room for historical and genealogical information. William Henry Sargeant was head librarian from 1895 until his death in 1917. He started the extensive collection of Norfolk and Virginia materials in the 1890s, and it included census records (Virginia, 1810–1910; North Carolina, 1800–1910; and other holdings); newspapers from 1736; "how-to" books on genealogy; magazines of historical and genealogical interest; photographs of buildings, people, and places from the late 1800s to the present; early postcard scenes of Norfolk (particularly the 1907 Jamestown Exposition); Norfolk directories from 1801; assorted high school and college yearbooks from the early 1900s; and much more. All of this can help your historical and genealogical research. Of course, if you have materials such as old pictures or telephone books or family histories and would like to find a safe place to keep them, the librarian will be delighted to accept your gift.

The Kirn Library, at 301 East City Hall Avenue, is open Monday through Thursday 10:00 A.M. to 9:00 P.M., Friday from 10:00 A.M. to 5:30 P.M., Saturday from 10:00 A.M. to 5:00 P.M., and Sunday from 1:00 to 5:00 P.M. The Sargeant Room is open Monday, Tuesday, Thursday, and Saturday 10:00 A.M. to 5:00 P.M., Wednesday from 10:00 A.M. to 9:00 P.M., and Sunday 1:00 to 5:00 P.M. For more information call (757) 664–READ; www.npl.lib.va.us.

Anyone who's spent any time in Norfolk is sure to mention **Doumar's Drive-in.** Abe Doumar created the ice-cream cone at the 1904 St. Louis Exposition. He originally called his rolled-up wafer that contained ice cream the "ice-cream cornucopia." After that he opened a concession at Coney Island in 1905 and visited state fairs (President Teddy Roosevelt had a cone at Raleigh, North Carolina). In 1907 a shop was opened in Ocean View, Virginia, where in 1925 his brother George and crew sold 22,600 cones in a single day. After the 1933 hurricane destroyed much of Ocean View Park, George opened the Doumar Drive-in at Nineteenth and Monticello Streets in Norfolk. It was the first and is now one of the last curbside restaurants in Virginia.

Although many people claim the credit for making the first ice-cream cone, Doumar's story stands up the best. The Smithsonian Institution has collected some of his pictures and memorabilia to add to an exhibit in the Museum of American History in Washington, D.C.

Doumar's is open 8:00 A.M. to 11:00 P.M. Monday through Thursday and 8:00 A.M. to 12:30 A.M. weekends. It is located at 1919 Monticello Avenue, Norfolk; (757) 627–4163; www.doumars.com.

In 1912 a grand lady, the **Wells Theatre,** now the **Virginia Stage Company at the Wells Theatre,** opened to a capacity house with the musical *The Merry Countess*. The theater was converted into a movie house in 1935 after such stars as Billie Burke, Douglas Fairbanks, Fred and Adele Astaire, Will Rogers, and others had trod her boards. As at other theaters of the time, the sixties brought the garish light of X-rated flicks, and a bar was built where the stage had been. The fair damsel was saved from such distress when the Virginia Stage Company took over in October 1979 and the bar was removed. The thrust stage was built, and the lobby was returned to its approximate original size. The interior and exterior were scrubbed clean, paint was applied, seats were reupholstered, new carpet was laid, and productions once again were mounted.

The Virginia Stage Company presents a handful of plays each year, usually worth seeing, but the amazing artistry that went into this steel-reinforced concrete structure of the pre–Beaux Arts period is a command performance. The Wells Theatre is at 108–114 East Tazewell Street, Norfolk; (757) 627–1234; www.vastage.com.

The fifty-five-acre **Virginia Zoological Park** has been established to accurately reflect an entire habitat for its more than 320 animals and birds, so when you visit you will find plants in the animal exhibits and animals in the plant exhibits. With the monkeys are vines and assorted habitat plants; with the cats are jungle flora. This is such an important part of the operation that visitors receive a *Botanical Conservatory Guide* to help you through the zoo.

Three special planting areas—Gardens for the Mentally Retarded, Gardens for the Blind, and the 4-H Children's Garden—are grouped around the conservatory, which was built in 1907. Also there are more than 3,000 blooming

cannonballrun

Well, actually it's the *Cannonball Trail* winding its way along historic sites in downtown Norfolk. The walk-it-yourself tour is a storytelling stage for interpreting 400 years of Norfolk's history with forty stops along the way. Begin your sojourn at the Freemason Street Reception Center, 401 East Freemason Street, Norfolk; (757) 664-6620 or (800) 368-3097; www.norfolkcvb.com.

annuals and 150 hanging baskets. The rose garden has beds of floribunda, hybrid tea, and climbing varieties. Although the zoo has been known (adversely) for its outdated exhibits, there's a large campaign to improve the situation. Signs of improvement include two new, rare red-ruffed lemurs, which were acquired a few years ago by donations under the Species Survival Plan. In March 2005, the Indianapolis Zoo donated Cita, an African elephant.

The zoo is open 10:00 A.M. to 5:00 P.M. daily except Thanksgiving, Christmas, and New Year's Days. Admission is $7.00 for adults and $5.00 for children under twelve; children under two get in free. The park is at 3500 Granby Street, Norfolk; (757) 441–2374; www.virginiazoo.org.

The **d'ART Center** (Dockside Art Review of Tidewater), long housed on College Place, has moved to the heart of downtown's historic Selden Arcade. The complex features 1930s Art deco–style architecture and houses fifty artists (sculptors, painters, jewelers, potters, etc.) who create, display, and sell their works. Free studio tours are available, and children's and adult classes and workshops are offered. Five galleries hold changing exhibits of local, regional, and national artists.

Open 10:00 A.M. to 6:00 P.M. Tuesday through Saturday, and 1:00 to 5:00 P.M. on Sunday, there's no admission charge so you should be able to afford a wonderful souvenir that you wouldn't find anywhere else. 208 East Main Street, Selden Arcade, Norfolk; (757) 625–4211; www.d-artcenter.org.

inhonorandmemory

On October 12, 2001, a memorial was dedicated to the victims of the bombing of the **USS Cole** and to the crew members who saved the ship from sinking. The memorial, comprising seventeen granite slabs encircling a 10-foot-tall monolith, is on the grounds of the Naval Station, Norfolk; (757) 444–7955 or (757) 322–2330; www.navstanorva.navy.mil.

We all "know" that milk comes from stores, not cows. And, unless your children have watched or helped you put up jams and jellies, one can only assume that the little ones think these things come from stores, too.

So, take your school-age children to **Rowena's** to watch them make jams and jellies, and pound cakes, cooking sauces, and other items. Carrot jam is a Rowena's specialty. The kitchen boasts two extra-large mixers that used to be on the US *United States*. Rowena Fullinwider started this operation in 1983 and now is doing a million-dollar business shipping food to such exotic places as Guam and Finland. Take the paper tour hat, try some samples, and receive a placemat children can color. Tours are available from January through mid-

October, Monday through Wednesday (closed holidays), from 9:00 A.M. through 3:00 P.M. Call for reservations, please; allow thirty minutes, plus time in the gift shop where you can buy cakes, sauces, foods produced for Colonial Williamsburg, recipes, and children's story cookbooks *The Adventures of Rowena and the Wonderful Jam and Jelly Factory* and *The Adventures of Rowena and Carrot Jam the Rabbit*. Remember, the factory can get very warm during the summer months. The store is open all year, and a catalog is available, 758 West Twenty-second Street, Norfolk; (800) 980–CAKE or (757) 627– 8699; www.rowenas.com.

Not everything is old in Virginia, although it may cover historic material. ***Nauticus, the National Maritime Center*** (1 Waterside Drive, Norfolk), is a hands-on entertainment and education center with scores of interesting exhibits about the exploration of the world's oceans. This is a wonderful place to learn how vast the influences of water are on our lives, for it encompasses marine biology and oceanography, commercial shipping, naval technology, shipbuilding, and energy exploration. Whether your fascination is with science, technology, commerce, or the siren call of the deep, you'll see how the sea connects to our existence—and it's fun.

What does all this mean? Simply that you can sit in the captain's chair in the Navy pilothouse and observe the harbor from the bridge. You can plot ships in the harbor on the live Nauticus radar. How would you like to land your plane (F-14 or prop) on an aircraft carrier (videogame) or be a weatherman and conduct your own television show? One of my favorites in any marine exhibit is the touch pool, where you can feel the creatures of the sea, and Nauticus has one. Kids of various ages love periscopes, so they can check this one out and target in on a ship in the harbor.

This $52 million project is set on three levels at Norfolk's Waterside complex, at the west end of the waterfront, adjacent to Town Point Park. There's

Home Port

As part of the U.S. Navy's 225th anniversary in late fall 2000, the battleship **USS Wisconsin** was located adjacent to Nauticus. Launched December 7, 1943, the warship—at 888 feet one of the longest ever built—was one of the last four battleships built by the United States for service in World War II. It also saw action during the Korean conflict and the Persian Gulf action. Norfolk was the home port of the *Wisconsin* during most of its active-duty career. Included in locating the ship here was the building of a berth and a connecting walkway to the museum. The main deck and 01–03 levels are open, free of charge. www.thenmc.org/wisconsin.

Home Porting

Home porting is the phrase used by the cruise industry as cruise ships are based in various ports around the country, eliminating the need for travelers to fly to somewhere to get somewhere.

Holland America's *Maasdam* has been calling Norfolk home for a while, and occasionally other ships sail from here as well. So, Norfolk decided to give the ships and passengers a new home with a $36 million ship terminal due to open in the fall of 2006. The 80,000-square-foot two-story terminal, located between Nauticus and Town Point Park, is made of corrugated steel and glass that gives it a smooth, nautical look. It's the first cruise terminal in the nation to fully comply with Homeland Security standards.

If you think that's a steep price to pay just to make you feel comfortable, realize that they expect each passenger will spend $104 on land purchases (hotel, restaurant, gas, souvenirs) and that more than 105,000 passengers and 34,000 crewmembers spent an estimated $15,000,000 in 2005. And there's about $1.2 million in passenger head tax, parking revenues, and dockage fees.

Norfolk certainly knows its starboard from its port.

docking space on the water for research ships and active Navy ships, which you may visit.

The Aegis Theater tests your reactions and defense mechanisms, but it's a lot like what the "kids" say about the Fox television network, "If it's too loud, you're too old." The Aegis was too loud for me, but the younger set really seems to like it.

Exhibits have been assembled with the assistance of the Coast Guard, Navy, Old Dominion University, Norfolk State University, the College of William and Mary's Institute of Marine Science, and the National Oceanic and Atmospheric Administration. In addition, the Hampton Roads Naval Museum has been relocated to this spot. There is no charge to visit this museum. Nauticus is open daily 10:00 A.M. to 6:00 P.M. May through Labor Day 30; 10:00 A.M. to 5:00 P.M. Tuesday through Saturday and noon to 5:00 P.M. Sunday the rest of the year. Admission is $9.95 for adults and $7.50 for children.

Parking is across the street (and down the street and around the block), and if you're taking children (even adult-age children), make sure you plan to stay a very long time, for it's incredibly interesting. For additional information call Nauticus at (757) 644–1000 or (800) 664–1080; www.nauticus.org. For more information about the Hampton Roads Naval Museum, call (757) 444–8971.

Portsmouth

West of Norfolk in the town of Portsmouth, Herb Simpson said, "Virginia has an outstanding record of producing great athletes," when he started the *Virginia Sports Hall of Fame and Museum* here. After a look at the Texas Sports Hall of Fame in Dallas, he thought Virginia should honor its talent, too, so he helped organize the Hall of Fame in 1966, and in March 1972 the first induction banquet was held in Portsmouth. It opened in Olde Towne on April 3, 1977. A 35,000-square-foot facility opened in April 2005, and it has a digital theater with a 16-foot-high definition project screen to show Virginia's sports traditions and televised games. That's where you can see uniforms, trophies, and other memorabilia highlighting the careers and records of Cy Young, Sam Snead, Arthur Ashe, Norman Snead, and Shelly Mann. Recipients must have been born in Virginia or have made significant contributions to their sport(s) in Virginia.

The Virginia Sports Hall of Fame and Museum honors 208 Virginia athletes, representing twenty sports, and is one of only sixteen official state Sports Halls of Fame in the country. The architectural team, van Dijk Pace Westlake, is known for its work with both the cultural arts and nonprofit organizations across the country. Among the twenty-plus designs that helped earn the firm the Portsmouth project are the Cleveland Museum of Art, Cleveland Museum of Natural History, Temple Hoyne Buell Theatre in Denver, The Orpheum Theatre in Phoenix, Wausau ArtsBlock in Wisconsin, and Museum of Progress in Scottsdale, Arizona. Even if you aren't eligible, you can try your skills at basketball, baseball, football, soccer, and auto racing. From Labor Day through Memorial Day, the Hall is open from 9:00 A.M. to 5:00 P.M. Monday through Thursday, 9:00 A.M. to 7:00 P.M. on Saturday, and 11:00 A.M. to 5:00 P.M. on Sunday. It's closed on Monday the rest of the year. Admission is $6.00 per person. Children four and under are free. The hall is located at 206 High Street, Portsmouth; for more information call (757) 393–8031; www.virginiasportshalloffame.com.

ferrymeback tooldvirginny

The first ferry service in America was established in 1636 on the Elizabeth River between Portsmouth and Norfolk. The *Gosport,* the first steam-powered ferry, was christened in 1832 and crossed the Elizabeth River in five minutes.

Bordering downtown Portsmouth's Olde Towne historic district, the museum is easily reachable by car or public transportation and is just a short walk from the Elizabeth River passenger ferry, the Renaissance Hotel and Waterfront Conference Center, and the Riverfront Performing Arts Center.

The "Path of History" will link two of the nation's oldest Navy facilities, the Naval Medical center and the Naval Shipyard, both in Portsmouth, some time in 2007. A one-acre park sits at the south end of the path, near the shipyard, and features brick walkways and two 75,000-pound propellers from naval supply ships. A dozen signs featuring key milestones in the shipyard's 200-plus-year history and various artifacts will be erected throughout the park.

A three-acre park at the north end, at the entrance to the country's first Navy hospital (built in 1830), will also feature artifacts and historical signs of the hospital's history.

The ***Children's Museum of Virginia*** is more than 54,000 square feet of foot-stomping, bubble-blowing, music-making educational fun. Located in Olde Towne Portsmouth, the museum is based on the philosophy that children learn by doing. With more than ninety interactive exhibits (making it the largest interactive children's museum in Virginia) dedicated to enhancing the cultural, educational, and recreational development of children, the museum encourages a lifelong love of learning.

Inside the candy-colored walls of the museum, you'll find a sixty-four-seat planetarium with wheelchair access; a bubble machine that lets children explore surface tension, refraction, reflection, and geometry through bubbles; and a science circus that encourages scientific discovery through the manipulation of mazes, hydraulic lifts, pulleys, and perpetual-motion machines. There's also a "Rock Climb," an operable crane for early construction lessons, and a quiet room for family time-out.

Phase II of this museum includes a train collection that's a must-see for children of all ages. The $1 million train collection is said to be the largest on the East Coast. Admission is $6.00 for anyone over the age of two. The museum is open Tuesday through Saturday 9:00 A.M. to 5:00 P.M. and on Sunday from 11:00 A.M. to 5:00 P.M. in the winter. From Memorial Day to Labor Day, it's open Monday through Saturday from 9:00 A.M. to 5:00 P.M. and on Sunday from 11:00 A.M. to 5:00 P.M. It's located at 221 High Street; for more information call (757) 393–5238; www.childrensmuseumva.com.

While you're in Portsmouth's Olde Towne, take the long (one-hour) or short (fifteen-minute) walking tour along the brick sidewalks through this oldest portion of Portsmouth. Land patents were granted as early as 1659. Look for Historic Portsmouth markers on the streetlamps, which indicate stopping points. Pick up information at the ***Portsmouth Visitor Information Center,*** 6 Crawford Parkway, Portsmouth 23704, North Landing (at the foot of High Street); (800) 767–8782 or (757) 393–5111; www.portsmouth.va.us/tourism.

Along the way you'll see the ***Cassell House,*** with its hand-carved arched doorway and stone lintels and sills at the windows; the Old Courthouse, built in 1846; Trinity Church, the oldest church in Portsmouth, dating back to 1761; and numerous other buildings that represent a variety of architectural styles and influences including Dutch colonial, English basement, Gothic Revival, Victorian, Federal, and Romanesque Revival.

Additional information about Portsmouth's architecture is available for a slight charge at the Office of City Planning, One High Street. The walking-tour brochure is free. Portsmouth Convention and Visitors Bureau is located at 505 Crawford Street, Portsmouth. Call (757) 393–5327 or (800) PORTS–VA for more information.

Isle of Wight

The active *Isle of Wight Tourism Bureau* invites you to stop by before you start wandering the lovely streets of town. The Visitors Center is located at 335 Main Street, Smithfield, and it offers a six-minute video of the area. The docents are very knowledgeable about all the attractions and surrounding areas. Call (757) 357–5182 or (800) 365–9339 for additional information or visit www.smithfield-virginia.com.

William A. Cheever's 1941 painting *Captain John Smith Trading with the Indians* is the **WPA mural** on the Smithfield Post Office wall at 234 Main Street. It's said to be a scene from life at Burwell's Bay, 6 miles north on Route 10 out of Smithfield off Route 621.

Smithfield may be the "Ham Capital of the World," but that doesn't mean you can tour the Smithfield or Gwaltney (P. D. Gwaltney Sr. started his curing process in 1870) ham processing plants.

The Smithfield curing process is protected by law, and only a ham cured within the Smithfield town limits can bear the name. You can, however, smell the delicious aroma for miles around, and you can tour the *Isle of Wight Museum* to see exhibits on the Civil War and Indian artifacts, as well as a display about the history of ham. There's also a reproduction of an old country store.

The Isle of Wight Museum, at 103 Main Street, Smithfield, is free and open Tuesday through Saturday from 10:00 A.M. to 4:00 P.M. and Sunday from 1:00 to 5:00 P.M. For further details call the museum at (757) 357-7459 or the Isle of

funfacts

When you stop by the Isle of Wight Museum, take a look at the interactive exhibit of a one-ton-plus ham biscuit. A Guinness World Record was awarded for this super-size edible created in honor of Smithfield's 250th anniversary. You can also see Smithfield Ham's oldest ham—more than one hundred years old—protected in a glass case.

Wight Convention and Visitors Bureau at (757) 357–5182 or (800) 365–9339 or visit www.smithfield-virginia.com.

Pick up the brochure for the scenic Smithfield ***Historic Old Town Walking Tour*** and proceed past buildings dating from the mid- and late-1750s (the completely restored Old Courthouse—which is one of the state's oldest operating courthouses—and Clerk's Office at 130 Main Street and Pollard House at 108 Cary, the Old Jail at 106 North Mason, the Eason-Whitley House at 220 South Church, and others) up to pre–Civil War times. The mix of housing styles is almost eclectic. Early residents either tore down or updated their homes to make way for the newest styles (keeping up with the Smiths rather than the Joneses, if you will). Therefore, as you stroll around, you'll see Colonial, Federal, and Victorian styles. Fifteen homes and four buildings, fourteen of which predate the Revolutionary War, are authentically eighteenth century. You can also view the four identical Victorian houses on Main Street and the Gingerbread Cottage on Grace Street. You can spend at least ninety minutes on this walk and expand it to three hours. For information call (757) 357–5182 or (800) 365–9339.

Guided walking tours are offered by the Tourism Bureau. Group tours are available and must be scheduled in advance. Agricultural tours also are available, in season, to see peanuts from seeds to shelling and grading and cotton from plants to ginning. For additional information call the Tourism Bureau at (757) 357–5182 or (800) 365–9339.

Gracious lodging is available at the ***Smithfield Inn and Tavern Bed and Breakfast,*** said to be one of the town's most enduring landmarks. It's been providing lodging in its five rooms (some with fireplaces) and serving meals since 1752, with slight interruptions when it was used as a rectory for the Christ Episcopal Church and for a period after the Civil War when it was uninhabitable. The inn is located at 112 Main Street, Smithfield; (757) 357–1752; www.smithfieldinn.com.

Those who love to wander the waters around the James River and find their way to Pagan River have been delighted with ***Smithfield Station Waterfront Inn and Marina,*** at the junction of the two creeks that form the river. Run by Ron and Tina Pack, it's a carefree place dedicated to those who want to pull up to a dock, be greeted by the owners, and not have to worry about "dressing" for dinner. The specialties at the restaurant are, naturally enough, seafood and pork, including Smithfield "Lean Generation Pork." Entertainment and special events are held on the boardwalk adjacent to the restaurant. Newlyweds and anniversary celebrants might enjoy the Cape Chesapeake Bay–style lighthouse building with honeymoon suites.

Stay a day or two and rent a bicycle or canoe to really "sit back" and relax.

Then head out and go crabbing or look for osprey and eagles, deer, and muskrat; 415 South Church Street; (757) 357–7700; www.smithfieldstation.com.

About 2 miles south of Smithfield on Route 10 is historic **St. Luke's Church (or St. Luke's Shrine),** known also as the "Old Brick Church," the nation's oldest original Gothic church. The construction date is pegged at 1632, although the style is perhaps that of seventy-five years earlier. On the other hand, the earliest Anglican records date several decades after the 1630s. One theory says that the church was built by members of the Lost Colony of Roanoke Island, even before the settlement of Jamestown. At the entrance you'll find a wicket door within a larger door. Inside are a mid-seventeenth-century communion table and chairs, a seventeenth-century silver baptismal basin, original Gothic tracery windows, and a 1665 English organ.

The church, at 14477 Benn's Church Boulevard, Smithfield, is open Tuesday through Sunday, except for major holidays and the month of January. Tours are scheduled from 9:30 A.M. through 4:00 P.M. Tuesday through Saturday and from 1:00 to 3:30 P.M. on Sunday. For more information call (757) 357–3367; www.historicstlukes.org.

Fort Boykin Historic Park, on the high cliffs over the James River (which is navigable to Richmond), has been around since 1623 and has been involved in every military campaign fought on American soil. It first protected the colonists against the "Spaniards by sea and the Indians by land" and then was refortified during the Revolutionary War. It is named in honor of Major Francis Boykin, a member of General George Washington's staff. Its current seven-pointed star shape was created during the War of 1812, but much of the property was destroyed by a Union landing party. While the American poet Sidney Lanier was stationed here during the Civil War, he wrote "Hoe Cakes" and "Beautiful Ladies" and started his novel *Tiger Lilies.* The property had pretty much returned to nature until 1908, when Mr. and Mrs. Herbert Greer bought it and started landscaping the grounds. Picnickers are welcome.

Located at 7410 Ft. Boykin Trail, Smithfield, the park is open daily 8:00 A.M. to dusk; (757) 357–5182 or (800) 365–9339; www.smithfield-virginia.com /attractions.

Just the name of the **Great Dismal Swamp National Wildlife Refuge** sounds depressing, but nature lovers should jump for joy. This 111,000-acre swamp suffered some damage during Hurricane Isabel, but all that humans can and should do has been done. Wander along the 140 miles of hiking and biking trails and you'll see bald cypress, shady creeks, and maybe barred owls, otters, bats, raccoons, and bears. Canoe and kayak access to Lake Drummond is via the feeder ditch near Chesapeake. There are no entrance fees.

The headquarters is open from 7:30 A.M. to 4:00 P.M. Monday through

Friday. 3100 Desert Road, Suffolk; (757) 986–3705; http://greatdismalswamp
.fws.gov.

Surry

Bacon's Castle in Surry doesn't exactly look like a castle, and Nathaniel Bacon
(for whom it's named) probably never visited, but the 1665 high Jacobean-style
structure is said to be the oldest known brick dwelling in North America, and it
has given its name to the area. Built by Arthur Allen, it was seized and occupied
for three months in 1676 by troops who supported the rebel Nathaniel Bacon in
an event known as Bacon's Rebellion. The building has Dutch-gabled ends and
triple diamond stack chimneys on each end, and it has been purchased by the
Association for the Preservation of Virginia Antiquities. Two rooms are furnished
from the original inventory, and there are archaeological and architectural
exhibits offered, as well as a slide show. One of the digs has uncovered an old
trash pit with an "AA" (for Arthur Allen) bottle seal on it.

Guided tours are available 10:00 A.M. to 4:00 P.M. Tuesday through Saturday
and noon to 4:00 P.M. Sunday from April through October and by appointment.
November and March it is open only on weekends, and by appointment
December through February. Admission is $7.00 for adults, $5.00 for seniors,
and $4.00 for children six through seventeen. Bacon's Castle is just off the
intersection of Routes 10 and 31 at 465 Bacon's Castle Trail, Surry. For details
call (757) 357–5976 or visit www/apva.org/baconscastle.

Somehow it wouldn't seem right if you left Surry County without stopping
in at the **Surrey House Restaurant** on Route 31 (757–294–3389, 800–200–
4977; www.surreyhouserestaurant.com), a favorite destination for Williamsburg
residents, especially on a sunny Sunday after church. In operation since 1954,
the Surrey House specializes in ham, seafood, pork, and poultry dishes as well
as other regional fare—it's Southern cooking at its best! I recommend that you
begin your meal with peanut soup, a creamy delicacy full of chunky bits of
world-famous Virginia peanuts. As a main dish, the Surrey House Surf and Turf
is typically Virginian, featuring a combination of ham and crab cakes. Other
regional dishes include delicious hamhocks, great Southern fried chicken, and
homemade desserts. For the latter, I prefer the peanut raisin pie, a proudly
served local variation on the South's ubiquitous pecan pie. It's delicious. This
restaurant has a waiting list on weekends and holidays, so reservations are
recommended.

The free **Scotland-Jamestown Ferry,** or the Jamestown-Scotland Ferry
(clearance 12 feet, 6 inches), connects Route 31 over the James River and is
the only twenty-four-hour state-run ferry operation in Virginia. Four ferries

(*Virginia, Williamsburg, Surry,* and *Pocahontas*) can carry from twenty-eight to seventy cars. Call (757) 294–3354 or (800) VA–FERRY for additional information or visit www.virginiadot.org/comtravel/ferry-jamestown.asp.

Williamsburg

Now it's time to head east-northeast, and then west-northwest, traveling along Route 58 as the most direct route. Then pick up Interstate 664 to take the Monitor-Merrimac Memorial Bridge Tunnel and go toward the historic triangle of Jamestown, Yorktown, and Colonial Williamsburg.

In 1984 a 92,000-square-foot reception center was opened for ***Carter's Grove.*** Located about 6 miles east of Colonial Williamsburg, this was once a 300,000-acre plantation where Robert "King" Carter's grandson built a mansion in the 1750s. The facility has a ticket and information desk, a one-hundred-seat theater, an exhibit gallery, a gift shop, a vending area, and restrooms.

After a brief orientation film, shown about every twenty minutes (last showing is at 4:20 P.M.), you cross a deep, wooded ravine via a footbridge to the mansion or to an overlook for an introductory presentation of the archaeological dig of the site of Wolstenholme Towne, an early seventeenth-century settlement that was destroyed by Indians in 1622. From there you can hear descriptions at nine barrel-housed stations around the grounds about the items that have been found and how they are used to document the partial reconstruction of palisades, fences, and buildings. Most of these sites were explored between 1976 and 1981, but diggers are still working the site, waiting for it to reveal its historical significance.

Operating hours vary, and the area is closed from January through mid-March. It's also closed on Monday in season. Call (800) HISTORY for further details. Admission is $18.00 for adults and $9.25 for children for a one-day pass to all the exhibits at Carter's Grove. You can purchase tickets to all of the exhibits at the ***Colonial Williamsburg Visitor's Center.*** There are several ticket options for touring Colonial Williamsburg and Carter's Grove. The Freedom Pass is $59 for adults and $29 for youths ages six through seventeen; it includes unlimited visits for an entire year plus free admission to events held exclusively for Freedom Pass Holders, discounts at two dozen stores in the area, and other area benefits. A quarterly newsletter is included, and you receive special visitor services at the Freedom Pass Hospitality Center. Special rates are available from January through mid-March in connection with stays at Colonial Williamsburg hotels (757–220–7205; www.history.org).

The ***Jamestown Island, Yorktown Battlefield,*** and ***Cape Henry Memorial*** are administered by the Colonial National Historical Park.

Jamestown represents the first permanent English settlement (1607) and Yorktown covers the last major engagement of the American Revolutionary War (1781), thus defining the beginning and the end of English Colonial America.

The historic triangle is connected via the 23-mile scenic Colonial Parkway (757–898–3400).

All national park grounds close daily at sunset. Jamestown Entrance Station is open 8:30 A.M. to 4:30 P.M. daily throughout the year; closed December 25. The Jamestown Visitor Center is open 9:00 A.M. to 5:00 P.M. daily throughout the year; closed December 25. The Yorktown Visitor Center is open daily: 8:30 A.M. to 5:00 P.M. from early April through mid-June and mid-August through late October; 8:30 A.M. to 5:30 P.M. in summer; and 9:00 A.M. to 5:00 P.M. in winter from late October through early April. It is closed December 25.

Admission fees for Yorktown are $5.00 for adults; Jamestown is $8.00 for adults; and both are free for children sixteen and under. A combined ticket is $10.00 for adults and is good for a seven-day period. The yearly park pass, Golden Age, Golden Eagle, and Golden Access passports are honored.

At the ***Jamestown Visitor Center*** there's a glasshouse where you can watch glassblowing demonstrations by costumed crafters. Ruins of the original glass furnace are nearby. The reconstructed Jamestown Church is here, and you can see the 1639 Church Tower (great photographs), plus statues of Pocahontas and Captain John Smith. There's a bookstore and museum.

Take time to see the fifteen-minute film at the visitor center and to take the walking tour, which takes about thirty minutes. This is where you'll learn the interesting points of life back then, such as what the native Indians did with bear grease. A 5-mile trail is perfect for a leisurely walk or jog on a comfortable afternoon (757–229–1733). Several seasons of excavations at the APVA Jamestown Rediscovery Archaeological Project, Jamestown Colonial National

It's a New World

The New World, an epic film written and directed by Terrence Malick and starring Colin Farrell as John Smith, Christian Bale as John Rolfe, Christopher Plummer as Christopher Newport, August Schellenberg as Chief Powhatan, and Q'orianka Kilcher as Pocahontas, opened in movie theaters in January 2006 and portrays the adventure of the first encounter of European and Virginia Indian cultures during the founding of Jamestown settlement in 1607. What a great advertising campaign New Line Cinema created for the Jamestown 2007 celebration! *The New World* shot for six months in Charles City and James City Counties, in Richmond, at the Chicohominy Wildlife Management Area.

Historical Park (1367 Colonial Parkway, Jamestown; 757–229–0412; www.apva
.org) have uncovered more than 160,000 artifacts dating from the first half of
the seventeenth century. Nearly half the objects date to the first years of
English settlement. They've also uncovered more than 170 feet of palisade line,
the east bulwark, three large trash pits, and a building—all part of James Fort.
Contrary to some opinion, the evidence uncovered indicates that James Fort
was not washed into the river. The dig is open daily 8:30 A.M. to 4:30 P.M., and
children are admitted free.

At the *Yorktown Battlefield Museum* (757–898–3400) there's a bookstore, original and reconstructed eighteenth- and nineteenth-century earthworks, Surrender Field, original eighteenth-century buildings such as the
Moore House and Nelson House, the Victory Monument, French Memorial,
and Yorktown National Cemetery (Civil War era).

For some reason, when many people visit this historic triangle, the
Yorktown Victory Center seems to be omitted, which is good for you, as it
means that the center isn't as crowded as it might be. It's not good for the others because they miss the important lessons the center has to tell. Start by
viewing the documentary *The Road to Yorktown,* in which the sights and
sounds of the naval Battle of the Capes and subsequent events at Yorktown
are brought to life. "The American and British Foot Soldier, 1775–1785"
explores—through original artifacts, period graphics, and documents—life as
led by soldiers in training and the women who lived during this era. Visit a
surgeon's tent, see how meals were prepared, or watch a carpenter prepare
wood for finishing the construction of an eighteenth-century–style tobacco
barn in post–Revolutionary War days

"The Legacy of Yorktown: A Nation of Immigrants" is a new long-term
exhibition at the Yorktown Victory Center that chronicles immigration to
Virginia from before the 1607 founding of Jamestown to modern times. It
focuses on the Constitution and the Bill of Rights as a result of the American
Revolution. Among the considerations for crossing the Atlantic that are covered
are economic, political, and religious. The Witnesses to the Revolution gallery
explores the Declaration as a radical document that made people decide
whether to side with the Americans, the British, or remain neutral. (757–898–
3400, 757–253–4838; www.historyisfun.org). Admission to Yorktown Victory
Center is $8.25 per adult and $4.00 per child or $17.00 per adult and $8.75 per
child for a combination ticket to Yorktown and Jameston Settlement.

As a child, my visits to *Jamestown Settlement,* previously Jamestown
Festival Park, were at least an annual treat. It's amazing how much things have
changed over the years as historians have learned more about what happened
here and how people lived here 300 years ago.

Stockades used to be a feature; they aren't now, because historians determined that stockades weren't used in Colonial Jamestown.

Costumed guides no longer talk in first person because they found it off-putting for some people who didn't know how to ask questions and difficult to stay in character when confronted with a question about cameras, for example. The guides still wear what was worn, to some extent, but you'll also find guys with earrings, and one would suspect that the early settlers didn't do that.

This is the place to explore bark- and mat-covered dwellings, a garden, tanning deerskin hides, and preparing meals. Board the re-created *Susan Constant,* the *Discovery,* or the *Godspeed* to see how small these ships were that brought the original colonists here in a four-month journey. Try on armor and see military training and drills. Visit the church, the storehouse, and the guardhouse to learn why each was so important to the early settlement.

Starting in the fall of 2006, a 30,000-square-foot exhibit area will have a 250-seat theater showing an introductory film about seventeenth-century Virginia through the cultures of the Powhatan Indian, England, and western-central Africa. Historical knowledge in an innovative design set the stage for the founding of America's first permanent English colony in 1607 and explores the impact of the Jamestown settlement. More than 500 artifacts from seventeenth-century Europe and Africa, including portraits, documents, furnishings, tools, weapons, ceremonial and decorative objects, and hundreds of Virginia archaeological items, are displayed in the galleries.

The Jamestown Settlement, at Route 31 and Colonial Parkway, is open daily except Christmas and New Year's Days. A living-history museum depicts life in America's first permanent English colony, featuring replicas of three ships, a palisaded fort, and an Indian village. Exhibition galleries and film tell the history of the Jamestown and the Powhatan Indians. It's open daily except Christmas and New Year's Days (757–253–4838, 888–593–4682; www .historyisfun.org) from 9:00 A.M. to 5:00 P.M. Admission fees are $11.25 for adults and $5.50 for children from six through twelve. Parking is free. A combination ticket for Jamestown Settlement and Yorktown Victory Center is $16.75 for adults and $8.25 for children.

It's said the Williamsburg Pottery (outlet center) has more visitors than **Colonial Williamsburg** does, perhaps because history is history, but a good bargain is hard to beat. Nevertheless, I promote repeat visits to this restored portion of Williamsburg, for displays change, seasons change, and your perspective changes.

Some differences are more subtle than others. During winter some furniture may be covered or some pieces may be displayed that wouldn't be covered or displayed in the summer heat. During fall you can watch or even participate in grape stomping, something you won't find in spring or summer.

In recent years more emphasis has been placed on making the Colonial experience accessible to those with hearing, vision, or maneuverability limitations. Some places are accessible, some places have portable wheelchair ramps available, and slide programs about inaccessible areas of some of the buildings are being created.

morepeace,please

The **Moore House,** part of the Colonial National Historical Park, at Yorktown, is the site where the terms of surrender for the British army were negotiated in 1781. The house is restored and decorated with eighteenth-century–style furnishings. It's open from 1:00 to 4:30 P.M. weekends in the spring and fall and 10:00 A.M. to 5:00 P.M. daily during the summer. (757) 898–2410; www.co.york.va.us/ychc/virtour/moorehouse.htm.

On the other hand, there are few curbs in the restored city, and automobiles are not permitted on the main streets during the day. An escorted walking tour is available for the visually impaired, and a special tour of the Powell-Waller House can be arranged. Free publications for the hearing impaired are available, as are discount tickets for some programs. For a copy of the *Colonial Williamsburg Guide for the Handicapped,* write to P.O. Box C, Williamsburg 23187, or call (757) 229–1000.

The Governor's Palace has undergone a remarkable makeover to show the lifestyle of Lord Dunmore, the last royal governor of Virginia, and his family. The Lord issued a proclamation in 1775 calling for all able-bodied men to assist him in defense of the British colony, including slaves who were promised their freedom in exchange for service in the King's Army. This was very controversial at the time, especially among slaveholders, who feared a mass slave rebellion. But the proclamation proved successful and within a month Dunmore had more than 800 soldiers.

Other changes over the years include exhibits and tours featuring "The Other Half" of the population, for during the eighteenth century half the population of Williamsburg was black. Some of these African-Americans, both slave and free, were cooks, maids, footmen, and drivers; others were skilled carpenters, blacksmiths, coopers, wheelwrights, and spinners. Take the Other Half tour, or pick up a brochure to learn how they influenced life in Colonial Williamsburg.

As a marker of time passing, when this book was first published, the **DeWitt Wallace Decorative Art Museum** had just opened. It's now been around long enough that it's been redone and once again is open for your

Sign on the Dotted Line . . .

The *Nelson House,* on Main Street in Yorktown, was the home of Thomas Nelson Jr., a signer of the Declaration of Independence, a governor of Virginia, and commander of the Virginia Militia during the siege of Yorktown. The Georgian mansion has been restored, and you can tour it from 10:00 A.M. to 5:00 P.M. Memorial Day through Labor Day and as staffing permits from 1:00 to 4:00 P.M. the rest of the year. Admission is included in the Yorktown Visitors Pass; (757) 898–2410; www.york county.gov/tourism.

enjoyment and astonishment at the beautiful things housed there. You'll find finely crafted seventeenth- to nineteenth-century household items here. The Abby Aldrich Rockefeller Folk Art Museum, in its expanded facility, features America's premier collection of works created by unschooled American artists, so this is the place to visit if you like rough-hewn toys, weather vanes, and painted furniture.

Evening programs have expanded, so you don't have to stay in your hotel room watching the television as if you weren't even on vacation. Family tours, shows, and concerts explore Colonial Williamsburg at night, and topics might include what frightened people out of their breeches and how they explained the unexplainable.

My recommendation to Williamsburg visitors is to buy a Freedom Pass. It's only a few dollars more than a one-day pass, and because it's good for a year, it might encourage you to stay another day or come back in a different season. And, as mentioned earlier, it's good for admission to Carter's Grove.

For additional information contact the **Williamsburg Visitor Center** at (800) HISTORY or visit www.williamsburg.com.

After a year of extensive renovations completed in 2001, the **Williams-burg Inn** boasts brilliantly refurbished chandeliers and a new tearoom and bar lounge. The sixty-two guest rooms and suites in the main building have been decorated in an elegant English Regency style, as originally directed by Mr. and Mrs. John D. Rockefeller Jr., and all guest rooms have been enlarged and include elaborate baths.

The inn has been host to a wealth of heads of state, and with its renowned pampering service, you may feel you're one of the Royals. Gourmet dining, clay tennis courts, award-winning golf (well, the course is award-winning— there's no guarantee how you'll do), a spring-fed pool, and a fitness club with spa services make this an experience worth the trip. If those activities aren't enough, try lawn bowling or croquet.

Charles City County

A short drive west of Williamsburg (or east of Richmond), in rural Charles City County, **Piney Grove at Southall's Plantation** offers bed-and-breakfast–style lodging and keeps you in the mood while you're visiting the nearby colonial sights. Depending on the season, your visit begins with mint juleps on the front porch or hot toddies by a roaring fire. Another option is a bottle of Virginia wine or cider from the Piney Grove wine cellar selection, including vintages from the Williamsburg Winery.

In the 1857 Ladysmith House the guest rooms are furnished with antiques and modern conveniences. Outside, there's a pool, gazebo, nature trail, and lawn games for those times when you just can't spend one more minute in a shop or tour another historic site. Animals occupy the barnyard.

You might not want to think about sleeping in, though, for the farm bell announces your plantation candlelight breakfast in the 1790 log room.

House and garden tours are available, either on a separate ticket or as a package with other local plantations. Piney Grove at Southall's Plantation, 16920 Southall Plantation Lane, Charles City; (804) 829–2480; www.pineygrove.com.

All that sightseeing and shopping can make one hungry, but not everyone wants to stop for food. Helen and Ike Sisane, the proprietors of the **Williamsburg Sampler Bed & Breakfast,** help solve that problem with Ike's "Skip Lunch" breakfast. It started when a former Penn State football player stayed over, and Ike decided the guy needed a little extra food for breakfast. The former football player described it as a "skip lunch meal" and the name stuck. A typical meal includes orange juice, fruit platter, eggs, meat and potatoes, muffins, and beverage.

partypartyparty

Big plans are under way for a year 2007 exhibit celebrating the 400th anniversary of the founding of America's first settlement. In the meantime, you can view a display of more than fifty recent additions to the Jamestown Settlement collection. Among the mostly seventeenth-century artifacts are clothing, paintings, military items, toys, documents, and vessels of silver, glass, and ceramic.

The home is a stately three-story, eighteenth-century plantation-style building with six bedrooms, including a two-room suite. 922 Jamestown Road, Williamsburg; (757) 253–0398 or (800) 722–1169; www.williamsburgsampler.com.

You've no doubt heard that Virginia is the mother of presidents, and John Tyler, tenth president of the United States, lived from 1842 until his death in 1862 at **Sherwood Forest.**

This classic example of Virginia Tidewater design has been elegantly restored and furnished with Tyler's possessions and shows the lifestyle of this mid-nineteenth-century family. The home is situated on twenty-five acres of terraced gardens and lawns, woods, and landscape and surrounded by six original outbuildings. The home is still owned by the Tyler family, and his great-grandson, who still resides at the plantation with his wife, oversaw the important restoration in the mid-1970s.

The house and grounds are open for tours 9:00 A.M. to 5:00 P.M. daily, except Thanksgiving and Christmas Days. Admission is $5.00 per person or $4.00 with AAA membership. There is also a gift shop. Sherwood Forest is located on Route 5, 14501 John Tyler Highway, Charles City; (804) 829–5377; www.sherwoodforest.org.

DelMarVa

One way or another, you have to cross the Chesapeake Bay Bridge, or the **Chesapeake Bay Bridge-Tunnel** officially called the Lucius J. Kelkew Jr. Bridge-Tunnel, to get from the main part of Virginia to the Eastern Shore, the southern part of the DelMarVa (Delaware, Maryland, Virginia) Peninsula.

From this area, the easiest and shortest way is via the bridge-tunnel. Before the time of the bridge-tunnel, there was the ferry. There's still a 26-mile rail/barge ferry service running, but it's for the Eastern Shore Railroad between Cape Charles and Virginia Beach.

funfacts

John Tyler was the first vice president to ascend to the presidency when he assumed the office after the death of William Henry Harrison, ninth president of the United States.

The bridge-tunnel, at 20 miles, is the world's longest bridge-tunnel complex. There are two mile-long tunnels, more than 12 miles of trestled railway, two bridges, nearly 2 miles of causeway, four man-made islands, and 5½ miles of approach roads.

At Island 1 (the one closest to Virginia Beach), you can eat at the **Seagull Pier** restaurant (open 7:00 A.M. to 6:00 P.M. October through March and 6:00 A.M. to 10:00 P.M. April through September). Take a minute or two to watch the ships coming into and going out of the harbor; drown a line for bluefish, trout, croaker, flounder, shark, and other species from the 625-foot fishing pier (bait and tackle are available); or shop at the Seashell and Gift Shop.

Whether you stop to visit or go from one side to the other, it's sure a marvelous way to see the magnificent confluence of the Chesapeake Bay and the

Atlantic Ocean. A forty-five-minute film about the bridge-tunnel is available for viewing by appointment.

The toll is $12.00 (for automobiles) each way with a $5.00 charge if you return within twenty-four hours and show your receipt; if, however, you tell the toll taker that you're going out to the island and will be returning without going all the way across the bay, you

funfacts

Sherwood Forest, at more than 300 feet long, is reported to be the longest frame house in America. Tyler added a 68-foot ballroom in 1845 to accommodate the popular dance of his time, the Virginia Reel.

will be charged only once. If you don't do this ahead of time, you will be charged a second $12 toll for coming back the other direction. For more information call (757) 331–2960 or visit www.cbbt.com.

Just before you travel the bridge-tunnel (or in case you really don't want to travel it), the western tunnel entrance is great for watching the bay shipping traffic navigate the waterways. You might see a submarine come booming out of the water (they can't traverse the bay submerged) or an aircraft carrier, but you're almost certain to see something interesting. So, grab a cup of coffee and sit a few minutes; perhaps you'll have a tale to tell your friends and family for years to come.

As mentioned in the introduction, two Virginia counties are located on the Eastern Shore of the DelMarVa Peninsula. Normally, thousands of people just drive north or south on Route 13 and never bother to see what's on either side of them. Fortunately, for those who like to get off that beaten path, there's a lot happening here.

Some of the "happenings" are very today and tomorrow. Sometimes the FedEx pickup and delivery depends on the winds across the Bridge Tunnel. Some things tell their old tales. For instance, the two counties have the oldest consecutive court records in the entire United States of America.

There's a time capsule buried in Eastville with a legend on it that says EASTVILLE COURT RECORDS TIME CAPSULE COMMEMORATING 365 YEARS OF THE OLDEST CONTINUOUS COURT RECORDS IN THE UNITED STATES. DEDICATED SEPTEMBER 20, 1997. TO BE OPENED EVERY 25 YEARS. So mark your calendar for a return visit in 2022.

For those who participate in the annual Christmas bird count, you'll gladly have your pinfeathers pulled when you learn that more than 150 species have been spotted. That's one of the highest counts north of Florida. Monarch butterflies migrate through here, and birders have been known to band everything from bald eagles to hummingbirds.

Could any place be more idyllic?

Oh, you say, birds and butterflies don't mean anything to you. You want to fish! Be one on one with nature and the deep. Okay, this is the place for you: You can try your luck catching—are you ready?—amberjack, Atlantic, Spanish, and king mackerel, black and red drum, blue and white marlin, bluefin and yellowfin tuna, bluefish, croaker, dolphin, flounder, gray trout, sea bass, spot, striped bass, tautog, and wahoo.

Many years ago, my family and about a half-dozen other families went camping at Cherrystone Family Camping Resort (www.cherrystoneva.com), just north of Cape Charles, on the Chesapeake Bay, for a week. We raked oysters off the campground coastline and went to Oyster (on the Atlantic side of the peninsula) to get clams. We found a guy there who was really, seriously upset because his crab trap was filled with blowfish (probably the one creature that really scares crabs), so we took them off his hands and carefully filleted them and understood why they're called the "chicken of the sea." My uncle had a boat in Hampton Roads and Sunday morning was "guy day," so he took all the guys out fishing and they came back with a bunch of palm-size spot that were perfect for breakfast cooked over the fire. One of the guys had brought some venison, so we did have a little variety in our meals, but basically, except for some prepackaged cereal to keep the children happy, we lived off the land for the entire week. Of course, the mosquitoes lived off us, so maybe that was Mother Nature's way of evening the score.

Northampton

The two Virginia counties on the Eastern Shore are Accomac and Northampton. The dozens of hamlets in these two counties are known for their surf and deepwater fishing, seafood, crafters, sweet potatoes, chicken, and a grand welcome to those who are "come heres" (families who have been in Virginia for less than three generations).

Almost all directions are given as "off Route 13," for that is the main highway through this area. There are several "searoads," which basically parallel the highway, such as Route 316 on the bay (Chesapeake) side and Routes 600 and 604 on the sea (Atlantic Ocean) side. It's along these roads that you'll find some of the unique Eastern Shore architecture, including homes with four different roof levels referred to as "big house, little house, colonnade, and kitchen."

Many people come for the most popular draw, or at least the best known, the pony roundup and penning at Chincoteague. Others want sun and sand or the antiques and the duck decoys. They're all available here. My advice on buying decoys is to look at quite a few first so that you can compare them and then decide what you want. There are decorative decoys (they look pretty) and working decoys (those that were hollowed out and had weights placed on the bottom for balance in the water and were used to lure ducks to the blinds). Some are brand-new and machine turned (you can even assemble and paint them yourself), some have intricately carved feather structures, and some are old and drab looking. You can expect to pay from $50 to $700 or more.

We'll start our tour at the southern end of the peninsula, then head north.

At the southern tip of the DelMarVa Peninsula is the **Eastern Shore of Virginia National Wildlife Refuge.** It features a variety of habitats ideal for millions of migrant birds including warblers, tree swallows, and other songbirds and thousands of raptors as they travel on their journey south, starting in late August and peaking around mid-November. Before that, the monarch butterfly migration goes through October. They come to stage (gather in large groups) until the winds and weather are favorable for an easy flight over the Bay.

According to the U.S. Fish and Wildlife Service, this land was known as Fort John Custis, and during World War II there were radar towers and large bunkers housing 16-inch guns to protect the naval bases and shipyards of Virginia Beach and Norfolk.

Within the 1,123 acres of maritime forest, myrtle and bayberry thickets, grasslands, croplands, and fresh and brackish ponds, there's even a place for you—there are trails and a photo blind. On Saturday afternoons from October through March, the service offers free tours (4-mile walking tour) to Fisherman Island, an area otherwise closed to the public. No entrance fee. Stop by the welcome station for detailed information. 5003 Hallett Circle, Cape Charles; (757) 331–2760; http://easternshore.fws.gov.

About 10 miles north of the Bridge Tunnel is **Cape Charles,** where the Northampton Chamber of Commerce has information about places to go,

Birding from the Bridge

Fishing, dining, and traveling between the eastern and western shores of Virginia are not the only uses for the Chesapeake Bay bridge-tunnel. Birders flock here to see black-tailed gulls, harlequin ducks, king eiders, loons, marbled godwits, oystercatchers, purple sandpipers, red-breasted mergansers, and tricolored herons. Some of these birds are attracted to the small fish and mollusks that gather around the man-made islands; others are migratory fowl traveling between arctic Canada and Greenland and points south. It's one of the top birding spots on the East Coast. A fee is charged and you must arrange a fixed time and date for your visit, so check in with the bridge-tunnel office (32386 Lankford Highway, Box 111, Cape Charles 23310; 757-331-2960) and avoid the extra toll. www.cbbt.com/birding.

things to see and do, and where to stay and eat. Stop by the office or contact them at 109 Mason Avenue, Suite A, Cape Charles; (737) 331–2304; www .northamptoncountychamber.com.

Wander around the town and see one of the largest concentrations of late-Victorian and turn-of-the-century buildings on the East Coast. The homes were built for the expanding merchant class and the executives of the Pennsylvania Railroad, for Cape Charles was established as the railroad's southern terminus, from which steamships carried passengers and freight to Norfolk. The town received Historic District designation in 1989 and was placed on the National Register of Historic Places in 1991.

The town took a huge hit when the ferry to Norfolk stopped running. Businesses shuttered and, well, you know how some small towns just get smaller and smaller. Now it's changing and businesses are opening with nary a chain store in sight. Yet.

Southeast Expeditions sells a variety of boating and sea life essentials and nonessentials in their store, including a bench made from two surfboards, CROCS shoes, and sundries. They also offer kayaking adventures (for the experienced and inexperienced) through the Bay marshes or along the coastal barrier islands. Or you can sign up for a three-day kite surfing school, dolphin spotting, fishing and clamming, aquaculture adventure, wild clam wrangling, and so much more. 32218 Lankford Highway, Cape Charles; (757) 331–2660; www.sekayak.com.

Coffee has come to town with the opening of the *Cape Charles Coffee Company,* located in a 1910 bank building. Paneled wood walls and chandeliers are the setting for espressos, lattes, and the signature Café Cape Charles (coffee, hazelnut, caramel, and melted chocolate). Food's available. The cafe is open from 9:00 A.M. to 9:00 P.M. weekdays and 8:00 A.M. to 10:00 P.M. on weekends. 241 Mason Avenue, Cape Charles; (757) 331–1880; www.capecharles coffee.com

Mary Ann McDevitt has opened the *Kellogg House Bed and Breakfast.* This Colonial Revival home has been restored to its original glory (and maybe a little more), retaining the original plaster walls, 10-foot ceilings, crown molding, and hardwood floors. Choose from the Kellogg room or the three-room Virginia Suite with two bedrooms and outside porch (or you can just use the front bedroom with the connecting bath). A three-course gourmet breakfast is served daily. All is not historic, for there's also wireless Internet access, individual climate control, and feather-topped beds and down comforters, 400-count Egyptian cotton sheets, and more. The Kellogg House is within walking distance of downtown and within half a mile of the beach and the Bay Creek golf course.

The Kellogg House is located at 644 Monroe Avenue, Cape Charles; (757) 331–2767; www.kellogghouse.com.

The *Cape Charles Hotel Historic Inn & Shoppes* was built as a hotel in 1884, one of the town's first commercial establishments. Richard Wagner is the owner, who spent four years renovating this seventeen-room hotel filled with memorabilia, photos, arts, and other treasures. This historic-district hotel that opened in July 2005 is centrally located for exploring. Each room has its own personality and private bath, air-conditioning, cable, phone, and Internet. Some rooms have water views, are ADA compliant, have adjoining rooms, or private terrace. A complimentary continental breakfast is included, and golf packages are available.

A cafe, art gallery, and retail space are on the first floor. 235 Mason Avenue, Cape Charles; (757) 331–3130; www.capecharleshotel.com.

Bay Creek Golf and Marina Resort may be in a still-sleepy area, but it's sure getting a lot of buzz. The 2,000-acre year-round planned community offers a marina (natch), shopping, restaurants, water sports, tennis, pools, a replica of a nineteenth-century lighthouse, a beach, and two 18-hole intersecting golf courses designed by Arnold Palmer *and* Jack Nicklaus. Foxes and sea birds nest along the courses that are lined with old-growth woods, magnolias, roses, and native beach grasses. The resort stretches along 3-plus miles of the Bay on one side and the Old Plantation Creek on the other.

Boaters can stay aboard their boats in Bay Creek's marina, which can accommodate boats up to 150 feet long (7-foot-deep low tide channel) with access to the intracoastal waterway, the Bay, and the Atlantic Ocean. Boat and kayak rentals are available.

Homes range from long- and short-term condominiums (you can rent for a week), and privately owned, single-family home rentals. 3335 Stone Road, Cape Charles; (757) 331–2200; www.bay-creek.com.

North of Cape Charles is *Eastville,* the Northampton County seat where the aforementioned time capsule is. It has a population of about 200 people, depending on the season and who's counting. Take time to stroll around the town, see the old courthouse (1731), the new courthouse, the prison (1814), Christ Episcopal Church (1741), and the attractive homes that line the streets of this quiet town.

Chef Charles Thann, a graduate with honors of the prestigious Johnson & Wales University, is the master of the meal at the *Eastville Inn.* Thann Shannon Price opened the lower-floor dining room of this old stagecoach hotel, built in 1780, as a restaurant in 2004. Fish, fresh fish, is the specialty (I've heard the flounder is magnificent), but there are plenty of other options, including salads, sandwiches, and entrees. It's open for lunch and dinner

Thursday through Monday. 16422 Courthouse Road, Eastville; (757) 678–5745; www.eastvilleinn.com.

On my most recent visit to Eastville, I stopped by **The Gallery at Eastville,** owned by award-winning designers Mary Miller and David Bruce Handschur. If I had my druthers, I'd probably still be wandering through the selection of 100 percent hand-loomed earthdesign® sweaters, one-of-a-kind jewelry pieces, wooden fish (for desk or tabletop, mantel, or windowsill), paintings, block prints, fused art glass, posters, and more. The Gallery is located in a restored 1908 Sears house (Queen Anne Victorian style) in the historic Courthouse District.

The Gallery is often open from 11:00 A.M. to 5:00 P.M., Friday through Monday. However, you should call to confirm the hours. 16319 Courthouse Road, Eastville; (757) 678–7532; www.thegalleryateastville.com.

Accomac County

Traveling north off Route 13 and then Route 605, you'll find Wach-apreague, which bills itself as the **The Little City by the Sea.** This fishing resort is said to have the state's largest charter boat marina, with all the wonderful fishing tournaments that accompany so many people involved in such a delightful sport. Call the town office, 6 Main Street, Wachapreague; (757) 787–7117 for details; www.wachapreague.org.

Elvis Ate Here, Sorta

The Exmore Diner, originally in New Jersey, has been in Exmore since P. C. Kellam had it trucked to town in 1953. In the trucking business, he'd gone to see a Yankees game in New York, stopped by the diner for a bite to eat, and saw the FOR SALE sign. He realized he had a hundred truckers a day coming to his place, and there was no restaurant in town. He had his wife wire the $5,000 to him, and he owned a diner.

According to waitress Ann Adams, Elvis Presley ate in the diner when it was in New Jersey, but she doesn't know where he sat or what he ordered.

A bright neon clock highlights the stainless steel exterior; the interior has four tables and twenty-four stools. Historians and historic preservationists think it's one of the most delicious-looking diners in the state. According to Evelyn Pruitt, who was working here as a waitress for ten years before she took over the business in 1991, the patrons go for the chicken and dumplings, chipped beef, butterfly shrimp, and hamburger steak.

The diner, located on old Route 13 on the south side of Exmore (almost where it rejoins US 13) is open 5:00 A.M. to 8:00 P.M. Monday through Thursday, 5:00 A.M. to 8:30 P.M. Friday and Saturday, and 6:00 A.M. to noon on Sunday (757–442–2313).

The picturesque harbor town of Onancock, on Chesapeake Bay 2 miles west of US 13 via Highway 179, is delightfully typical of Eastern Shore towns. A short walking tour of more than a dozen historical homes and churches begins at **Kerr Place** at 69 Market Street, Onancock, the 1799 home of the **Eastern Shore Historical Society.** Be impressed with an exhibit of how an ancient boat-carving technique changed five large logs into a boat used for oystering, crabbing, and fishing. It's open 10:00 A.M. to 4:00 P.M. Tuesday through Saturday; admission is $5.00, $4.00 for AAA members and $2.00 for children under seventeen. Kerr Place is closed January and February except for special events. (757) 787–8012, www.kerrplace.org.

It's said that **Accomac** is the second-largest restored town next to Williamsburg—or maybe it's the second-largest colonial-period city after Annapolis. In any case it certainly shouldn't be mistaken for the tourist attraction that either Williamsburg or Annapolis has become. It does, however, have a lot of colonial-period buildings. The chamber of commerce (now in Melfa) used to occupy the Customs House (ca. 1816), a historic landmark; (757) 787–8012.

Another historic landmark in Accomac, on Route 764, is the **Debtors' Prison** (ca. 1783), a two-story-and-loft building with a high pitched roof and Flemish Bond pattern to the brickwork. The west chimney is an inside unit to conserve heat. Make an appointment for a tour, or stop by the county clerk's office across the street to pick up the key.

funfacts

At the very southern tip of the DelMarVa Peninsula is **Kiptopeke State Park;** its 375 acres offer a variety of outdoor recreational and conservation activities, (757) 331–2267 or (800) 933–7275. There's a charge, but this is a great area for camping, boating, swimming, picnicking, and fishing. Kiptopeke is a Native American word for "big water." The site was named in honor of the younger brother of a king of the Accawmack Indians who befriended early settlers in the area. The Web site is at www.dcr .state.va.us/parks/kiptopek.htm.

Even if the building isn't open, you can peek in the windows to see the two rooms on the first floor. One room has been furnished as it might have been when John Snead, the resident jailer, and his family lived there between 1806 and 1815. The other will recall days when the building was a prison for debtors. After the General Assembly prohibited the jailing of debtors, the building was used for a variety of purposes including storage, a public library (1911–1927), scout headquarters, and WPA workroom, until 1953, when the Drummondtown Branch of the Association for the Preservation of Virginia Antiquities received custody of the building and repaired and restored it as a museum. Call (757) 789–3247; www.apua.org/debtorsprison.

Parksley's Railroad Depot was acquired in 1988 from Nancy Shield of Accomac. Now it's the *Eastern Shore Railway Museum.* The original depot was here in the late sixties and was a little larger than this 60-foot version, but the town is grateful because it is in such good condition.

Dozens of citizens donated their time to clean the site and paint and electrify the station; they also donated a potbellied stove, a railroad safe, a spike hammer, railroad lanterns, a railroad jack, a depot ceiling fan, and more than $20,000 for the museum. A 1943 caboose was donated by the Norfolk Southern Corporation, and the Tidewater chapter of the National Historical Railway Society promised a railway baggage car. All of this celebrates the history of the train on the Eastern Shore when that was the principal form of transportation and the only way to ship things in and out of the area. Located at 18468 Dunne Avenue, Parksley, the museum is open 10:30 A.M. to 4:00 P.M. Monday through Saturday and 1:00 to 4:00 P.M. Sunday (757–665–RAIL). It is closed on Monday from November through March.

There's also the *Accomack-Northampton Antique Car Museum* to complement the Railway Museum. Started by the late Melvin Shreves, the museum has received numerous items from local families, including neon car dealership signs and other memorabilia from old Hudson, Studebaker, Nash, and Durant auto dealers. There are also gas station signs, pedal cars, antique toy cars, and a rotating supply of old cars. Stop by and you might see a 1935 Auburn Cabriolet, a 1922 Durant Touring car, a 1964 Plymouth, and that classic, a 1956 Thunderbird convertible. The museum is open from noon to 4:00 P.M. Wednesday through Sunday. If you have any items you would like to donate or display in the museum, or if you have any questions or need directions to the museum, please contact Frank Russell at (757) 665–6161; www.parksley.com/seeus.shtml.

Wallops Island is occupied by the *National Aeronautics and Space Administration's (NASA) Visitor Center.* This was the nation's first rocket-firing and testing station, and nineteen satellites have been launched from Wallops Island, sixteen of which remain in orbit. It's possible that the flight center could be used for commercial satellite launches in the future. The site is geared toward small launchings, making it less expensive and easier for private firms to use than the Kennedy Space Center in Florida. Patented to John Wallop in 1672, Wallops Island became a National Advisory Committee

funfacts

Wallops Island is named after John Wallop, a seventeenth-century surveyor and original owner of the island.

for Aeronautics (NACA) site for aerodynamic research, while part of it was leased to the navy for aviation ordnance testing. The NACA eventually became NASA, which took over the site when the nearby Chincoteague Naval Air Station closed at the end of World War II.

You're invited inside the NASA museum for a self-guided tour that can last from fifteen minutes to several hours. (Groups of more than twenty are asked to make advance reservations.) There's an Apollo 17 moon-rock sample collected by astronaut Jack Schmitt from near the landing site in the Taurus–Littrow Valley region of the moon. Films, one on the forty-year history of Wallops Island and one on space highlights, are shown on a regular basis. Unlike at some other space and government areas, cameras are encouraged at this facility. The gift shop sells postcards, plates, cups, mugs, books, T-shirts, patches, and other space flight souvenirs. There are 100 to 150 space launches a year from Wallops, but there's little or no advance schedule; you have to stay several miles away, and some of them go up so fast they're off the ground and out of sight before you've blinked your eyes. Call (757) 824–2050 for launch information. Model rocket launches are held the first Saturday of every month.

To get to Wallops Island, Chincoteague, and Assateague Island, turn east off Route 13 at T's Corner, onto Route 175.

The museum is open 10:00 A.M. to 4:00 P.M. daily in July and August, Thursday through Monday (closed Tuesday and Wednesday) the rest of the year. It is closed Thanksgiving, Christmas, and New Year's Days. For general information call (757) 824–2298; www.wff.nasa.gov/~wvc.

After your NASA visit, you're ready to drive the last few miles to Chincoteague ("beautiful land across the water") and nearby Assateague Island. Once in Chincoteague you'll find lots of places to shop and eat and do a variety of other activities (if your visit is scheduled around Easter weekend, you can attend the yearly Chincoteague Decoy Festival), but the main attractions are the Chincoteague National Wildlife Refuge and Assateague Island National Seashore.

Is there a soul alive who has not read the book, seen the movie, or in some way heard about *Misty,* Marguerite Henry's famed horse from Chincoteague? Yes, the miniature horses still exist, and every year since 1925, there's an ***Annual Pony Swim and Auction*** held to sell off some of the horses to keep the herd at a manageable size. Thousands attend this event at the carnival grounds, held the last Wednesday and Thursday of July.

The wild ponies, which are assumed to be descended from mustangs that swam ashore from a wrecked Spanish ship in the sixteenth century, are auctioned by members of the volunteer fire department on Chincoteague. The members dress up in cowboy garb and corral the ponies, then carefully super-

funfacts

The Misty of Chincoteague Foundation has been purchasing land originally known as Misty's Meadow and plans to establish a permanent landmark and visitors' site on the property. A life-size bronze statue of Misty of Chincoteague was commissioned by noted equine sculptor Brian Maughan. The unveiling of this original artwork was held on July 29, 1997, the fiftieth anniversary of the book. Statue replicas can be ordered, $3,000 each. An education museum on Chincoteague will be dedicated to the legend's history (757–974–1089); www.mistyof chincoteague.org.

vise them as the horses swim to Chincoteague, where they can sell for more than $2,000 each. How nice to be able to visit Misty's relatives and stroll alongside them as they munch the grass of this seashore wildlife refuge that is their home. For more information contact the Chamber of Commerce, P.O. Box 258, Chincoteague Island 23336; (757) 336–6161; www.assateague.com.

Throughout the refuge you can take hikes, ride bikes, sit in the sun, and enjoy yourself. There's a 3½-mile bicycle/hiking loop open dawn to dusk for pedestrians and bikes (no mopeds allowed) and on which autos are allowed from 3:00 P.M. to dusk. Some 250 different birds fly by, and snow geese can be seen most of fall and winter. The refuge is a major resting and feeding area for the endangered peregrine falcon. Forest underbrush has been cleared in some areas, and nesting boxes have been constructed for the endangered DelMarVa fox squirrel. Scattered throughout the refuge are the sika (an oriental elk), Virginia white-tailed deer, and, of course, small bands of wild ponies. Tour bus service is available daily during the summer and on weekends the rest of the year, $12 for adults. (757) 336–3696; www.assateague.com.

Going back toward Route 13, you can see a huge selection of working duck decoys at the *Refuge Waterfowl Museum.* In addition to weapons, boats, traps, art, and items related to the life of the watermen, you'll see some magnificent duck decoy carvings. You might find the work of artisans Paul E. Fisher (Suffolk), Penny Miller (Reston), Reggie Birch (Chincoteague), J. D. Sprankle (Annapolis, Maryland), Paul Nock (Salisbury, Maryland), Tim Gorman (Machipongo), David and Ann-Marie Bundick (Modest Town), Walter W. Oler Sr. (Chincoteague), and noted master carver Grayson Chesser. Delbert "Cigar" Daisey is the resident carver.

Among the exhibits are backbay and canvas-covered Canada geese decoys, sink box decoys made of cast iron and used as weights on a sink box to make it float with a low profile, and a table with signatures from the Swan Club. You'll also find a model of a reed-and-feathers decoy made by Indians almost 1,000 years ago, handcrafted by Dr. H. S. Doolittle.

John Maddox owns the museum, which opened in 1978. Wyle Maddox, builder of the bridge to Assateague and the person for whom Maddox Boulevard is named, rode with the fire department in the Annual July Roundup and appeared in the movie *Misty* in his real-life role as leader of the cowboys. Wyle loved to hunt duck and was instrumental in the museum's acquiring this site for its building and collection.

The museum is open 10:00 A.M. to 5:00 P.M. daily, but hours can vary according to the season. Admission is $2.50 for adults and $1.00 for children twelve and under. It's located at 7059 Maddox Boulevard, Chincoteague. For more information call (757) 336–5800.

The **Oyster and Maritime Museum of Chincoteague** is said to be the only one of its kind in the United States. Since 1972 it has featured live marine exhibits of clams, oysters, crabs, sea stars, sea horses, and other marine specimens, as well as historical and maritime artifacts, shell specimens, implements of the seafood industry and of the shucking process, and an area diorama with lights and sound. The Oyster Museum covers a history of the Chincoteague and Assateague area and preserves the culture of the islands and of Eastern Shore oystering (the prime industry of the island) from the 1600s to the present. It holds the Maddox Library papers on marine life.

The museum, at 7125 Maddox Boulevard, Chincoteague, along the Assateague Beach Road, is open 11:00 A.M. to 5:00 P.M. daily during summer months; open weekends only during early spring and fall. Admission is $3.00 for adults and $1.00 for children. For more information call (757) 336–6117 or visit www.chincoteaguechamber.com/oyster/omn.html.

There may not be a better combination than getting away to someplace "remote" and finding it has almost all the conveniences of home, particularly if you're on a business trip. That's what you can find at the **Island Motor Inn,** which has all waterfront guest bedrooms, an indoor pool, exercise rooms, and a conference room with large windows overhanging and overlooking the waterfront. Oh, and add Ann Stubbs as a most gracious hostess. The inn is located at 4391 Main Street, Chincoteague; (757) 336–3141; www.islandmotor inn.com.

The **Locustville Academy Museum,** on Route 605 in the Academy Building, Locustville, is the only remaining school of higher learning of about a dozen that existed on the Eastern Shore during the 1800s, and the weatherboarding, brick foundations, and interior are intact. The school provided advanced studies for college-bound students or those entering business at a far lower cost than boarding schools. Advanced courses included Latin, Greek, and French, and in 1862 tuition did not exceed $20 for a semester. The school operated from the fall in 1859 until 1879 (except for brief periods during the

Civil War) and apparently looks much as it did when it was in operation, although the original entrance road has been closed. Inside are an old teacher's desk and student's desk, old textbooks, photographs, documents, and historical artifacts from the area. It's open by appointment. Call (757) 787–2460 for more information.

Where to Stay in Eastern Virginia

BELLE HAVEN

Bay View Waterfront
5350 Copes Drive
(757) 442–6963 or (800) 442–6966

CAPE CHARLES

Cape Charles House Bed-and-Breakfast
645 Tazewell Avenue
(757) 331–4920

CHINCOTEAGUE

1848 Island Manor House
4160 Main Street
(757) 336–5436
or (800) 852–1505

Channel Bass Inn
6228 Church Street
(757) 336–6148 or (800) 249–0818

Miss Molly's Inn
4141 Main Street
(757) 336–6686
or (800) 221–5620

Refuge Inn
7058 Maddox Boulevard
(757) 336–3469
or (888) 831–0600

CHURCH VIEW

Dragon Run Inn
35 Wares Bridge Road
(804) 758–5719

GLOUCESTER

Inn at Warner Hall
4750 Warner Hall Road
(804) 695–9565
or (866) 847–4887

HARBORTON

Harborton House
28044 Harborton Road
(757) 442–6800
or (800) 882–0922

MATHEWS

Buckley Hall Inn
11293 Buckley Hall Road
(804) 725–1900 or (888) 450–9145

MONTROSS

Montross Inn & Restaurant
21 Polk Street
(804) 493–0573

NEWPORT NEWS

Mulberry Inn
16890 Warwick Boulevard
(757) 887–3000

NORFOLK

Freemason Inn
411 West York Street
(757) 963–7000
or (866) 388–1897

Page House Inn
323 Fairfax Avenue
(757) 625–5033
or (800) 599–7659

ONANCOCK

Charlotte Hotel & Restaurant
7 North Street
(757) 787–7400

ONLEY

Bay View Waterfront
(757) 442–6963
or (800) 442–6966

REEDVILLE

Fleeton Fields Bed and Breakfast
2783 Fleeton Road
(804) 453–5014
or (800) 497–8215

TAPPAHANNOCK

Essex Inn Bed and Breakfast
203 Duke Street
(804) 443–9900
or (866) ESSEX VA

VIRGINIA BEACH

Angie's Guest Cottage
302 24th Street
(757) 428–4690

Barclay Cottage Bed & Breakfast
400 16th Street
(757) 422–1956

Cavalier Hotel
4201 Atlantic Avenue
(757) 425–8555
or (800) 422–8725

Colonial Inn
2809 Atlantic Avenue
(757) 428–5370 or (800) 344–3342

Schooner Inn
215 Atlantic Avenue
(757) 425–5222
or (800) 283–7263

WILLIAMSBURG

Black Badger Inn
720 College Terrace
(757) 253–0202
or (877) 334–0641

Fife & Drum Inn
441 Prince George Street
(757) 345–1776
or (888) 838–1783

Great Wolf Lodge
549 East Rochambeau Drive
(757) 229–9700
or (800) 551–9653

Kingsmill Resort
1010 Kingsmill Road
(757) 253–1703
or (800) 982–2892

Newport House
710 South Henry Street
(757) 229–1775
or (877) 565–1775

Where to Eat in Eastern Virginia

CAPE CHARLES

Chesapeake
307 Mason Avenue
(757) 331–2505

Pelican Pub
32246 Lankford Highway
(757) 331–4229

CHINCOTEAGUE

Chincoteague Inn Seafood
6262 Marlin Street
(757) 336–6110

Don's Seafood Market & Restaurant
4113 Main Street
(757) 336–5715

Steamers Seafood
6251 Maddox Boulevard
(757) 336–6236

EXMORE

Trawler Seafood
2555 Lankford Highway
(757) 442–2092

MACHIPONGO

Great Machipongo Clam Shack
13037 Lankford Highway
(757) 678–5759

MELFA

Tammy & Johnny's Fried Chicken
27352 Lankford Highway
(757) 787–1122

NORFOLK

Blue Hippo
147 Granby Street
(757) 533–9664

Grate Steak
235 North Military Highway
(757) 461–5501

La Galleria
120 College Place
(757) 623–3939

Monastery
443 Granby Street
(757) 625–8193

ONANCOCK

Bizzotto's Gallery
41 Market Street
(757) 787–3103

Blarney Stone Pub & Restaurant
10 North Street
(757) 302–0300

REEDVILLE

Crazy Crab
902 Main Street
(804) 453–6789

VIRGINIA BEACH

Lighthouse Oceanfront
96 Atlantic Avenue
(757) 428–7974

WACHAPREAGUE

Henry's Marina Restaurant
15 Atlantic Avenue
(757) 787–4110

Island House
17 Atlantic Avenue
(757) 787–4242

WILLIAMSBURG

BackFin Seafood
3701 Strawberry Plains Road
(757) 565–5430

Captain George's
5363 Richmond Road
(757) 565–2323

Cascades
Visitor Center Drive
(757) 229–2141

Fireside Steakhouse & Seafood
1995 Richmond Road
(757) 229–3310

Jamestown Settlement Café
1760 Jamestown Road
(757) 253–2571

Kingsmill Restaurants
1010 Kingsmill Road
(757) 253–3900

Shields Tavern
Duke of Gloucester
(757) 229–1000

Central Virginia

The central portion of Virginia is a huge mix of the cosmopolitan Richmond-Petersburg area and an almost nineteenth-century feeling of people still practicing rural folk ways. This is the proverbial breadbasket, the source of such products as tobacco, cantaloupe, grains, forage, and tomatoes. You'll also see beef and dairy products. Here you'll travel through miles and miles of moderately rolling piedmont dotted with gracious plantations. The area is surrounded by the Blue Ridge Mountains on the west and northwest and the Tidewater on the east. A look at a topographical map makes you think this is the palm of someone's hand that is protecting the people and their interests.

This is where you'll find Tiffany windows, museums, peanuts, fishing, boating, fine restaurants, good shopping, and what advertisers and marketing specialists call a great quality of life. This area is home to a nationally renowned amusement theme park and county fairs.

Traversing the central area can be done via several interstate highways, including Interstate 95, Interstate 85, both running north and south, and Interstate 64, running east and west. There are several other scenic routes, including U.S. Highways 29, 15, 160, and 360/58.

CENTRAL VIRGINIA

Richmond

Richmond is as good a place to start as you can find, and many of the suggested stops can be made in a day's drive. Others will be done more easily if you plan an overnight stop.

A lot of the Civil War was fought in Virginia, and a look at a map shows just how strategic it was. Richmond, the capital of the Confederacy, was under frequent attack from 1861 to 1865. The ***Richmond National Battlefield Park*** commemorates eleven sites involved in three battles that came within miles of the city. These include skirmishes at Gaines' Mill, Malvern Hill, and Cold Harbor. Stop by the park visitor center on East Broad Street; park rangers will provide maps so that you can tour the battlefield.

Within Gaines Mill, Cold Harbor, Malvern Hill, Fort Harrison, and Drewry's Bluff, there are interpretive walking trails, with ranger-guided tours, scheduled talks, living history programs, and summer season youth programs (also at other times by request). Cold Harbor and Fort Harrison have tour roads, and their visitor centers have exhibits about the battles. In May, June, July, and September, there are activities that coincide with the anniversary of one of the park's major battles.

Within the Chimborazo Visitor Center are a scale model of the Chimborazo hospital (the Confederacy's largest) and Civil War artifacts. A twenty-two-minute motion picture depicts the battles that took place near the city. Some research facilities are available.

The contact station at Chimborazo Park is open all year, but the ones at Cold Harbor, Glendale Cemetery, and Fort Harrison are open subject to staff availability.

AUTHOR'S FAVORITES IN CENTRAL VIRGINIA

Central Virginia Scottish Festival and Games, May, Ashland, (804) 883–6917

Historic Garden Week, April, statewide, (804) 643–7141
www.vagardenweek.org

James River Batteau Festival, June, Appomattox, (804) 352–2621

Jeffersonian Thanksgiving Festival, November, Charlottesville, (804) 296–7864

Lewis Ginter Botanical Gardens, Richmond, (804) 262–9887
www.lewisginter.org

Montpelier, Montpelier Station, (504) 672–2728; www.montpelier.org

Old Blandford Church and Cemetery, Petersburg, (804) 733–2400

Science Museum of Virginia, Richmond, (804) 367–6552
www.smv.org

Camera, Lights, Action

Richmond was an even busier movie/TV shoot in 2004 with the filming of *Cry Wolf*, with Jeff Wadlow, a Charlottesville native, as writer and director of this horror/thriller flick. Scenes were shot at Collegiate School, 103 North Mooreland Road, St. Joseph's Villa, 8000 Brook Road, and the University of Richmond, 28 Westhampton Way.

The pilot for the TV show *Commander in Chief*, starring Geena Davis, also used the University of Richmond and New Millennium Studios in Petersburg.

Virginia Film Tours offers a Saturday morning bus tour for an insider's look at the many sites used for Hollywood movies and TV shows made in Richmond. Or you can sign up for an interactive weekend tour that includes makeup and a screen debut for your fifteen minutes of fame (take the video home to show your friends and family). There's also a one-day Civil War movie tour. Numerous pickup points around the city. 401 North Third Street, Richmond; (804) 744–1718; www.virginiafilmtours.com.

To find out which is open when and where to find them, and to pick up a cassette tape that explains the defense of Richmond for your self-guided driving tour, stop by the visitor center first. It is open 9:00 A.M. to 5:00 P.M. daily, and the parks are accessible to people in wheelchairs. There's no admission fee, but donations are accepted, and there's a bookstore at the visitor center. It is closed on Thanksgiving, Christmas, and New Year's Days. The park headquarters is located at 3215 East Broad Street, Richmond; (804) 226–1981; www.nps.gov/rich.

The state's oldest institution preserving Virginia's history and culture is the *Library of Virginia,* 800 East Broad Street, Richmond. Within its walls you'll find artwork, books, manuscripts, maps, and genealogical information covering nearly 400 years of history. A rotating schedule of exhibits highlights different aspects of Virginia's history and the collection.

seacreatures

Embedded in the black limestone squares of the checkerboard-patterned floors around the rotunda and halls of the capitol in Richmond, you can see snails (including a giant marine snail shell from the Ordovician period), nautiloid, shell, sea lily, coral, and algae fossils.

The public reading rooms are open 9:00 A.M. to 5:00 P.M. Monday through Saturday, holidays excepted; (804) 692–3500; www.lva.lib.va.us.

The *American Civil War Center at Historic Tredegar* is the first museum in the nation to tell the Civil War story from the perspectives of the Union, Confederate, and African-American men, women, and children whose lives were

When Is a Bank Not a Bank?

The Federal Reserve Bank of Richmond, at 701 East Byrd Street, Richmond, is a bank, but it cannot cash your check, accept your deposit, transfer funds for you, or make a loan.

And now for your lesson in economics. The Reserve Bank of Richmond is one of twelve in the United States. Because it is the central bank of the United States, the directors of each reserve bank, who are private citizens, establish the discount rates charged by their banks on collateralized loans. The Federal Reserve Bank of Richmond was incorporated on May 18, 1914, and serves the Fifth Federal Reserve District, which comprises the District of Columbia, Maryland, Virginia, North Carolina, South Carolina, and most of West Virginia. On average, about 40,000 transactions, with a value of approximately $130 billion, are made here daily. In other words, they regulate the money supply and maintain the soundness of the banking industry.

On display in its unique museum are exhibits devoted to the different items civilizations have used as "money," from the British colonies of North America (including wampum) and the United States. There are utensils, weapons, and jewelry, as well as conventional coins and notes from the Far East to the New World. Some are as old as thirty centuries, and some are less than thirty years. Twelve exhibits tell the story of money in our country, from Colonial days to the present. For the numismatist there are Federal Reserve notes in $500, $1,000, $5,000, and $10,000 denominations, a sheet of twelve $100,000 gold certificates, and a gold bar.

Stop by for a more detailed explanation and to learn what the bank does and can do, and visit the money museum and its art collection, or see the bank's wire transfer room. The money museum is open daily from 9:30 A.M. to 3:30 P.M. Individual, group, and art tours are offered weekdays between 10:00 A.M. and 2:00 P.M. Three weeks' notice is requested for some tours. Call (804) 697–8110 for regular tours and (804) 697–8466 for art tours, or visit www.rich.frb.org.

forever changed by this powerful event. This new (summer/fall 2006) 10,000-square-foot center incorporates artifacts, media, and interactive features so you'll be engaged and enlightened. The tour starts with the causes for the war, moves into the war years, and then finishes with the legacies it left. 490 Tredegar Street, Richmond; (804) 788–6480; www.tredegar.org.

For pure architectural and historical enjoyment of a structured nature, visit *Richmond's Fan District,* bordered by Monroe Park, the Boulevard, and Monument Avenue on the north and Cary Street on the south. The Fan District, with about 2,000 town houses, is said to be the largest intact Victorian neighborhood in the United States. The aptly named Monument Avenue has monuments to Confederate generals Robert E. Lee, Thomas "Stonewall" Jackson, and J. E. B. Stuart; Confederate president Jefferson Davis; Commodore Matthew

Fontaine Maury, "Pathfinder of the Seas"; and tennis legend Arthur Ashe. A suburb of this bustling town back in the 1890s, the Fan District is now incorporated into the city of Richmond.

At one time the height of fashion, later nearly abandoned, it's once more the place to be. The mile-square, tree-lined district of streets radiates, or fans out, and a map of the district slightly resembles the fashionable accessory Southern ladies are so noted for—and surely, as modern as Richmond has become, she is still a Southern lady. The town houses carry Victorian, Greek Revival, Italianate, Tudor, and Georgian touches. They're joined by party walls or separated by narrow walkways. Call (804) 782–2777 for walking and driving tour maps.

A visit and tour of the 1790 *Capitol* is a special treat, particularly the hidden dome, which Thomas Jefferson designed, in the Italian-architecture–inspired building. Beneath that dome is the only statue of George Washington that was modeled from life. Sculptor Jean Antoine Houdon visited Washington at Mount Vernon to mold his head in a gooey plaster mix and measured his body as accurately as a tailor would. Such details as the vein in his thumb and the stitching in the cloak facing are included. This Washington does not look like the Washington of the ubiquitous Gilbert Stuart painting, and most likely it's a much more accurate interpretation of his appearance.

The Capitol is closed through late 2006. Outdoor tours are available. Free tours will resume after the renovations are completed; they are given by docents Monday through Friday from 9:00 A.M. to 5:00 P.M., Saturday from 10:00 A.M. to 4:00 P.M., and Sunday (from November to March only) from 1:00 to 5:00 P.M. To take the last full tour, plan on arriving an hour before tour hours end. You'll also receive a free booklet about the Capitol. The large equestrian statue of George Washington in the northwest corner of the square was constructed to be his final resting place, before his body was buried at Mount Vernon. If you're interested and can find an agreeable guard, you can climb up the inside of the statue. The Capitol is at Ninth and Grace Streets, Richmond. Call (804) 698–1788 for more information.

The Virginia *Governor's Mansion,* on Capitol Square, is the oldest continuously occupied governor's residence in the United States. Virginia governors and their families have occupied the Federal-style structure since 1813. As a Virginia and National Historic Landmark, the mansion recently underwent a multimillion-dollar renovation and features many original examples of the woodwork, plaster cornices, and ornamental ceilings. Tours are available Tuesday through Thursday from 10:00 A.M. to noon and 2:00 to 4:00 P.M. There is no charge; (804) 371–2642.

Of course, there is the option of doing nothing, or almost nothing, and a great place to do that is at the *Lewis Ginter Botanical Garden* (1800

Lakeside Avenue, Richmond). Ginter made his first fortune in dry goods, his second in the stock market, his third in tobacco (he sold the rights to his cigarette-paper rolling invention to Duke, figuring it would never fly), and his fourth fortune in real estate development. The obvious and correct implication here is that he lost his fortunes in between earning them. It was through the real estate fortune that he most directly affected Richmond. Among other things he built the Jefferson Hotel, Ginter Park (Richmond's first suburb), and a number of buildings that house Virginia Commonwealth University.

This world-class botanical garden contains the three-and-one-half-acre Henry M. Flagler Perennial Garden, one of the largest on the East Coast. The Ginter garden people aren't aware of any connection between Flagler and Ginter; although surely Ginter would have known of Flagler, they aren't sure if Flagler knew of Ginter. Nevertheless, the Flagler people donated this garden. It is the largest single display, with some 12,000 plants and with 4,000 species planted within bordered walkways and meandering streams. It is unique in size and in its kaleidoscopic colorations. Changes are noticeable daily, and the garden is appealing even into the deepest of winter because there is either something blooming all the time or because of the interesting foliage.

Groups of children (not necessarily school groups, but at least fifteen) are encouraged to come through the Children's Garden, where they can learn that flowers come from the ground, not from the florist shop or the street corner vendors. The programs are participatory, and the children are allowed to dig in the garden, harvest flowers and vegetables, and learn about the ecology of the garden and animals found there. Call (804) 262–9887 for reservations.

The Lucy Payne Minor Garden features daffodils, daylilies, and true lilies, so you can see the different varieties next to one another. Installation of a bog or an island garden is in the works. In all there is a twenty-year master plan,

It's a Grave Matter

Richmond's **Hollywood Cemetery** was designed by John Notman, who pioneered romantically landscaped cemeteries. A Gothic Revival chapel marks the entrance, and outstanding examples of Victorian monuments and ornamental ironwork can be found almost everywhere. A 90-foot pyramid honors the 18,000 Confederate soldiers buried on the property. U.S. presidents James Monroe and John Tyler and Confederate president Jefferson Davis are also buried here. Oh, and the name Hollywood is for the large holly trees that grace the ground; not that city out in California; 412 South Cherry Street, Richmond; (804) 648–8501; www.hollywood cemetery.org.

OTHER PLACES TO SEE

Ashland
Scotchtown, Home of Patrick Henry
(804) 227–3500 or (800) 897–1479
www.apva.org/scotchtown

Charlottesville
Monticello
(434) 984–9800
www.monticello.org
Virginia Discovery Museum
(434) 977–1025
www.vadm.org

Danville
Danville Museum of Fine Arts & History
(434) 793–5644
www.danvillemuseum.org

Doswell
Paramount's Kings Dominion
(804) 876–5000
www.kingsdominion.com

Richmond
Children's Museum of Richmond
(804) 474–CMOR or (877) 295–CMOR
www.c-mor.org
Richmond Braves
(804) 359–4444
www.rbraves.com
Valentine Richmond History Center
(804) 649–0711
www.richmondhistorycenter.com

which includes an azalea garden and walk, production greenhouses, and an education facility and library. Geoffrey Raush, of Environmental Planning and Design in Pittsburgh, created the overall design of the garden. (The firm also is responsible for beautiful work in Chicago and St. Louis.) There's also a Japanese teahouse.

The 23,000-square-foot E. Claiborne Robins Visitor Center opened in March 1999. The classic, Georgian-style building features an exhibit hall, garden shop, meeting and banquet room, and cafe.

Spring highlights include tulip week, beginning about April 16 or a week before Virginia's Garden Week on April 23. The Ginter garden sponsors a plant sale in the last full week of April and a Mother's Day concert in early May, complete with food.

The garden is open 9:00 A.M. to 5:00 P.M. daily. Admission is $9.00 for adults, $5.00 for children, and $8.00 for seniors. The visitor center has the same hours except on Sunday, when it's open from 12:30 to 4:30 P.M. The gardens are closed on Thanksgiving, Christmas, and New Year's Days. For more information call (804) 262–9887; www.lewisginter.org.

If you haven't been to Richmond in a while, and you love nature, the **Robbins Nature and Visitor Center at Maymont** is for you. This one-hundred-acre park was the country home of Richmond financier James H. Dooley and his wife. They had no heirs, so they willed the land to the city in

For the Kids

Children's museums are hot, hot, hot.

The **Children's Museum of Richmond,** 2626 West Broad Street, Richmond, is designed for children twelve and younger. The museum provides exhibits, programs, performances, and demonstrations. In its 42,000 square feet of exhibit space, children can climb trees, explore an eagle's nest, and discover how food travels through the human body. A stage, art studio, and "how-it-works" area allows families to work and create together. Call (804) 474–CMOR or (877) 295–CMOR; www.c-mor.org.

The **Amazement Square, the Rightmire Children's Museum** opened in fall 2000 at 27 Ninth Street, Lynchburg. Eight galleries include a giant climbing tower, a 50-foot working model of the James River, and an architecture gallery complete with an operating crane. Call (804) 845–1888; www.amazementsquare.org

1926. The thirty-three-room Victorian mansion has been restored to its glory days, and there are formal Italian and Japanese gardens, an arboretum, a children's farm, and a petting zoo. All attractions are open to the public and free, although there is a $4.00 suggested donation.

Within the center is a state-of-the-art complex that houses thirteen aquaria that follow the life and ecosystems of the James River, including shallow pools, open water, backwaters, a turtle pool, estuaries, and channel runs. Along with lots of fish, there are snapping turtles (in the turtle pool, of course) and even two otters, the center's mascots, in an indoor-outdoor tank.

Children eight and up can explore the natural world with microscopes and other lab equipment. A discovery room is available for younger children, and there's an area that explores night life, not of discos and bars, but of such nocturnal animals as owls, meadow voles, and white-footed mice. There's also a gift shop with science-related items and a cafe for a brief bite to eat.

The Robbins Nature and Visitor Center at Maymont is at 2201 Shields Lake Drive, Richmond. The Nature Center, Maymont House, children's farm, and gift shop are open noon to 5:00 P.M. Tuesday through Sunday. The visitor center, grounds, and gardens are open daily 10:00 A.M. to 5:00 P.M. A tram runs noon to 5:00 P.M., weather permitting, and is $3.00 for adults and $2.00 for children. Carriage rides are available on Sunday noon to 4:00 P.M., weather permitting, and are $3.00 for adults and $2.00 for children. Call (804) 358–7166; www.maymont.org.

A superb overlook of the city is off East Broad Street, west up Twenty-third Street, with a right turn on Grace Street until it dead-ends, where you can

cooookies

The wonderful aroma you smell along the 900 block of Terminal Place is from the Interbake Foods bakery, where they produce some one million pounds of cookies a week. Some of your Girl Scout cookies are produced here.

view downtown Richmond. It is particularly beautiful on a clear night.

The *Science Museum of Virginia* features, among many things, the Ethyl IMAX Dome, a tilted hemispherical projection dome, 23 meters in diameter and almost five stories tall.

Within the dome is an Omnimax projection system manufactured by the Imax Corporation of Canada. This 280-seat auditorium has a hemispheric 76-foot-diameter screen that visually envelops you with its projections.

The dome also houses a Digistar 2 planetarium system. This system, from the Evans & Sutherland Corporation, uses a Sun computer and Evans & Sutherland graphics system to project the stars, planets, and moons of our solar system. The Digistar 2 system was installed in January 1997 to replace the original Digistar system, the world's first permanently installed such system.

The dome six-channel audio system has thirty-four three-way speaker systems and six subwoofers driven by fifty-four BGW amplifiers capable of a combined output power of more than 13,000 watts.

Shows are presented daily (except Thanksgiving and Christmas Days and during changeover periods). Occasional lectures, concerts, and laser light shows are also presented. Call (804) 367–6552 or (800) 659–1727 for current information on program offerings and schedule. There's also an aquarium displaying the various fish of the James River.

This is definitely a hands-on museum, and you're invited to discover and explore the scientific world in language and displays that reach all levels. Other attractions at the museum are the computer works sections, where you can pick up the basics or go one-on-one against the superbrains. After you've played mind games, head for the visual perception area and play games with your eyesight with mirrors and other optical illusions. Five crystal-shaped structures fill the rotunda floor, and these crystals house a complete display on the formation of crystals and their importance.

The science museum is located in the historic former Broad Street Railroad Station. Originally opened in 1919, the building was designed by John Russell Pope.

As if the former train station weren't impressive enough, there's a five-story-tall DNA strand to welcome you at the entrance. No ordinary molecule, this one is a trillion times larger than life! It's part of the new permanent Bioscape exhibit that begins in the Very Small Gallery of cells and DNA where

TOP ANNUAL EVENTS

April
Historic Garden Week, statewide
(804) 653–7141

June
Hanover Tomato Festival, Mechanicsville
(804) 752–6766

July
Hanover Tomato Festival,
Mechanicsville; (804) 365–4695;
www.cohanover.va.us
Virginia Cantaloupe Festival, South
Boston; (804) 572–3085

September
Natural History Weekend, Wintergreen
(434) 325–8169
State Fair of Virginia, Richmond
(804) 228–3200
Taste of the Mountains Main Street
Festival, Madison; (540) 948–4455;
www.madison-va.com
Virginia Peanut Festival, Emporia
(434) 634–9441

October
Monticello Wine and Food Festival,
Charlottesville (434) 296–4188
Virginia Garlic Festival, Amherst County
(434) 946–5168

you can investigate genes, traits, and heredity. A Science Sleuth Theater, funded partially by novelist Patricia Cornwell, lets you be her Dr. Kay Scarpetta by examining such evidence as a drop of blood or a fallen hair. The My Size Gallery features multisensory explorations of human biology and health science so you can see how joints work when you manipulate a human skeleton. The Really Big Gallery presents an environmental science display, including a giant smallmouth bass, and a look at mutation and evolution.

The exhibits are open 9:30 A.M. to 5:00 P.M. Monday through Saturday, and 11:30 A.M. to 5:00 P.M. Sunday. The Planetarium and Space Theater are open 11:00 A.M. to 5:00 P.M. Monday through Thursday, 11:00 A.M. to 9:00 P.M. Friday and Saturday, and noon to 5:00 P.M. Sunday. Admission prices to the exhibits are $10.00 for adults; $9.00 for seniors (sixty and over); and $9.00 for children (four through twelve). Combination tickets are available. Children three and younger and museum members are admitted free.

The museum is at 2500 West Broad Street, Richmond (804–864–1400 or 800–659–1727); for information about the planetarium, call (804) 25–STARS; www.smv.org.

Planted firmly in mid-tap at Leigh and Adams Streets is the *statue of Bill "Bojangles" Robinson,* noted tap dancer and entertainer, by Ashland sculptor Jack Witt. Robinson was born at 915 North Third Street in Richmond's Jackson Ward neighborhood. He gave money for a traffic signal at this corner to help the neighborhood children safely cross the street and to a variety of other charitable causes, and in 1973 the city of Richmond erected this statue in his honor. He's portrayed as we all remember him, tap dancing down (or up) a flight of stairs. (Witt has another life-size sculpture, a bronze of a street jester, in front of the Grace Street entrance to the Sixth Street Marketplace.)

The 1895 *Jefferson Hotel,* a massive, white-brick hotel blending Louis XVI and Colonial Renaissance styles, was once the finest hostelry in the South. It burned in 1901 and again in 1944. A few years ago it enjoyed an estimated $40 million renovation and restoration, and the glorious colors of the magnificent stained-glass dome once again radiate into the Palm Court lobby below. Live alligators lived in the two reflecting pools in the Palm Court lobby from the early 1900s until 1948, with "Old Poppy" being one of particular note. Several of the bellhops of that period told stories of finding the alligators crawling on the upholstered chairs in the lobby and having to chase them back into their pools.

The alligators are now enshrined in bronze, permanently situated at the foot of the Thomas Jefferson statue; however, when the Ringling Brothers, Barnum and Bailey Circus came to town a few years ago, they brought a real alligator to the Jefferson for some publicity photographs. You never know what you'll find here. Just be sure when you put your feet up on a footstool that it doesn't walk away.

The grand staircase, which legend says was the model for the staircase in *Gone with the Wind,* is back. Film buffs might recognize the hotel from the film *My Dinner with André,* which was shot at this location.

The hotel is at Franklin and Adams Streets, Richmond. Call (804) 788–8000 for more information; or visit www.jeffersonhotel.com.

April 1997 saw the completion of the first phase of the Virginia *Holocaust Museum* in Richmond, the first in the state. The museum is conceived as a tribute to Richmond Holocaust survivors and a unique hands-on children's museum specifically geared for students in the eighth through tenth grades. The first five exhibit rooms cover Kristallnacht (the Night of Broken Glass), life in the Jewish ghetto, and other significant elements from the history of the Holocaust. A time line features the story of Jay Ipson and his parents, Richmond residents since 1947. During the Holocaust the family lived in Lithuania in a 9-by-12-by-4-foot area hidden under a potato field. Donations and loans of Holocaust and World War II memorabilia are being sought to add to the collection. The museum is open from 9:00 A.M. to 5:00 P.M. Monday through Friday, 11:00 A.M. to 5:00 P.M. Saturday and Sunday. Guided tours are offered at 1:00 P.M. on Friday. The museum is at 2000 East Casy Street, Richmond, adjacent to Temple Beth El; (804) 257–5400; www .va-holocaust.com.

At the ***Virginia Aviation Museum*** (a division of the Science Museum of Virginia) by the Richmond International Airport is the Shannon collection of historic airplanes. The exhibit offers you an hour's walk through aviation history. Here you can see Captain Dick Merrill's 1930s open-cockpit mail plane, examine aircraft engines from the pioneering days (aviation pioneering, not Daniel Boone pioneering), take a memorable close look at a World War I SPAD, stroll past exhibits of aviation artifacts, and see the special exhibit dedicated to Virginia's legendary Admiral Richard E. Byrd. A small gift shop is open in the lobby.

The museum is open 9:30 A.M. to 5:00 P.M. Monday through Saturday and noon to 5:00 P.M. on Sunday, except Thanksgiving and Christmas Days. Admission prices are $6.00 for adults, $5.00 for seniors (sixty and over), and $4.00 for children (four through twelve). Children three and under are admitted free. The address is 5701 Huntsman Road, Sandston. For more information call (804) 236–3622, or visit www.vam.smv.org.

For additional tourism information write to the ***Metropolitan Richmond Convention and Visitors Bureau,*** 401 North Third Street, Richmond 23219, or call (800) 370–9004; www.visit.richmond.com.

Hanover County

Traveling north a bit, you come to Hanover, the Hanover County seat, where the historic ***Hanover Tavern*** has reopened after an eighteen-month restoration. The tavern was given a license as an ordinary (tavern) in 1733. Patrick Henry, Virginia's first governor, and his wife, Sarah Shelton Henry, lived here, as did George Washington and Lord Cornwallis. Time, the automobile, Prohibitions, and any number of other factors led to its decline and disuse. It saw a rebirth in 1953 when an acting troupe opened Barksdale Theatre, combining dinner with a show (not at the same time), and then they moved on to other projects.

By 1990, the Hanover Tavern Foundation acquired the property and set about the massive task of restoration. A second phase was completed in 2005, and the tavern now has refinished interior flooring and painting, two dining rooms, and a restored theater that seats 156 people. A brick terrace has been laid, with an accessible ramp, and now serves as the new entrance. The space is used for art shows, lectures, and as an educational center promoting Virginia history. 13181 Hanover Courthouse Road, Hanover; (804) 537–5050; www.hanovertavern.org.

Michelle's at Hanover Tavern is open for lunch daily and for dinner Tuesday through Saturday, with chef Michelle Williams and her partner Jeffery Ferris offering a Southern grill menu. (804) 537–5250; www.michellesathanovertavern.com.

Check out the ***Bellwood Flea Market,*** 9201 Jefferson Davis Highway (the Willis Road exit off I–95), just south of Richmond. It is Virginia's largest outdoor flea market, in continuous weekend operation since 1970. This outdoor market is open every Saturday and Sunday, weather permitting, starting at 6:00 A.M. Admission for buyers twelve and over is $1.00. Call (804) 275–1187 or (800) 793–0707.

Travel south on I–95 and branch off on Route 10 to ***Hopewell and City Point Historic District,*** where you can view the confluence of the Appomattox and James Rivers. This small, bustling town adjacent to Fort Lee had a population of 40,000 during World War I, with an additional 65,000 at the then Camp Lee. The DuPont Nemours plant was known for making guncotton for dynamite. At the end of the war, Hopewell's population returned to 1,369, about the same as after the Civil War. Local historian Mary M. Calos prepared a walking- and driving-tour brochure. There's also a driving tour of the Sears, Roebuck homes that were purchased from the catalog, shipped to the home site, and assembled.

st.dennischapel

St. Dennis Chapel's "City Point Early History Museum and Gardens" is Hopewell's first museum. It features a time line from 1635 through World War I, when Hopewell became a city. The museum is located at 600 Brown Avenue, Hopewell; (540) 458–4682.

If you've been tracing the trail of the ***WPA murals*** and sculptures through the two dozen post office buildings in Virginia, you've noticed a similarity in style and execution even though the paintings were created by many different artists. Now look at Edmund Archer's painting, *Captain Francis Eppes Making Friends with the Appomattox Indians,* at the Hopewell Post Office at 117 West Pythress Street. The gesture of friendship is melodramatic and physically impossible—try to imitate the postures of the two men and see if you can keep your balance (perhaps you should not do this in the post office, though). Reportedly, Captain Eppes arrived on the ship *Hopewell,* which gave the city its name.

A little farther east (off Route 10 and then 639) is ***Flowerdew Hundred Foundation Museum,*** where the cultural history of the plantation and its region is studied and interpreted. The area surrounding Flowerdew was one of the earliest English settlements and was inhabited by American Indians before that. More than sixty-five sites have been explored through archaeological digs since 1971, and more than 200,000 items, some dating from 9000 B.C., have been uncovered, and many are on display in the museum. The eighteenth-century–style windmill has been reconstructed and is operational.

Reproductions, cornmeal ground at the windmill, and other items are for sale at the museum shop and bookstore.

The exhibits (housed in an 1850 schoolhouse), which focus on aspects of life at Flowerdew, are about the original inhabitants, the clash of cultures, the introduction of tobacco, world commerce, the burgeoning middle class, the Industrial Revolution that brought cultural changes, evidence of conspicuous consumption, Flowerdew Through the Nineteenth Century, and Grants Crossing. Maps, photographs, documents, prints, and objects are on display.

Flowerdew Hundred is located at 1617 Flowerdew Hundred Road, Hopewell, and is open 10:00 A.M. to 4:00 P.M. Monday through Friday, with the last tour stopping at 3:30 P.M., April 1 through November 15; it is closed on New Year's, President's Day, Memorial Day, Fourth of July, Labor Day, Thanksgiving, and Christmas. Admission is $8.00 for adults, $5.00 for children six to twelve, and free for those under six. For more information call (804) 541–8897; www.flowerdew.org.

Write to the Hopewell Visitor Center, 4100 Oaklawn Boulevard, Hopewell 23860, or call (804) 541–2461 or (800) 836–8687; www.historichopewell.org.

Petersburg

Even though Petersburg is nicely promoted and directly off I–95 and I–85, there are a few things that are still off the beaten path, and some that should be noted. First off, stop by the **Petersburg Visitors Center,** 425 Cockade Alley, in the McIlwaine House in Old Towne Petersburg. The center is open daily from 9:00 A.M. to 5:00 P.M. For specific information, call (804) 733–2400 or (800) 368–3595. A second visitor center is located along I–95 at the Carson rest area. It, too, is open daily from 9:00 A.M. to 5:00 P.M.; (434) 246–2145; www.petersburg-va.com.

There are two **WPA murals** in Petersburg, both in the post office at 29 Franklin Street, Petersburg. One, *Riding to Hounds,* by Edwin S. Lewis, is about fox hunting (he did the mural in the Berryville Post Office), and supposedly his wife is portrayed as the central figure in this painting. The second, on the east wall, is by William Calfee (who did the Tazewell and Phoebus murals as well); it's more pastoral and entitled *Agriculture Scenes in Virginia,* with tobacco on one side

virginia's ninth president

Although many think eight presidents were from Virginia, there's actually a ninth—Joseph Jenkins Roberts—first president of Liberia. Born in Norfolk (1809–1876) and raised in Petersburg, Roberts served six terms and is credited with obtaining the recognition of the republic by many European powers.

trivia

Included in the University of Virginia library collections are letters written to American novelist John Dos Passos. The gift was donated by Elizabeth Dos Passos, widow of the "lost generation" writer. Letters by poets e. e. cummings and Archibald MacLeish, critic Edmund Wilson, and Ernest Hemingway (which include gossip about mutual friends and tell about life in Key West) are also part of the collection. The collection also has the manuscripts and typescripts of the author's novels, histories, works of journalism, poetry, and most of his short stories. Dos Passos was a writer-in-residence at the university and an admirer of the university's founder, Thomas Jefferson.

and peanuts on the other. Also in the post office, in one of the display boxes, is a history of the Petersburg postal service that dates back to 1773, which includes a list of all eighteen postmasters who served (some served multiple terms) in this Petersburg office up to the present.

The *Old Blandford Church and Cemetery*, is the highest spot in the Petersburg area. Embark on your tour of the church and cemetery at the interpretation center with a free eighteen-minute slide show that runs about every thirty minutes.

Not only is the church, with its inverse ship's hull ceiling design, a Confederate memorial, it's also one of the art treasures of the country. It's known for its fifteen magnificent Louis Comfort Tiffany stained-glass windows. The church was built in 1735, and they say it's the only building in the country with every window an original Tiffany production. The original plan called for windows to represent each of the Confederate states, each depicting one of the Apostles, and smaller ones for the states whose sympathies had been divided. The windows took eight years to complete, and each cost between $100 (for the smaller Maryland window) and $400, including shipping. The Cross of Jewels window was donated by Tiffany.

If possible, you might want to see the church twice or even three times: the first when there isn't much sun, the second when there's a brilliant sun, and the third at sunset, to see the magnificent beauty of the Cross of Jewels. The work really is gorgeous, and some of the detail is beyond description and belief. The windows change almost moment by moment, with a three-dimensional effect coming from the Tiffany talents. Three visits may seem a large demand on your time, but these windows are worth it. The church was restored in 1901 through the efforts of the Ladies Memorial Association of Petersburg, whose remembrances of the war dead launched our Memorial Day tradition. Reportedly a Union general's wife saw "Miss Nora" Davidson and schoolchildren placing flowers on Confederate graves. The general persuaded Congress to declare a national holiday to honor the war dead.

The cemetery began before the church building was constructed, and the oldest known grave dates to 1702. Some of the finest examples of cast and wrought iron in the nation are found here. Many locals are buried here, along with 30,000 Confederate soldiers who were brought in from other areas. William Phillips, British general, was buried here secretly—the only British general to have been buried in American soil for many, many years. But the Blandford cemetery is not just for Civil War casualties. Joseph Cotton —actor, Petersburg native, and narrator of the film at the Siege Museum—is interred here.

The church, 111 Rochelle Lane, Petersburg, is open 10:00 A.M. to 5:00 P.M. daily. A donation for touring the church and grounds is $5.00 for adults and $4.00 for seniors, group members, and children. Residents of Petersburg are admitted free. Services are held here about once a month, and the newspapers are supposed to carry notice of the exact dates and times. Blandford Church Memorial Day services are held on June 9 each year. For more information call (804) 733–2396; www.petersburg-va.org.

Over in Old Towne Petersburg (which was referred to as Old Towne years ago) is the Petersburg tour's second most outstanding attraction, the *Siege Museum,* which tells the tale of life in Petersburg during the ten months the city was under attack, the longest siege of any city during the Civil War. The museum is in the former Bank of Petersburg, and it, like the other 800 buildings in the city, was under attack for two to three hours a day. Conditions were terrible, and the museum shows the war's effect on the economy, industry, and the people themselves. View the film first, shown every hour on the hour, and then wander through to learn how the women were the real heroes. Learn how ladies' hoop skirts hid food, supplies, and ammunition for the defenders. You'll see two bullets that met in midair and fused. Also on display is one of only two revolving cannons ever built—the first exploded when it was fired, and the second was never fired. View the photographs, eyewitness descriptions, and artifacts. Admission fees are $5.00 for adults and $4.00 for seniors and group members. The museum is open 10:00 A.M. to 5:00 P.M. daily

aquadrilateralhaving notwosidesparallel

Recall your math to define what a trapezium is, or be satisfied to know that Charles O'Hara built his home at 244 North Market Street in 1817 without parallel walls. Legend says his West Indian servant told him evil spirits could not reside in such a building. Or it could be O'Hara just had an unusually shaped lot on which to build. The Trapezium House is open during some community events. Call the Siege Museum for specific information. (804) 733–2400 or (800) 368–3595.

funfacts

except Thanksgiving Day, December 24 and 25, and New Year's Day. The museum is at 15 West Bank Street, Petersburg; call (804) 733–2404 for information; www.petersburg-va.org.

A Block Pass is good for admission to three sites (Blandford Church, Centre Hill Mansion, and Siege Museum) for $11.00 for adults and $9.00 for seniors (sixty and older), active miltary, and children from seven to twelve.

Think of Civil War battlefields, and you most likely think of the National Park Service. But just south of Petersburg, between I–95 and I–85, there's a privately owned attraction called ***Pamplin Historical Park and the National Museum of the Civil War Soldier.*** This is where the "beginning of the end" occurred as Federal troops outnumbered a small brigade of North Carolinians. Within a week, Lee surrendered at Appomattox. In private hands since then, the area was ignored and overgrown.

A highly dramatic-looking $10 million museum and interpretive center with an unusual design replicates (interpretively) the shape of the Confederate defensive line. You can see exhibits of Civil War artifacts and relics and learn at the interactive stations. You can follow the breakthrough from April 2, 1865, via maps, a diorama, and a state-of-the-art fiberoptics battle map.

Outside, there are $1\frac{1}{10}$ miles of walking trails among the trees and original earthworks fortifications (some 12 feet high) built to protect Petersburg. Along the trail is a reconstructed soldiers' hut of the kind used by Confederates in the winter of 1864–1865. Park guides provide tours, and special programs explain the life, weapons, and uniforms of the era from spring to fall.

Nearly three million men served in the American Civil War. More than 620,000 of them never returned home, giving their lives for the causes they fought for. The National Museum of the Civil War Soldier, a 25,000-square-foot, $16 million facility, includes an exhibit in the main gallery, Duty Called Me Here, where you select a "soldier comrade" from a group of thirteen real Civil War soldiers. Wearing a personal audio device, you become intimately acquainted with your comrade as you tour the gallery, hearing his own words taken from diaries and letters. By the end of the gallery tour, the real-life fate of your comrade is revealed, making the experience of the Civil War soldier a very personal one for you. Children may choose as their comrade thirteen-year-old drummer boy Delevan Miller, whose story is central to the Discovery Trail, the park's tour designed especially for children. The National Museum of the Civil War Soldier is also home to the Hardtack and Coffee Cafe, providing hearty fare for hungry troops, and the Civil War Store, one of the finest Civil War book and gift shops in the country.

Tudor Hall, on an additional sixty-eight acres, is an 1812 plantation owned by the Boisseau family until 1864, when the opposing armies turned their farm into a battle and camping ground. It was a descendant of this family, Dr. Robert B. Pamplin Jr. (a great-great-nephew), and the Pamplin Foundation that funded the purchase of the property as it was about to be sold for lumbering. The home has been restored and is open for exhibition.

The Pamplin Park Civil War Site is at 6125 Boydton Park Road, Petersburg. It's open 9:00 A.M. to 5:00 P.M. in winter and until 6:00 P.M. June 14 through August 17. The admission fee is $13.50 for adults, $12.00 for seniors sixty-two and over, and $7.50 for children to age eleven. Call (804) 861–2408 or (877) PAMPLIN; www.pamplinpark.org.

The U.S. Army Quartermaster Corps is the branch of the service that supplies food, clothing, and military equipment to our armed forces. The ***U.S. Army Quartermaster Museum*** at Fort Lee (formerly Camp Lee) shows life-size exhibits of colorful uniforms, weapons, Pershing's office furniture, General Patton's jeep, and furniture from Eisenhower's and Kennedy's offices. You'll also see a drum used in President Kennedy's funeral cortege and the architect's original model for Arlington National Cemetery's Tomb of the Unknowns.

There is no admission charge, but you must have a photo ID to enter the base. The museum is open 10:00 A.M. to 5:00 P.M. Tuesday through Friday and 11:00 A.M. to 5:00 P.M. Saturday, Sunday, and holidays; closed Monday and Thanksgiving, Christmas, and New Year's Days. Take Route 36 east 5 miles from Petersburg. The museum is in building 5218 on A Avenue and Twenty-second Street, Petersburg. Call (804) 734–4203 for more information; www.qmmuseum.lee.army.mil.

When Fort McClellan, Alabama, was closed, the Women's Army Corps Museum there was closed too. Fort Lee, where members of the WAC were trained from 1948 to 1954, was chosen as the new site for the museum because

funfacts

North of Richmond in Glen Allen is the Hohner, Inc. harmonica (and other instruments and harmonica-themed jewelry) manufacturer who supplied dozens and dozens of harmonicas to the troops in Operation Desert Shield so that they would feel more "at home"; 1000 Technology Park Drive, Glen Allen; (804) 515–1900; www.hohnerusa.com.

of its historical ties to the WAC. Today hundreds of Army women are trained at Fort Lee.

The newly renamed **U.S. Army Women's Museum** depicts the day-to-day service and duties of women in the military from Revolutionary days through Desert Storm. There are forty exhibits, thousands of artifacts and archival materials, and more than 300 videos in the 13,325-square-foot museum. It is open from 10:00 A.M. to 5:00 P.M. Tuesday through Friday and 11:00 A.M. to 4:30 P.M. weekends. There is no admission charge, but you must present a photo identification to the gate personnel. U.S. Army Women's Museum, at P-5219 A Avenue and Twenty-second Street, next to the Quartermaster Museum at Fort Lee, Petersburg; (804) 734–4327; www.awm.lee.army.mil.

Prince Edward County

West of Petersburg is Farmville, the home of the **Robert Russa Moton Museum and the Center for the Study of Civil Rights in Education.** In 1951 this was the site of the first nonviolent student demonstration that became part of the 1954 *Brown vs. Board of Education* case heard before the U.S. Supreme Court. That case led to the mandate of equal education for all Americans, not just separate but equal. Located in the Moton High School, the center is considered a nationally significant part of the history of the civil rights movement. Two rooms are dedicated to the court actions and another to the history of the school and the student strike. The museum rooms are open from 1:00 to 5:00 P.M. Tuesday through Friday and noon to 4:00 P.M. on Saturday; 111 South Street, Third Floor, P.O. Box 908, Farmville 23901; (434) 315–8775; http://motonmuseum.org.

To the northwest of Petersburg is Colonial Heights, home of Violet Bank (the name Violet Bank seems to have come from the profusion of violets growing on the hillside), a spreading cucumber tree (planted in 1833, it's one of the largest in the world and very rare east of the Blue Ridge Mountains), and Lee's headquarters for five months beginning June 8, 1864 (he had to leave when the falling leaves bared his position). The **Violet Bank Museum** here boasts an autographed photograph of "Stonewall" Jackson and other items of interest to Civil War buffs. The Colonial Heights Federated Women's Club is responsible for the restoration of the ornamented ceilings and the 1815 reproduction furniture.

The museum is open 10:00 A.M. to 5:00 P.M. Tuesday through Saturday and 1:00 to 6:00 P.M. Sunday. A donation is requested. It's at 303 Virginia Avenue, 1 block off Route 1/301 in Colonial Heights. For more information call (804) 520–9395; www.colonial.heights.com.

Sussex

The first commercial peanut crop grown in Virginia was grown in Sussex County, southeast of Petersburg on Route 450, in 1844. Today peanuts represent a multimillion-dollar industry in the state, so it's not surprising that you'll find "peanut this" and "peanut that" all along Route 460 and throughout the southside. The peanut, filled with protein, is the basis for several cookbooklets, which include recipes for crunchy chicken bits, cookies, glazed peanut bread, peanut-stuffed squash, peanut party biscuits, wine-cheese logs, cream of peanut soup, peanut broccoli salad, peanut spinach balls, Oriental crepes, peachy peanut spread, and, of course, peanut butter pie. Write to Production Promotion, Division of Markets, Virginia Department of Agriculture and Consumer Services, P.O. Box 1163, Richmond 23209 for a copy.

On Route 460 West, near the intersection with Route 40 in Waverly, is the **First Peanut Museum** in the United States, just about 4 miles from where Dr. Matthew Harris grew the first commercial crop. Inside the museum (a converted coal shed) are pictures of early planting and harvesting techniques, and displays including a carved elm-wood peanut by John Thornton, a Goodrich peanut digger, and other antique farm machinery and equipment.

Outside, if you arrive during growing season, you might see some peanut plants. A peanut harvest is conducted the first Saturday in November.

The museum is open 2:00 to 5:00 P.M. Thursday through Monday at the **Miles B. Carpenter Museum Complex** (Victorian house and folk art) at 201 Hunter Street, Waverly. There's no admission charge, but donations are accepted (804–834–2969). Also at the complex is an exhibit of work by internationally renowned folk wood-carver Miles B. Carpenter and crafts from other nearby artisans. There are also outhouses built during the Franklin D. Roosevelt era, a nature trail, an amphitheater, and more. The museum Web site is located at www.sussex.K12.va.us/Sussex_County/Miles_B_Carpenter_Museum.

For miles along Route 460 before you come to Wakefield, you see billboards announcing how many miles it is to the **Virginia Diner,** noted for its treatment of peanuts. It's an old 125-seat diner that is singularly unimpressive in appearance, but don't let that deceive you. It started life in 1929 as a refurbished 1860 train car and has grown ever since. Owner Bill Galloway has Virginia Fancy and Virginia Jumbo peanuts, which he first boils in water, then roasts in his special vegetable oil (he says the peanuts blister, giving them extra crunch). Remember to visit the diner's gift shop for all those ham and peanut needs. The diner is open daily, except December 25, from 6:00 A.M. to 9:00 P.M. in summer and until 8:00 P.M. in winter. Write P.O. Box 310, Wakefield 23888, or call (757) 899–3106 or (888) VA–DINER; www.vadiner.com.

Across the street is **Plantation Peanuts,** with a select variety of nuts chosen for their classic style and flavor. Each batch is slightly cooked and hand salted (ask them how they salt peanuts in the shell), and it's all done in the back room, except for the candied or sugared nuts, which are prepared elsewhere. Write P.O. Box 128, Wakefield 23888, or call (757) 899–8407 or (800) 233–8788; www.plantationpeanuts.com.

There are two other peanut museums in Virginia that you may wish to visit. In 1837 Mills Riddick built an impressive Greek Revival house, a style fairly common in the Midwest but rarely seen this far south, and it was immediately labeled **Riddick's Folly.** As with most follies that still stand, he was proven right over the years. The carved cypress woodwork survives, as do the decorative medallions that crown the 14-foot ceilings.

The rooms that housed five generations of his descendants are now home to gallery space for changing and semipermanent exhibits, lectures, and art workshops; a gift shop where local artists and crafters sell their work; and the archives of the Suffolk Nansemond Historical Society.

Riddick's Folly is open 10:00 A.M. to 5:00 P.M. Wednesday through Friday, 10:00 A.M. to 4:00 P.M. on Saturday, and 1:00 to 5:00 P.M. Sunday. It's closed on Monday, Tuesday, and on major holidays. There is no admission charge, but a suggested donation is $4.00 for adults and $2.00 for children. It is partially accessible to the handicapped and located at 510 North Main Street, Suffolk. For more information call (757) 934–1390; www.riddicksfolly.org.

Another museum that has early farm equipment and a focus on peanuts is the Southampton Agriculture and Forestry Museum in Courtland. It's open Sunday and Wednesday from 1:00 to 4:00 P.M. from March through November; 26315 Heritage Lane, Courtland. For information call (757) 653–9554.

Andree Ruellan created the 1941 **WPA post office mural** *Country Sawmill* at 109 South Main Street, Emporia. The sawmill depicted is a real one that belonged to the Daughtry and Davis sawmill, which was replaced by a shopping center.

Amelia County

The last major battle of the Civil War was fought in Amelia County at **Sayler's Creek** (or Sailor's Creek), called the "Black Thursday of the Confederacy," and **Battlefield Historical State Park** commemorates the Confederate Army's crippling defeat on April 6, 1865, which led to General Lee's surrender at Appomattox seventy-two hours later. Reenactments are held here on the Sunday closest to April 6 unless it falls on Easter Sunday, in which case the re-creation is held the following Sunday. Interpretive driving tours, called Lee's

Retreat, are available in April from Petersburg to Appomattox. Call (800) 6–RETREAT or (804) 733–2400 for a brochure and map. There's a nice genealogical library and a small museum open 10:00 A.M. to 4:00 P.M. Monday, Wednesday, and Friday. Contact Twin Lakes State Park, Box 70, Green Bay 23942; www.saylerscreek.org or www.der.state.va.us/parks/sailorcr.

Charlottesville

Going northwest out of Richmond along I–64, you can stay in this direction and go to Charlottesville, or you can turn north to Gordonsville.

We'll head for Charlottesville first, home of Thomas Jefferson's Monticello, the University of Virginia, and so much more. But you should begin your visit at the **Monticello Visitor Center,** with the offices of the Charlottesville/Albemarle Convention and Visitors Bureau.

First, it's in a lovely setting, particularly in the fall.

Second, there's an interesting exhibit that shows the life of Jefferson (particularly good if you're not taking time for Monticello).

Third, you can buy a combination ticket, the Presidents' Pass ($26 for persons twelve and up), for Monticello, Ash Lawn–Highland, and Michie Tavern.

It may be the only information center for which you should allow an hour for your visit (because of the exhibits). The center is open 9:00 A.M. to 5:30 P.M. from March 1 through October 31 and 9:00 A.M. to 5:00 P.M. November 1 through February 28; closed Thanksgiving, Christmas, and New Year's Days. It's at 600 College Drive on Route 20, south of I–64, Charlottesville; (804) 977–1783 or (877) 386–1102; www.charlottesvilletourism.org.

You can take a walking tour of Historic Downtown Charlottesville along the pedestrian mall with 30 restaurants, 120 shops, and flowering fountains, set in and around historic buildings. For your entertainment there are street performers, free concerts in an open air amphitheater, an ice park, and other diversions. The Charlottesville Municipal Band performs free concerts from May through August (rain location is in the Lane Auditorium, 4010 McIntire Road); (434) 296–8548.

I love historic theaters, particularly those built in the golden age of movie palaces, before the multiplex was invented. The **Paramount Theater** in Charlottesville was constructed with a Georgian facade, an elegant lobby, chandeliers, and eighteenth-century–style scenes painted on silk panels. When constructed in 1931, it was one of the last of these fine theaters. It had remarkable sight lines and astonishing acoustics. It quickly became a landmark that lasted for the next four decades. By mid-1974 it had been shuttered and was threatened with demolition several times (to be replaced with the ubiquitous parking garage or retail office building).

whataboutbob?

If you're stopping by Smith Mountain Lake for fishing, you may realize that this is where the movie *What About Bob* was shot (with Bill Murray and Richard Dreyfuss). The story goes that the location scout loved the lake but needed a small town next to it. There's no small town next to Smith Mountain Lake, but Virginia Film Commission people took care of that by showing them a nearby town and suggesting that people could drive by on power lawn movers with sail masts attached and bobbing around in the background. The production company bought the idea. So when you next watch the movie, check the shot of Bill Murray with the sail masts "floating" behind him while he's in town.

Fortunately, some community leaders bought the theater in 1992, had it renovated and expanded, so the old 12-foot-deep stage is now 36 feet deep, and there's fly space above the stage for curtains, lighting, and scenery. There's also rehearsal rooms and scene shops. The orchestra pit in front of the stage has a hydraulic lift to raise the theater's Mighty Wurlitzer Theatre Organ to stage level. So, now the Paramount is alive and well and doing what it's supposed to be doing—providing live entertainment, including Yo Yo Ma, Chick Corea and Touchstone, *Swan Lake,* and *The Prisoner of Second Avenue*—in the center of Charlottesville's Downtown Mall. 215 East Main Street; (434) 979–1333 or (434) 979–1922; www.theparamount.net.

The **Boar's Head Inn's** history started with an 1834 waterwheel gristmill that survived the Civil War, ran for sixty years, and then, when John B. Rogan bought it in the early 1960s, was dismantled. Rogan had the pieces numbered and reconstructed on the Boar's Head Inn property. Fieldstones from the mill's original foundation were used in the inn's fireplace and in the arched stone entrance below the ordinary (a public house or tavern). The blue boar's head was a symbol of hospitality in Elizabethan England and is well translated at the inn.

Besides fresh mountain air, stunning scenery, proximity to the University of Virginia, gracious hospitality, spa services, sports and fitness facilities, and fine dining in the Old Mill Room, you can take a champagne hot air balloon ride daily (weather permitting) between March and December with Pilot Rick Behr at the controls. Ride over the foothills of the Blue Ridge, see deer running in and around the woods and farmlands, watch people enjoying breakfast on their backyard patios. Even though you might catch them in their pajamas, they'll extend a friendly wave to you. When you're through with your hour-long ride, there's the traditional champagne celebration. Think of it as bed-and-breakfast and ballooning; 200 Ednam Drive, Charlottesville. Call (434) 296–2181 or (800) 476–1988 for reservations; www.boarsheadinn.com.

If you're feeling presidential (from your visits to the University of Virginia and Monticello) and you want to continue in this vein, then visit *Ash Lawn,* home of President James Monroe and called Highland when it was owned by the Monroe family (Monroe lived here from 1799 to 1826). Do leave your UVA feelings in your car; Monroe attended the College of William and Mary, and they are in charge of preserving and restoring the estate. Oh, and leave any "stuffy" feelings in the car as well. Depending on the time of the year, you'll see people (and one hopes you will join them) flying kites, enjoying the Summer Festival of children's shows, listening to traditional music and opera in the Boxwood Gardens, and cutting their own Christmas trees.

Ash Lawn–Highland is open 9:00 A.M. to 6:00 P.M. April through October and 11:00 A.M. to 5:00 P.M. November through March. It is closed on Thanksgiving, Christmas, and New Year's Days. Admission prices are $9.00 for adults, $8.00 for seniors and AAA members, and $5.00 for children ages six through eleven. Local residents pay $3.00—or nothing if they bring paying guests. Ash Lawn is located at 1000 James Monroe Parkway, Charlottesville. For additional information call (434) 293–9539 or visit www.ashlawnhighland.org; for Summer Festival information call (434) 293–4500.

Wendy Martin of Richmond was kind enough to send a reminder about *Crozet Pizza.* Twelve miles west of Charlottesville, Crozet Pizza is the reason people drive out of their way when they're visiting Charlottesville (the burgeoning arts community and arts festival are other reasons). It's an eatery with red clapboard exterior, a wood stove in the middle of the restaurant, and lace curtains covering the country windows. The lines form early, and on Saturday takeout must be ordered hours in advance; but should you find yourself waiting, take a look at the wall with business cards from around the world, or catch a look at family photos or the world map with pushpins indicating where patrons have been—all wearing the Crozet Pizza T-shirts. For lovers of nontraditional pizza, try such seasonal toppings as asparagus spears or snow peas, just two of the almost three dozen toppings available. Closed Sunday and Monday. 5794 Three Notched Road, Route 240, Crozet; (434) 823–2132.

Orange County

Virginia has a number of vineyards, and most of them are eager to have you stop by for a sample or maybe even to buy some of their wines. One of the more unusual ones is *Horton Cellars Winery* in Gordonsville, where Dennis Horton has created a winery that's "functional during the wine-making season, someplace wine lovers would visit again and again because of its beauty and atmosphere, and ideal for storage." The twenty-four-and-one-half acres of

Viognier grape acreage at Horton is one of the largest commitments to the grape in the country. Horton built underground cellars that fit the contour of the land and provide a constant temperature and humidity that's ideal for wine storage and a very energy-efficient building. Architect Angus McDonald created an Old English Tudor building that includes a spacious tasting room with an impressive fireplace. The Horton Cellars are open for tours and tasting. You're invited to stop by from 11:00 A.M. to 5:00 P.M.; 6399 Spotswood Trail, Gordonsville; (540) 832–7440 or (800) 829–4633; www.hvwine.com.

Back in Gordonsville, stop by the ***Exchange Hotel Civil War Museum*** to see an 1860 railroad hotel that served as a Civil War hospital for the sick and wounded. Some 23,000 men were treated in one year. In addition to medical artifacts and surgical tools, there are weapons, uniforms, and other personal items from Union and Confederate cavalrymen, artillerymen, and infantrymen. The museum is at 400 South Main Street, Gordonsville, (540) 832–2944, and is open 10:00 A.M. to 4:00 P.M. Monday through Saturday (except Wednesday) and 1:00 to 4:00 P.M. on Sunday from April through November. The last tour begins no later than 3:00 P.M. It's closed on Memorial Day, July Fourth, Labor Day, and Thanksgiving; www.hgiexchange.org. Admission is $3.00 for students, $5.00 for senior citizens, and $6.00 for adults.

Just minutes away is ***Montpelier*** (Montpelier Station), lifelong home of James Madison Jr., fourth president and "Father of the Constitution." Madison was a successful businessman, the primary author of the U.S. Constitution, one of the authors of the Federalist Papers, a key player in negotiating the Bill of Rights, a member of the U.S. Congress, and secretary of state under Thomas Jefferson. Now Montpelier is a mystery unfolding on a daily basis, an intricate tapestry of the lifestyles of two centuries. Archaeologists and historians are exploring every nook and cranny to learn more about this home and how its residents lived.

Madison's home was a commodious building, well worthy of entertaining the most important people of the country. The estate sat on some 5,000 acres of rolling countryside, woodland, pastures, and cropland. The first portion of the existing building was constructed about 1760. It was renovated, added to, modified, stuccoed, papered, gardened, farmed, and lived in. There was a previous house, but that's another story.

To pay debts incurred by Dolley Madison's son, Montpelier had to be sold, a transaction that could have led to disastrous results. The house changed hands six times until it was purchased in 1900 by William and Anna Rogers du Pont. They enlarged the house to fifty-five rooms, reestablished the gardens, and added new outbuildings, including barns from the Sears, Roebuck catalog and houses from Montgomery Ward. When its last inhabitant, Marion du Pont Scott (former wife of actor Randolph Scott), died, she left it to the National Trust for Historic Preservation.

The big news from Montpelier is that the mansion will be restored to the 1820s house that the Madisons called home. The project, started in 2003, and scheduled for a 2007 completion, will remove alterations made to the mansion after his death in 1836. That means removing the wings added by the du Pont family in the early 1990s and reducing the home to twenty-two rooms.

During the renovation, you'll still be able to see parts of the home, and you can sit in on an "insider's briefing" about the project, presented daily on the half-hour from 9:30 A.M. to 3:30 P.M. You also can take a guided behind-the-scenes "hard-hat" tour of the house under restoration. These tours are given from November through mid-March, every hour on the hour, from 10:00 A.M. to 3:00 P.M. The rest of the year, the tours will be offered every half-hour from 10:30 A.M. to 4:00 P.M. Space is limited so sign up as soon as you arrive.

A Montpelier Education Center will house Madison furniture, furnishings, and exhibits.

Activities are scheduled throughout the year, including a wine festival (usually late May), celebration of Dolley Madison's birthday, a hot-air balloon festival, and the Orange County Fair. Montpelier is open 9:30 A.M. to 5:30 P.M. daily April through October and to 4:30 P.M. the rest of the year. It is closed on Thanksgiving, Christmas, and New Year's Days and the first Saturday in November for the Montpelier Hunt Races. Admission is $11.00 for adults, $10.00 for seniors, and $6.00 for children from six through fourteen. A gift shop features books, handicrafts, and decorative items. For more information call (540) 672–2728; www.montpelier.org.

There's much more to explore in Orange County, much of it dealing with events of the eighteenth century and the Civil War.

Nearby, in the town of Orange, is the *James Madison Museum* (housed in a 1928 Nash automobile dealership), with exhibits that include possessions of James and Dolley Madison, including a campeachy chair, made from a type of mahogany grown in Mexico. The Hall of Agriculture contains antique farming tools and implements from the area. It naturally focuses on his interests in the Constitution, but it also features his involvement in agrarian reform, as illustrated in the eighteenth-century "cube" house contained in the agricultural display at the museum.

The museum, at 129 Caroline Street, Orange, is open 9:00 A.M. to 5:00 P.M. Monday through Friday all year and 10:00 A.M. to 5:00 P.M. Saturday and 1:00 to 5:00 P.M. Sunday from March through December. Admission is free to Orange County students and $4.00 for adults and $3.00 for seniors. Out-of-county students are admitted for $1.00, and adults are admitted free with a group (540–672–1776; www.jamesmadisonmuseum.org).

For lodging and dining in an eighteenth-century plantation steeped in history, try the *Willow Grove Inn,* complete with period furnishings. Owner and

gravestonesandmore

The **Old City Cemetery** (401 Taylor Street, Lynchburg) has a cemetery records research center; a display of nineteenth-century mourning clothing, jewelry, and artifacts; and a gift shop. An adjacent caretaker's museum features a display on gravestone carving, a turn-of-the-twentieth-century hearse, and nineteenth-century cemetery-maintenance tools and equipment. 401 Taylor Street, (434) 847–1465; www.gravegarden.org.

innkeeper Angela Mulloy-Brown and her accomplishments personify the Old South, with modern touches, of course. Willow Grove began as a modest frame structure built by Joseph Clark in 1778. His son added a brick portion in 1820, and the exterior is an example of Jefferson's Classical Revival style, with a more simple Federal-style interior. Set on thirty-seven acres of rolling hills and pastures, the plantation has been carefully preserved to look the way it would have naturally evolved. Hundreds of ancient trees, Victorian gardens, the original wide pine flooring, fireplace mantels, and wainscoting set the background for your long or short visit.

Dine in the elegant Dolley Madison dining room, enjoy the casual Clark's Tavern bar and pub, relax in the bright and sunny Jefferson Library, or contemplate nature from the antebellum veranda overlooking the Victorian gardens.

Douglas Gibson, general manager, uses local products to create such menu selections as potato pancakes with forest mushrooms, lobster-stuffed catfish, oyster fritters with caviar, and bourbon-maple-glazed duck breast with wild rice cakes.

The Willow Grove Inn is at 14079 Plantation Way, Orange; (540) 672–5982 or (800) WG9–1778; www.willowgroveinn.com.

Madison County

With nearly one hundred wineries now in Virginia, a place has to be exceptional to be known as exceptional, and **Prince Michel Vineyards and Winery** definitely qualifies. It's set in the heart of Virginia wine country, just east of the Blue Ridge foothills. You can take a self-guided tour of the winemaking facility, enjoy a picnic on the lawns, stroll through the vines, talk with the knowledgeable staff, and have a complimentary wine tasting of their award-winning wine in the "see-through" room atop the winery. Oh, and pets and children are welcomed. Prince Michel is open daily from 10:00 A.M. to 6:00 P.M. 154 Winery Lane, Leon; (800) 800–WINE or (540) 546–3707; www.princemichel.com

Amherst County

After a few years of residing in the 1891 jail, the **Amherst County Museum** is now in its own home where you can explore the county's history from the early Woodland Indians to the Civil War and beyond. A new permanent exhibit called Amherst County Pathways explores natural history, the bateaus, agriculture, and the Civil War. See Monacan projectile points, a copy of the original legislation creating Amherst County out of Albemarle County, and more. The museum and the genealogy library are free, but donations are accepted. The museum is open from 8:30 A.M. to 5:00 P.M. (closed from noon to 1:00 P.M.) Tuesday through Saturday; 154 South Main Street; (434) 946–9068; http://members.aol.com/achmuseum.

Bedford County

The Peaks of Otter overlook Bedford, "The World's Best Little Town" (population 6,000), as you take a western approach to the part of the state called Southside. Before entering the town you can hike up the 3,875-foot-high Sharp Top, said by Bedford residents to be Virginia's most famous mountain. A stone from the top of Sharp Top was Virginia's contribution to the Washington Monument in 1852. Milepost 86 on the Blue Ridge Parkway. (828) 298–0398; www.nps.gov/blri/peaks.

In the middle of the Bedford City Historical District is the **Bedford City/County Museum** (201 East Main Street), housed in the 1895 Masonic building on Main Street since 1979. It features two floors of displays, including old photographs, surgical instruments, a one-hundred-year-old wedding dress worn by Miss Anspaugh, daughter of Colonel David Anspaugh, and a Benjamin Franklin printing press used at the *Bedford Bulletin*. The only other press like it is at the Smithsonian Institution in Washington.

The museum's library of historical and genealogical materials is well used by those trying to find their family histories. Special lectures and films are shown in the evening. The library also has a file on the legendary Beale's treasure. There are some who say a treasure was buried in a cave near Montvale by a party of adventurers who returned from a trip to the west laden with gold and other valuables "long years prior to the War Between the States." Others say the treasure's been recovered, whereas still others say there wasn't any treasure in the first place. The directions to the treasure were left in a sealed box in a Lynchburg bank. When the box was opened, there were three intricate codes describing the treasure and its location. Reportedly, two of the codes have been deciphered, but so far no one seems to have broken the third code. You can come to your own conclusion after looking at the file and checking the maps.

Admission to the museum is free, but donations are accepted. It's open 10:00 A.M. to 5:00 P.M. Monday through Friday. For more information call (540) 586–4520 or visit www.bedfordvamuseum.org.

If you'd like to talk to some of the older residents of the county, visit the folks at the **Elks National Home,** where you can swap stories about Beale's treasure. This has been the national retirement home of the Fraternal Order of Elks since 1903. The home sits on 180 acres, and the biggest attraction is the Christmas lighting (thousands and thousands of light bulbs), which draws visitors from hundreds of miles around and gives Bedford its other title, "Christmas Capital of Virginia"; 931 Ashland Avenue, Bedford; (800) 552–4140; www.elks.org/elkshome.

The **National D-Day Memorial** was dedicated on June 6, 2001, the anniversary of the battle. Thirty-five Bedford residents went ashore at Normandy, and twenty-one of them died on the spot or soon after. It's said Bedford had the highest per capita loss of any city in the United States. Total town population at the time was about 3,500.

The sprawling monument sits atop eighty-one acres at the highest point in Bedford, with a sweeping 360-degree view of the Blue Ridge Mountains and surrounding countryside. It consists of two reflecting pools and an archway with a statue of a soldier titled *The Final Tribute* in the archway. Life-size statues, replicating soldiers approaching the beach, face a story wall that explains the unfolding battle. An education center has exhibits and work on an oral history project and is available for conferences and seminars. The memorial has been overwhelmingly more popular than even its staunchest supporters had imagined. Instead of 150,000 people a year, more than 200,000 had visited in the first months it was open. A gift shop has a variety of D-Day–related items. Other than on days of inclement weather, the memorial is open from 10:00 A.M. to 5:00 P.M. It is closed on Thanksgiving, Christmas, and New Year's Days. Admission is $5.00 for adults and $3.00 for children six through sixteen. A family pass is $25.00. The memorial is located at 202 East Main Street, Bedford; call (800) 351–DDAY or (540) 586–3329; www.dday.org.

Most people think of Monticello when they think of Thomas Jefferson, but there's another place he called home—the place he went to when he wanted to get away from the crowds of people who filled his Charlottesville home after his presidency. That place is **Poplar Forest,** a home he started constructing in 1806 while still in office. It's an octagonal plantation home, set on 4,800 acres, in Bedford County.

Guided forty-minute tours, covering such topics as the design and construction of the retreat, his landscaping design, the restoration, and the plantation community are offered from 10:00 A.M. to 4:00 P.M. Wednesday through Monday, April through November except Thanksgiving Day. Admission is $8.00 for adults, $6.00 for seniors, and $1.00 for children from six through sixteen; (434) 525–1806; www.poplarforest.org.

The new **Bedford Welcome Center,** opened October 29, 2004, has 10,700 square feet of exhibit, display, and meeting space. Large window walls offer views of the Peaks of Otter and the National D-Day memorial.

Besides the local pride, the new center received national recognition with a 2004 Crown Community Award, one of eight building projects nationwide.

Of interest to those with recreational vehicles, there are three hookup sites (for one night only) with water, electric, sewer, and Wi-Fi for $25. Permission is needed. Parking only, with no hookups, is $10 per night. Picnic tables are available on the north side of the center.

For more information about the center and Bedford County, call (877) Hi–PEAKS or (540) 587–5681 or go to www.visitbedford.com.

Appomattox County

One of the newest attractions around historic Appomattox is **Clover Hill Village,** a six-acre living-history rural village. Roy Varcoe and Nancy Murray led the development and preservation of Clover Hill Village. There is also a very well-stocked gift shop at the museum where you can purchase gifts and souvenirs. $2.00 admission fee. Open from 1:00 to 4:00 P.M. Thursday through Sunday, April through October, with guided building tours. The grounds are open daily until dusk. Call (434) 352–2007 for more information or visit www.appomattox.com/html/cloverhill_village.html. The village and museum are located on Route 627, approximately 3½ miles from Appomattox.

Franklin County

Visit the **Booker T. Washington National Monument,** which memorializes the slave childhood of the man who would educate himself and go on to found Tuskegee Institute in Alabama in 1881 and later become an important and controversial leader at a time when increasing racism in the United States made it necessary for African Americans to adjust themselves to a new era of legalized oppression. Visitors are invited to step back in time and experience firsthand the life and landscape of people who lived in an era when slavery

Booker T. Washington National Monument

was part of the fabric of American life. The cabin, one of several reconstructed buildings on the site, is a replica of the slave cabin that Washington lived in as a child.

Within the grounds are living-history demonstrations during the summer and occasionally some costumed interpretation programs. Park rangers offer guided walks of the historic area daily. They vary in length but are rarely two hours long. In the visitor center there are exhibits, an audiovisual program, and a bookstore. There is a living-history farm, trails, and a picnic area. The Plantation Trail is a quarter-mile walking trail through the historic area of the park. Jack-O-Lantern Branch Trail is a 1½-mile walk through woods and fields. The visitor center facilities are accessible to people in wheelchairs, and the historic area is partially accessible. One wheelchair is available for free loan on a first-come, first-served basis.

The park is open 9:00 A.M. to 5:00 P.M. daily, with no admission charge. The park is closed on Thanksgiving, Christmas, and New Year's Days. It is located at 12130 Booker T. Washington Highway, Hardy; (540) 721–2094; www .nps.gov/bowa/home.htm.

Look at a map and you'll realize it's a short ride to the ***Blue Ridge Parkway.*** Stop at one of the National Park Service stations for a detailed map of the Blue Ridge Parkway so that you know what you're seeing; otherwise, it tends to look like one bunch of trees after another bunch of trees. You should also find a Parkway Bloom calendar that lets you know that skunk cabbage and dandelions bloom in February, dwarf iris, spring beauty, mayapple, serviceberry, silver-bell tree, and more bloom in April, and the list continues through witch hazel in October; www.nps.gov/blri/vamap.htm.

The Crooked Road is a driving route that features some of Virginia's significant contributions to the music world. In promoting Appalachian Virginia's cultural heritage, it goes through Ferrum (Blue Ridge Institute and Museum) on the eastern end, through Floyd (Floyd Country Store and Country Records), Galax (Blue Ridge Music Center and the Old Fiddler's convention at the Rex Theater), Bristol (Birthplace of Country Music Alliance Museum), Hiltons (Carter Family Fold), Norton (Country Cabin), to Clintwood (Ralph Stanley Museum) on the northwestern end.

You can visit one or all depending on where you're driving or how you like your blend of gospel, bluegrass, and mountain music. Look for annual festivals, weekly concerts, live radio shows, and informal jam sessions throughout the area.

You'll also have a chance to appreciate (and buy, in some cases) traditional handcrafted woodwork, weaving, and pottery.

The Crooked Road, 851 French Moore, Jr. Boulevard, Suite 174, Abingdon, 24210; (866) MTN–MUSIC (686–6874); www.thecrookedroad.org.

Campbell County

In 1940 Herman Maril painted the **WPA mural** *The Growing Community* in the Altavista Post Office on Bedford Avenue and Seventh Street. It depicts the train station on the right and the Lane Furniture factory on the left. The Lane Furniture Company was opened in 1907 by John and Edward Lane when John Lane bought a box plant for $500. That box plant has grown into a company with nineteen plants in four states covering ninety-two acres of floor space and employing more than 5,000 people. The company developed the first known moving-conveyor assembly system in the furniture industry during World War I and became known through advertising in such national publications as the *Saturday Evening Post* and the "girl graduate program," which gave miniature cedar chests to some fifteen million female high-school graduates between 1930 and a few years ago.

Charlotte County

The **Red Hill Patrick Henry National Memorial** was Patrick Henry's last home and burial place. One of seven different homes he had, this was said to be his favorite as "one of the garden spots of the world." It's the home of the nation's oldest osage orange tree, estimated to be 350 to 400 years old, with a span of 90 feet and height of 54 feet. Red Hill Memorial is open daily 9:00 A.M.

to 5:00 P.M. April 1 through October 31; it closes at 4:00 P.M. the rest of the year. Admission is $6.00 for adults, and $2.00 for students and children. The memorial is at 1250 Red Mill Road (Route 2), Brookneal; to get there, drive 5 miles east of Brookneal on Route 600. Call (804) 376–2044 or visit www.redhill.org for more information.

Nelson County

Just a few miles southeast of Charlottesville, over the James River a touch, is the town of **Schuyler** (pronounced Sky-ler), the fictional home of television's Walton family and the original home of Earl Hamner Jr., on whose work the television program was based. With such a memorable time of our lives spent watching the trials and tribulations of John-Boy and Mary Ellen and the other Waltons, people just assumed there really was a Waltons Mountain. Visitors came to Schuyler in droves, sometimes as many as 500 a day. There's little resemblance between the real and the fictional town, but visitors wanted to see "Ike's" general store, the Baptist Church, the elementary school, and the Waltons' home.

Not able to do this, they'd stop by the old country store, owned by Rosie Snead, where they could buy a fact sheet detailing the history of the area, a postcard, or a color photograph of the Hamner home. She'd even stay open seven days a week until late at night during summer months. She purchased the store about the time the show went on the air, and no one would be surprised if she made more money from the souvenirs than she did from her general merchandise, but then in 1989 the store burned down.

Now, thanks to a grant from the state and local collections, there's a **Waltons Mountain Museum** (6484 Rockfish River Road, Schuyler) located in the old school, which also serves as a community center. Each of four classrooms holds a re-creation of one of the program's sets. There's the living room where, week after week, all the problems of the family were resolved with love and compassion. You'll also see the kitchen set and John-Boy's bedroom (his retreat and writing space). Each display has an audio interview with Hamner, and he talks about his growing up during the Depression; there are also video interviews with the actors.

funfacts

Patrick Henry, of "Give me liberty or give me death" fame, played the violin, flute, and pianoforte.

There are two models, one of the Waltons' house and one of the general store. In the school lobby there's a wall that's covered with newspaper articles of the press coverage of the museum's opening. On the other side local resident Barbara Marks has assembled a photographic history of the area. Naturally, you can purchase Walton memorabilia in the museum store. Proceeds of the sales and admission fees support the community center, whose activities are held in the other classrooms.

The museum is open daily 10:00 A.M. to 4:00 P.M. from the first Saturday in March through the last Sunday in November. It's closed on Easter, Thanksgiving, and the last Saturday in September, when the annual school reunion is celebrated. Admission is $6.00, free for children five and under. For more information call (800) 282–8223 or (434) 831–2000; www.waltonmuseum.org.

funfacts

James Monroe's younger daughter, Maria Hester Monroe, became the first presidential daughter to have a White House wedding.

Chesterfield County

The Ruritan Clubs of Chesterfield County, outside Richmond, established the *Chesterfield Museum* in the early 1950s. It features a reproduction of the original 1750 Chesterfield County Courthouse, the story of Chesterfield presented through narration and artifacts, a replica of an old-fashioned country store, the 1892 jail (in service through 1962), and, on the green, monuments to Baptist ministers imprisoned in 1773 and to Confederate soldiers. It's situated toward the back of the courthouse green, off Route 10 west of I–95 at 10011 Iron Bridge Road, Chesterfield. Visiting hours are 10:00 A.M. to 4:00 P.M. Monday through Friday and 1:00 to 4:00 P.M. Sunday. Suggested donations are $4.00 (including Magnolia Grange); call (804) 796–1479 for further details; www .chesterfieldhistory.com.

Across the courthouse green is the *Magnolia Grange Museum House.* Built in 1822, the plantation house is appropriately furnished and is one of the finest examples of Federal-period architecture in Virginia. Visiting hours are 10:00 A.M. to 4:00 P.M. Monday through Friday and 1:00 to 4:00 P.M. Sunday. It's closed on Saturday. Admission fees are $4.00, including the museum and jail. 10020 Iron Bridge Road, Chesterfield; (804) 777–9663.

Brunswick County

The *Brunswick County Museum,* located in the historic Courthouse Square of Lawrenceville, traces the nearly 300 years of written history (and several thousand of prehistory) of this area, covering just about everything from Native American relics (one arrowhead is estimated to be more than 4,000 years old) to Fort Christanna (1714–1718), from Saint Paul's College (founded in 1888) to the life and times of Albertis Sidney Harrison Jr., a local boy who grew up to be governor of Virginia from 1962 to 1966.

One of the more interesting exhibits is the Mrs. Alice Samford Room, which shows a buggy that belonged to a South Brunswick doctor in the late 1800s. Note that the headlamps were actually candles. Two saddles on display—a lady's side-saddle and a gentlemen's Texas saddle—are more than one hundred years old. A real charmer is the showcase of antique dolls wearing authentic clothing of the day. There's also a collection of Civil War artifacts, items from country schools, and household and farm implements.

The Brunswick County Museum is open 10:30 A.M. to 1:00 P.M. Tuesday and Thursday and 1:30 to 4:00 P.M. Saturday. There is no admission charge, but donations are accepted; (434) 848–2638.

Mecklenburg County

Buggs Island Lake, covering 50,000 acres (and 800 miles of shoreline), and straddling the North Carolina–Virginia border, was constructed by the U.S. Army Corps of Engineers between 1946 and 1953 as one of a series of dams along the Roanoke River. It's really the John H. Kerr Dam and Reservoir (named after a North Carolina congressman who supported its construction), and 169-acre Buggs Island is downstream of the dam. You can't tour the powerhouse, but you are welcome in the lobby, where you can see the generator and control room, or you can go to the Kerr Ridge Coffee Shoppe and Overlook. Besides 800 miles of shoreline, with the expected water fun of fishing (striped bass or rockfish, crappie, and largemouth black bass as well as hybrid muskie, bream, sunfish, carp, and gar), boating, and swimming, there are plenty of campgrounds and picnic and hunting areas. The activity that seems to be drawing the most attention here is the July Pontoon Boat Parade kicking off the annual Virginia Lake Festival (Lakefest). Decorated like parade floats, the boats look like anything from pirate ships to trains. The Lake County Chamber of Commerce is located at 105 Second Street, Clarksville; (800) 557–5582, (434) 374–2436; www.clarksvilleva.org.

The ***Kinderton Manor Bed and Breakfast*** in Clarksville, on Kerr (Buggs Island) Lake, is on a Donald Ross golf course (he designed Pinehurst #2), across from the Kinderton Country Club with swimming pool and tennis courts. A full country breakfast in the sunny dining room starts your morning. You might have to decide which is more important, though: golf, fishing, boating (a marina is nearby with boat rental if you don't bring your own), or swimming. And remember to visit Clarksville, the only town on the 50,000-acre lake, filled with artists and crafters. You may love this place enough to schedule your vacations, your seminars, a wedding, and who knows what else?

Peter and Gail Eaton are your host and hostess at Kinderton, a Georgian plantation home, built in 1834. Each of the four rooms is a spacious 20 feet by 20 feet, and each has a fireplace, television, phone, and private bath. Kinderton is at 850 Kinderton Road, Clarksville; (434) 374–8407.

fossilsinfocus

Virginia boasts one of the five top fossil sites in the world, a proliferation of dinosaur tracks, and modern animals found nowhere else on Earth. Many exhibits at the Virginia Museum of Natural History in Martinsville are the result of original research conducted by seven scientists on staff. Exhibits include Rock Hall of Fame, Age of Mammals, Age of Reptiles, and Dan River People. After years of being located in the old Joseph Martin elementary school, the museum is moving to new digs and 89,000 square feet of space in 2006. 21 Starling Avenue, Martinsville. Open from 10:00 A.M. to 5:00 P.M. Monday through Saturday and 1:00 to 5:00 P.M. Sunday. (276) 666–8600; www.vmnh.net.

Don't Return to Sender

East of Clarksville is **Valentines,** a small community of rural southside Virginia, with an internationally recognized name. Normally it's your typical sleepy country town, but beginning in mid-January every year, there's a certain buzz in the air, particularly at the post office. The story goes that William H. Valentine established the Valentines post office in 1887. In 1951 when Willie Wright became the postmaster of the office in the corner of Wright's General Store, he started stamping envelopes "With Love" and the tradition has grown since then. Business really started booming in 1955 when the "LOVE" stamp was unveiled here. Bags of mail came in shortly after the new year containing some 35,000 to 40,000 letters, all waiting for the postmark with a red heart and several dogwood flowers on the envelope before being sent to that special person; 23 Manning Drive, Valentines 23887; (804) 577–2456.

Halifax County

Still heading west on Route 360, about 100 miles from Richmond, you'll come to South Boston in Halifax County, the fourth-largest county in the state. The land varies from level to gently rolling and is filled with tobacco (Halifax County was for many years the largest tobacco-producing county in the country), commercial forests (the state's largest agricultural revenue producer), and large tracts of seemingly endless land. At one time there were 4,000 active farms, most of them small. Now there are also factories representing such companies as Westinghouse, Daystrom Furniture, Wabash Magnetics, Vulcan Materials, Presto Products, Clover Yarns, Rochester Button, South Boston Manufacturing, and Switzer Furniture.

The Halifax County Chamber of Commerce initiated an annual ***Virginia Cantaloupe Festival*** in 1981. The festival is held the fourth Wednesday of each July at the Halifax County Fairgrounds on Route 360 in South Boston. The fun runs from 4:00 to 9:30 P.M.

Cantaloupe was chosen because the local Turbeville variety is patented. Only seven people grow it. It can be grown only in this rich chocolate-brown soil (Wickham) in a narrow strip of land along the Dan River, and the cantaloupes are much larger and sweeter than other varieties. Although the festival technically begins at 4:00 P.M., the action clocks in much earlier with the start of the slow-roasted pulled pork taking many hours. It's much like a "big old homecoming," says the chamber of commerce's Nancy Pool. All you have to bring is your appetite, your lawn chair, and the cost of admission, which is $30 (2005 price), advance ticket sales only.

The cantaloupe is so delicious by itself that it seems logical it would make other foods taste even better, so a cantaloupe cutup recipe contest was held in 1985. The contest brought in recipes for melon with chicken, melon franks (slit a hot dog and stuff with a slice of melon, wrap with bacon, and secure with a toothpick before roasting on the grill), cantaloupe pancakes, melon with Chablis or piña colada mix, and cantaloupe preserves. For more information call (434) 572–3085 or (888) 458–1003; www.valopefest.com.

With so much history here (the county seat dates back to 1777 and two military campaigns—the Retreat to the Dan in the Revolutionary War and the Battle of Staunton River in the Civil War—culminated or occurred in Halifax County), it's natural to have a historical museum. In 1982 the Tuesday Women's Club established the ***South Boston–Halifax County Museum of Fine Arts and History,*** which houses the permanent collections and loans of items relating to Halifax, including Civil War artifacts, glassware, Indian artifacts, military uniforms, and memorabilia from Halifax County families. The museum is open 10:00 A.M. to 4:00 P.M. Wednesday through Saturday and 2:00 to 4:30 P.M. on Sunday. The building is at 1540 Wilborn Avenue, South Boston; (434) 572–9200; www.sbhcmuseum.org.

Nottoway County

Originally, **Blackstone** was the village of the Blacks and Whites. This was so because of a rivalry between two tavern keepers, Schwartz (which is German for black) and White, rather than because of race relations. In 1885 the citizens adopted the name of noted English jurist Blackstone. It was the thirteenth town in the United States to adopt the town manager form of government. Nearby Camp Picket helped swell the town's population to 15,000 during World War II, and many retired military families have located here. Blackstone celebrated its centennial in 1988 by restoring some of the best turn-of-the-century store-fronts and homes in Virginia. Awnings and period lampposts, representing Blackstone's Victorian heritage, edge the tree-lined street; (434) 292–1677; www.blackstoneva.com.

Patrick County

Two of the seven **covered bridges** remaining in Virginia are found in Patrick County, named for Patrick Henry. The Bob White Bridge is an 80-foot Theodore Burr–style bridge over the Smith River near Virginia Route 8, south of Woolwine. It was constructed in 1921 and served as the main link between Route 8 and a church on the south side of the river. It was used for more than a half century before it was replaced by a newer bridge, but you still can walk up to the old bridge, which has been kept as a landmark. Drive about 1½ miles south from Woolwine on Route 8 and then east 1 mile on Route 618 to Route 869, then south ¹⁄₁₀ mile.

Although it is called Jack's Creek Bridge, another covered bridge is over the Smith River on Route 615, just west of Virginia Route 8, about 2 miles south of Woolwine. You can see this 48-foot span from Route 8, where it intersects with Route 615, or travel about ²⁄₁₀ mile west on Route 615.

As an effort to preserve and promote the bridges, a covered bridge festival was started in 2005. The mid-June event is in Woolwine, with live bands, artists and crafters exhibiting and selling, food vendors, and carriage rides between the bridges. (276) 694–8367; www.visitpatrickcounty.org.

Pittsylvania County

The largest county in the state is Pittsylvania County, where eighteenth-century houses still stand (pick up a map at the Danville Area Chamber of Commerce and Visitors Center, 645 River Park Drive, Danville 24540; 434–793–4636) and where there were more than thirty water mills, with four—Tomahawk, Mt. Airy, Cedar Forest, and Stoney Mill—still in operation. History seems to be alive in this area, and if your group gives them enough notice, members of the local historical society will dress in Colonial costumes and entertain your busload at lunch. Genealogy can take on a new dimension in this county, for the courthouse records date from 1747, and the library has in-depth Virginia records and research tools. www.visitdanville.com.

Danville is the place where, on September 27, 1903, a southbound Southern Railroad express mail train left the tracks on a trestle and plunged into the ravine below, killing nine people. This incident was the inspiration for the song "The Wreck of the Old '97" and is recorded on a historical marker on Highway 58 between Locust Lane and North Main Street. A 46-foot by 74-foot canvas mural has been installed on the side of the Atrium Furniture building at the Gateway to downtown.

The *American Armoured Foundation Tank Museum* takes you to the beginning of military history. Stop here to see reenacters, military model shows, a military bicycle exhibit, and more.

Founded in 1981 and opened in May 2003, the museum has a mission to educate, collect, restore, preserve, and display as varied a collection of military tank and cavalry artifacts as is possible. There are 112 tanks and artillery pieces, the most extensive collection in the world. Some items date from 1509. You'll also find 150 machine guns, mortars, flamethrowers, recoilless rifles, rocket launchers, tank and artillery optical instruments, small arms, uniforms, and more. Stop by to see an exhibit dedicated to Elvis Presley during his military years and, perhaps by the time you read this, an exhibit devoted to women in the military. Timing on that exhibit is iffy as of this writing, for there are several other large displays to be established before the women's area can be created.

birthplaceofladyastor

Viscountess Nancy Astor, born in Danville May 19, 1879, was the first woman to sit in British Parliament. Her sister, Irene, inspired the famous "Gibson Girl" artwork done by her husband, artist Charles Dana Gibson. Their birthplace at 117 Broad Street is under renovation and tours are by appointment only, but a historical marker is located at the corner of Broad and Main Streets, Danville; (434) 793–4636.

Among the other facilities (research library, gift and hobby shop, class-room, etc.), the museum is home to the largest and only under-a-roof radio-controlled-tank battlefield in the world. At this time it's set up to represent a World War II–era town in France. Some exhibits are interactive, including a tank turret trainer with a machine gun attached and a gun sight that shoots out tennis balls using compressed air.

The museum is open from 10:00 A.M. to 5:00 P.M., Monday through Saturday, closed Thanksgiving and Christmas. Admission is $10.00 for adults, and $9.50 for children under twelve and adults over sixty. A.A.F. Tank Museum, 3401 U.S. Highway 29B, Danville; (434) 836–5323; www.aaftank museum.com.

The ***Danville Science Center*** occupies an 1899 train station and lets you experience science with hands-on exhibits where you can discover how things work. You can make sparks fly while discovering electricity. To understand orbits, you can launch balls. You can also see an astronaut's view of Danville.

If you visit the ***Butterfly Station*** at the Danville Science Center, you will learn that more than 160 species of butterflies inhabit Virginia. You can also learn that most adult butterflies live from twenty to forty days, they have foot-pads that act as taste buds, and butterflies and moths fold their wings differ-ently. You can also learn how to make your own butterfly garden and learn which caterpillar-host plants attract which butterfly species.

The Science Center is open 9:30 A.M. to 5:00 P.M. Monday through Saturday and 1:00 to 5:00 P.M. Sunday. It is closed Thanksgiving and Christmas Days. (The Butterfly Station is open in warm weather only.) Admission costs $5.00 for adults and $4.00 for seniors (sixty and over) and children ages four through twelve; children three and under admitted free; 677 Craghead Street, Danville; (434) 791–5160; www.dsc.smv.org.

As you drive through Danville, do take some time to drive or walk through ***Millionaire's Row,*** 8 blocks of one of the finest collections of Victorian and Edwardian architecture in the South. Look for such details as gables, ginger-bread scrollwork, columns, porticos, cupolas, and minarets.

Pick up a *Victorian Walking Tour* brochure at the visitor center. The homes are closed most of the year but are open the second Sunday in December for the Danville Historical Society's annual Christmas Walking Tour. (434) 793–4636.

Along your tour you'll see the 1857 Italian villa–style Sutherlin house, now the ***Danville Museum of Fine Arts and History,*** also known as the "Last Capitol of the Confederacy." Confederate president Jefferson Davis resided in this home during the final week of the Civil War, and it was here that Davis and his Confederate government received word that Lee had surrendered at nearby Appomattox. In 1870 the True Friends of Charity sealed a tin-box container in the wall of a department store. Renovation uncovered the box, whose contents reveal an unusual insight into a period of history, as displayed in the Time Capsule exhibit. Other exhibits depicting the history of the area and revolving art exhibits are featured. There's also a gift shop.

The museum is located at 975 Main Street, Danville. It is open 10:00 A.M. to 5:00 P.M. Tuesday through Friday and 2:00 to 5:00 P.M. on Saturday and Sunday. Call (434) 793–5644 for additional information; www.danvillemuseum.org.

Chatham, north of Danville on Route 29, has won several Keep Virginia Beautiful awards and has earned a reputation as the prettiest little town in the southside. The Pittsylvania County Historical Museum has artifacts from Revolutionary and Civil War days, with a series of five dioramas depicting General Nathanael Greene's immortal race to the Dan, which took place about 35 miles from Chatham. Call (434) 432–5031 for an appointment; www.pittced.com.

The Chatham Post Office at Main and Pitt Streets has another of the two dozen **New Deal murals** in the state, this one by Danville artist Carson Davenport. The murals were part of the Works Projects Administration, Roosevelt's New Deal program to keep unemployed artists working. Completed in 1938, the agricultural mural *Harvest Season in Southern Virginia* has Davenport's name on the tobacco packing crate on the right edge of the painting.

Stay on Route 29 for just a bit, and stop in Gretna to see that Williamsburg is not the only place to benefit from the donations of DeWitt Wallace (founder of *Reader's Digest*), for he also helped fund the restoration of the **Yates Tavern** in Gretna. Dating from about 1750, the basement has rock walls about 2 feet thick. The 10-inch front and back overhangs, known as jetties, provide additional upper living space and make the Yates Tavern the only such old dwelling with Elizabethan or Tudor overhangs in Virginia. In restoration, original eighteenth-century materials from a collapsing structure in Laurel Grove, an old cabin from Red Oak Hollow, and an old Danville structure were used rather than reproductions. Yates is open by appointment only. Call (434) 432–1650; www.pittced.com.

West of Danville is Martinsville, home of the **Piedmont Arts Association,** a Museum Partner of the Virginia Museum of Fine Arts. You never know what they'll be offering (well, you will if you call or check their Web site), but it might be an exhibit of paintings and graphics or three-dimensional works and installations in one or more of the five galleries. They also offer the opportunity to see (and purchase) one-of-a-kind craft items in the gift shop. Pottery, jewelry, carved wooden objects, dried flower wreaths, and more come from craftsmen from the region and across the country, with price ranges to fit every budget. Regional artists offer their work for sale in the Lynwood Artists' "Off the Wall" gallery, where visitors can purchase a painting "off the wall" and take it with them.

The Piedmont Arts Association is free and open to the public from 10:00 A.M. to 5:00 P.M. Tuesday through Friday, from 10:00 A.M. to 3:00 P.M. on Saturday, and from 1:30 to 4:30 P.M. on Sunday; 215 Starling Avenue, Martinsville; (276) 632–3221; www.piedmontarts.org.

Virginians have such a bent for history that it isn't surprising to find still another historical museum. The *Virginia Museum of Natural History* in Martinsville, under the direction of Drs. Noel T. and Dorothy Boaz, is a little different, as its focus deals with nature. Oceanography (mainly an exhibit of shells) and astronomy (mainly planets) are the subjects of the two permanent displays. Other exhibits rotate and might cover dinosaurs, American Indian heritage, rocks and minerals, holography, Ice Age Virginia, African explorations, botany, insects, rivers and streams, and reptiles and amphibians.

Of great interest to those who love bugs and insects is the donation of a collection of eleven million Virginia insects, from the National Museum of Natural History, Smithsonian Institution, to the museum. These critters were collected in Louisa, Essex, Fairfax, and Clarke Counties over a period of about ten years.

The museum is located at 1001 Douglas Avenue, Martinsville, and is open 10:00 A.M. to 5:00 P.M. Monday through Saturday, and 1:00 to 5:00 P.M. on Sunday. Admission is $5.00 for adults, $4.00 for senior citizens and students, and $3.00 for children three to eleven. There is a gift shop. Call (276) 666–8600 or visit www.vmnh.net for further details.

Head north out of Martinsville on Route 220 and, for information and exhibits about the traditional life and culture of the Blue Ridge and its inhabitants, stop by the Ferrum College's *Blue Ridge Institute and Museum.* The institute's programming has an international reputation. Offered are gallery exhibits and a living-history farm/museum of the day-to-day lifestyle of the German Americans who settled here in 1800.

Look for costumed interpreters cooking meals in an open hearth, baking bread in an outdoor bake oven, blacksmithing, and doing other house and farm chores. There are educational workshops, audio and video productions, and an annual folk festival. Historical breeds of sheep, chicken, horses, pigs, and cattle are in the farm buildings, and heirloom vegetables are grown in the gardens around the home and farm buildings. If you'd like, you can inquire about participating in visitor programs in which you wear the costumes and take part in the farm activities and village crafts.

The one-day fall celebration at the institute's Folklife Festival (10:00 A.M. to 5:00 P.M. on the fourth Saturday in October) shows old customs and competitions, with performers on three stages playing blues, gospel, and string band music. Dozens of artisans show their skills and sell crafts, and antique and contemporary quilts are displayed in the Mountain Comforts Quilt Show. You can also view restored automobiles and farm machines, and you might want to catch the horse pull and coon dog competitions. When you're ready for a bite to eat, try some of the dozens of regional specialties, but don't look for hot dogs or hamburgers. (540) 365–4416.

Located at Route 40, Ferrum, the Blue Ridge Museum is open for walk-in visitors 10:00 A.M. to 5:00 P.M. Saturday and 1:00 to 5:00 P.M. Sunday, mid-May through mid-August. Admission is $4.00 for adults and $3.00 for children and senior citizens. www.blueridgeinstitute.org.

Where to Stay in Central Virginia

AFTON

Afton Mountain
10273 Rockfish Valley Highway
(540) 456–6844 or (800) 769–6844

BEDFORD

Liberty House
602 Mountain Avenue
(540) 587–0966
or (888) 810–2903

Otter's Den
8578 Peaks Road
(540) 586–2204)
or (877) 968–8377

Peaks of Otter Lodge
85919 Blue Ridge Parkway
(540) 586–9263

Reba Farm Inn
1099 Reba Farm Lane
(540) 586–1906
or (888) 235–3574

BRODNAX

Three Angels Inn
236 Pleasant Grove Road
(434) 848–0830
or (877) 777–4265

CHARLOTTESVILLE

Boar's Head Inn
200 Ednam Drive
(800) 476–1988
or (434) 296–2181

English Inn
2000 Morton Drive
(434) 971–9900 or (800) 786–5400

Foxfield Inn
2280 Garth Road
(434) 923–8892
or (866) 369–3536
or (866) FOXFLDN

Inn at Monticello
1188 Scottsville Road
(434) 979–3593

DYKE

Cottages at Chesley Creek Farm
2390 Brokenback Mountain Road
(434) 985–7129 or (866) 709–9292

GORDONSVILLE

Shenandoah Crossing Resort
10 Shenandoah Crossing Road
(540) 832–9400

HARDY

Ashleigh Manor
430 Hartwell Drive
(540) 890–3332

KESWICK

Keswick Hall at Monticello
701 Club Drive
(804) 923–4388

LAWRENCEVILLE

Three Angels Inn
(434) 848–0830
or (877) 777–4265

LOUISA

Prospect Hill Plantation Inn
2887 Poindexter Road
(540) 967–0844
or (800) 277–0844

LYNCHBURG

Federal Crest Inn
1101 Federal Street
(434) 845–6155
or (800) 818–6155

Ivy Creek Farm
2812 Link Road
(434) 384–3802 (800)
689–7404

MADISON

Ebenezer House
122 Seville Road
(540) 948–3695
or (888) 948–3695

Ridge View
(540) 672–7024
or (866) 852–4261

MONETA

**Bernard's Landing Resort
& Conference Center**
775 Ashmeade Road
(540) 721–8870
or (800) 572–2048

NELLYSFORD

Mark Addy
641 Rodes Valley Drive
(434) 361–1101
or (800) 278–2154

ORANGE

Greenock House Inn
249 Caroline Street
(540) 672–3625
or (800) 841–1253

Holladay House
155 West Main Street
(540) 672–4893
or (800) 358–4422

Inn on Poplar Hill
278 Caroline Street
(540) 672–6840
or (866) 767–5274

Mayhurst Inn
12460 Mayhurst Lane
(540) 672–5597
or (888) 672–5597

RED OAK

CornerStone Farm
525 Barnes Road
(434) 735–0527
or (866) 977–3276

RICHMOND

Berkeley Hotel
100 East Cary Street
(804) 780–1300
or (888) 780–4422

Jefferson Hotel
101 West Franklin Street
(804) 788–8000
or (800) 424–8014

West Bocok House
1107 Grove Avenue
(804) 358–6174

William Miller House
1129 Floyd Avenue
(804) 254–2928

ROCHELLE

Ridge View
5407 South Blue Ridge
Turnpike
(540) 672–7024
or (866) 852–4261

SCOTTSVILLE

**High Meadows Vineyard
Inn & Restaurant**
55 High Meadows Lane
(800) 232–1832

SOUTH BOSTON

**Berry Hill Plantation
Resort**
3105 River Road

(434) 517–7000

STANARDSVILLE

Lafayette Inn
146 Main Street
(434) 985–6345

South River Country Inn
3003 South River Road
(434) 985–2901
or (877) 874–4473

WINTERGREEN

Wintergreen Resort
Route 664
(804) 325–2200
or (800) 266–2444

Where to Eat in Central Virginia

CHARLOTTESVILLE

Rococo's
2001 Commonwealth Drive
(804) 971–7371

LOUISA

Cooper Vineyards
13372 Shannon Hill Road
(540) 894–5253

PETERSBURG

Brickhouse Run
409 Cockade Alley
(804) 862–1815

Longstreet's
302 North Sycamore Street
(804) 722–4372

Outlaw's Bar & Grill
3729 South Crater Road
(804) 862–9277

RICHMOND

Bogart's
203 North Lombardy Street
(804) 353–9280

Buz and Ned's Real Barbecue
1119 North Boulevard
(804) 355–6055

Café Diem
600 North Sheppard Street
(804) 353–2500

Carlton's
2526 Floyd Avenue
(804) 359–3122

Corner Café
800 North Cleveland Street
(804) 355–1954

Frog and the Redneck
1423 East Cary Street
(804) 638–3764

Krispies' Fried Chicken
1625 Williamsburg Road
(804) 226–4831

Mrs. Marshall's Carytown Café
3215 West Cary Street
(804) 355–1305

SANDSTON

Ma and Pa's Diner
5600 Williamsburg Road
(804) 226–0329

WEST POINT

Tony and George's Seafood and Italian
2880 King William Avenue
(804) 843–4448

WILLIAMSBURG

A Carroll's Bistro
601 Prince George Street
(757) 258–8882

Berrets Seafood
199 South Boundary Street
(757) 253–1847

Blue Plate Diner
6380 Richmond Road
(757) 258–1924

Bones Select Chicken Beef & Ribs
351 York Street
(757) 564–7109

Giuseppe's Italian Café
5601 Richmond Road
(757) 565–1977

Jefferson Restaurant
1453 Richmond Road
(757) 229–2296

Old Chickahominy House
1211 Jamestown Road
(757) 229–4689

Trellis
403 West Duke of Gloucester Street
(757) 229–8610

Western Virginia

We'll explore the western part of Virginia from the northern part of the state and wander down the lush 200 miles of the Shenandoah Valley and mountains to Roanoke.

There are a lot of interesting aspects to the Shenandoah River. It runs "uphill," or from south to north. The valley was the main thoroughfare for settlers moving south from Pennsylvania. More major battles of the Civil War were fought in Virginia than any other state, and this lush, fruitful valley was a grand prize that changed hands dozens of times. Skyline Drive runs 105 miles through the 194,000-acre Shenandoah National Park. (*NOTE:* Admission is $10.00 per car plus $5.00 per pedestrian, bicyclist, or motorcyclist—good for seven consecutuve days, or get a Golden Eagle Passport, a Shenandoah Passport [currently $20.00 per private vehicle], Golden Access Passport, or a Golden Age Passport to enter the park; www.nps.gov/shen.) At its southern end it meets with the northern end of the 469-mile Blue Ridge Parkway as it winds along mountain crests toward the North Carolina border.

The valley is a monument to history and beauty, but it is also new and modern and exciting. The multimillion-dollar Virginia Horse Center in Lexington has become a major part of our country's horse culture. At the southern terminus is

WESTERN VIRGINIA

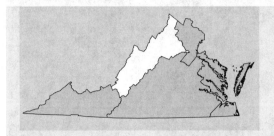

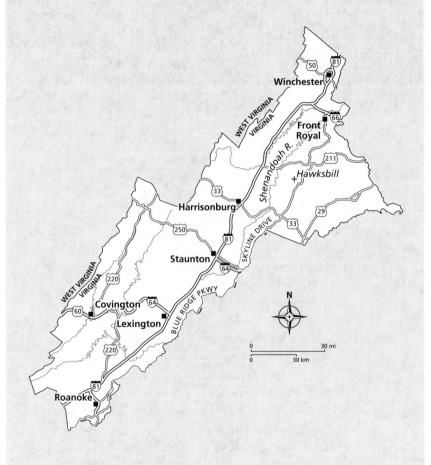

Roanoke, the cultural center of the valley, with its outstanding art, science, history, and transportation museums.

I call our Virginia mountains friendly because they invite the hiker, the stroller, the skier, the river rafter, and the explorer into their sanctuary, their tranquility. Perhaps most important to casual visitors, the scenery is breathtakingly beautiful, with each curve and bend in the road more extraordinary than the previous one.

There are four *skiing* resort areas in Virginia: Bryce Mountain, the Homestead, Massanutten, and Wintergreen.

Bryce Mountain has eight slopes and trails, a 500-foot vertical drop, and a long run of 3,500 feet. Bryce Resort also has a snow tubing park, grass skiing, and golf. Basye; (540) 856–2121 or (800) 821–1444; www.bryceresort.com.

The Homestead has nine slopes, a 700-foot vertical drop, and a long run of 4,200 feet. There's also snowboarding, an ice rink, and a two-lane tubing area open on weekends. Hot Springs; (540) 839–1776 or (866) 354–4653; www.thehomestead.com.

Massanutten has fourteen slopes, a 1,100-foot vertical drop, and a long run of 4,100 feet. All slopes are lit for night skiing. A six-lane tubing area has a 900-foot run, and snowboarding is available in the Terrain Park. Harrisonburg; (540) 289–9441; www.massresort.com.

Wintergreen has twenty trails, a 1,003-foot vertical drop, and a long run of 7,400 feet. The ski lift and top of the ski runs offer spectacular views of the Blue Ridge Mountains. Tubing and boarding options are available. Wintergreen; (434) 325–2200 or (800) 926–3723; www.wintergreenresort.com.

We'll travel parallel to Interstate 66, Interstate 81, and Interstate 64. Then we'll skirt and flirt with Skyline Drive and the activities and sights along its path. Stop here for covered bridges, antiques, handmade crafts, and Civil War and historical museums. Taste some of the most delicious apples anywhere, and they're not necessarily Delicious. You might want to stop by an inn filled with antiques or spend some time in a cloistered abbey. And while you're at it, you can catch music ranging from country to classical.

Clarke County

Leaving the northern area of Virginia, head west along Route 7 or Route 50, where you'll detour a smidgeon to enter the world of Clarke County and Berryville. Although still mostly bucolic, things have changed around here. Gone are the mortuary museum and a general store where your payment was put in a trolley that rode a pulley to the second floor office, and your change was placed in the trolley to be returned to you.

Generally, you might say people here like the status quo. In fact, it's said that one resident put a mock Civil War cemetery in his front yard to keep the state from taking his land for a road-widening project. Supposedly, they never asked him if it was a real cemetery, so he never told them otherwise.

What you can see in Berryville is the ***Old Clarke County Courthouse,*** designed and built by David Meade soon after Clarke County—named for George Rogers Clark (without the "e")—was formed from Frederick County in 1836. See items from a nineteenth-century dry goods store, a rare Goldsmith Chandlee tall case clock, and more. It's open from 1:00 to 4:00 P.M. Monday through Friday; 32 East Main Street. While you're in the courthouse neighborhood, you'll see the county jail, the sheriff's office, and a former clerk's office on the courthouse square; 102 North Church Street, Berryville; (540) 955–2600.

The bread and fruitcake (two pounds, four ounces each) from the cloistered Trappist ***Abbey of the Holy Cross Monastery*** is legendary. Locally, Safeway and Giant grocery stores carry the baked goods, free of preservatives and made from unbleached and stone-ground flours, spring water, and unsulfured molasses. Or you can order a cake for $25. The monastery is on the site of the historic Wormley Estate, a well-preserved, 200-year-old stone building.

What isn't as well known is that you can stay at the abbey. Accommodations are available for fifteen men and women, there are no scheduled activities other than meals, and three of them are included each day. Each room has a private bath and a large window that opens onto the scenic beauty of the Blue Ridge Mountains. This is a great, quiet retreat, and if you're going off the beaten path to escape, this is the place to do it. Oh, and there is a gift shop, open between 9:00 A.M. and noon and then from 1:30 to 5:00 P.M., where you can buy the aforementioned fruitcake. The abbey is on

Route 603; 901 Cool Spring Lane, Berryville; (540) 955–9494; www.monastery
fruitcake.org.

The **Burwell-Morgan Mill** is an operating overshot waterwheel with
wooden gears. It's made of stone and dates from 1785 (built by former Hessian
soldiers who were captured at the Battle of Saratoga in 1777); clapboard was
added in 1876. Lt. Col. Nathaniel Burwell and Brig. Gen. Daniel Morgan started
the operation, and during the Civil War flour and feed from the mill were sold
to both armies. It was an unusual mill in that the abundant water supply and
huge 20-foot-diameter wheel achieved forty-five horsepower, compared with
an average of only twenty horsepower. The mill remained in operation until
1953. After six years of extensive restoration work, the mill was rededicated on
July 4, 2001, with great fanfare and with more than 200 volunteers, patrons,
and dignitaries on hand. Charles Burwell, a descendant of Lt. Col. Burwell, was
there to celebrate the historical moment as red, white, and blue cornmeal was
ground in honor of the event and the day. Visit the mill on early Saturday afternoons and see one or more of the twenty volunteer millers who keep the
waterwheel and machinery going.

Located on Route 624, just north of Route 50/17 in Millwood, Burwell-
Morgan Mill is open 10:00 A.M. to 5:00 P.M. Thursday through Saturday, and
noon to 5:00 P.M. on Sunday. When the mill is operating, Saturday is grinding
day. For more information call (540) 837–1799 or (540) 955–2600; www.clarke
history.org/the_mill.htm.

It's not exactly in the same league as a historic mill, but for those who like
prehistoric stuff, **Dinosaur Land** (Route 1, Box 63A, White Post 22663) could
be the place to visit. Built in the mid-1960s, nearly three dozen nasty-looking
fiberglass critters, from allosaurus to yaleasaurus, roam (statue-wise) the woods
waiting to inform you and have their picture taken with you and your young-
sters. For your convenience, there's also a little store with souvenirs.

Dinosaur Land is open 9:30 A.M. to 5:30 P.M. March 1 to Memorial Day, 9:30
A.M. to 6:30 P.M. Memorial Day to Labor Day, 9:30 A.M. to 5:30 P.M. Labor Day to
November 1, and 9:30 A.M. to 5:00 P.M. November 1 to December 31. It is closed
in January and February. The admission price is $5.00 for folks ages eleven and
older and $4.00 for children ages two through ten; (540) 869–2222; www
.dinosaurland.com.

At the University of Virginia's **Blandy Experimental Farm and the
Orland E. White Arboretum** (which is the State Arboretum of Virginia) in
Boyce, you can enjoy a bucolic experience as you travel through 170 acres of
maintained landscapes and gardens featuring more than 1,000 varieties and
species of plants representing 100 generations and 50 families. View the most
extensive boxwood collection in North America. Feel free to drive the circular

apopulardish

The Mrs. Lauder's coleslaw you may find in Virginia grocery stores is made at Lauder's Restaurant (583 West Strasburg Road, Front Royal; 540–635–5121). They chop and mix about 350 pounds of cabbage five or six days a week, and that bumps up to half a ton for the Fourth of July weekend.

route or take a leisurely walk through a shady dogwood lane. Picnicking is allowed.

Among the types of activities planned by the staff here might be a bus trip to the Maymont Flower and Garden Show, an exhibit of wildflower pictures by Richmond photographer Hal Horwitz, book readings and signings, and an apprentice gardener workshop. Some of these events have an admission fee; some are free. The arboretum, at 400 Blandy Farm Lane, Boyce, is open to the public every day from dawn to dusk. There is no charge for admission; (540) 837–1758; www.virginia.edu/blandy.

Warren County

When you leave the metropolitan Washington, D.C., area on I–66, or more pastoral Route 55, you're driving through Warren County.

There's no doubt you're approaching apple country. One way to sample these succulent gifts of nature is by stopping at the *Apple House* in Linden. I dare you to resist the fragrant aroma and lure of the freshly baked apple-cinnamon donuts. I'm told the mountaintop orchards benefit from rare climatic conditions, and the high altitude produces apples "sweeter and more intensely flavored than valley-grown fruit." Take a taste of the nonalcoholic sparkling ciders (also no added sugar and no preservatives) they've named Alpenglow (a reddish glow seen near sunset or sunrise on the summit of mountains).

They offer the original Alpenglow (red Delicious and Winesap apples); mulled sparkling cider (apple pie in a bottle, they call it); sparkling scuppernong cider (wild grape muscadine from North Carolina and cider); classic blush (Virginia-grown rougeon grapes, muscadine, and various species of apples); and sparkling juice. Sampling is encouraged, they say, because "taste tells all." Apple House is just off I–66 at Route 55 exit 13, Linden. It's open 8:30 A.M. to 6:00 P.M.; (540) 636–6329 or (800) 462–1867; www.applehouseva.com.

Fauquier County

Almost before you're out of earshot of the planes from Dulles International Airport, you're in the area of The Plains, and that's where you'll find the *Rail*

Canoe Capital

Front Royal, northern gateway to Skyline Drive and Shenandoah National Park, has been officially granted the title "Canoe Capital" by the state because of the more than 40,000 people who annually explore the north and south forks of the Shenandoah River. If you want to join them, call the Front Royal Canoe Company (800–270–8808) and consider exploring the Andy Guest Shenandoah River State Park; www.frontroyal canoe.com.

Another canoe, tube, kayak, and raft rental place is Shenandoah River Outfitters, Inc. They also have river cabins and a tent campground; 6502 South Page Valley Road, Luray; (540) 743–4159 or (800) 6CANOE2; www.shenandoahriver.com.

Stop Restaurant. In this neat, old white building with random-width wooden floor boards.

Join the rest of the regulars, and those who've been sightseeing nearby, in one of the two main dining rooms, or reserve the Red Room, which can accommodate from two to six people. It's beautifully decorated and showcases the outstanding wine selection. You can choose from a special menu. Advance reservations are requested; they're required for the Red Room.

The Rail Stop is open for lunch Wednesday through Saturday, dinner Tuesday through Sunday, and brunch on Sunday; 6478 Main Street, The Plains; (540) 253–5644; www.railstoprestaurant.com.

Rappahannock County

If you're planning to stay in this area and you're looking for a base, try the *Flint Hill Public House,* where proprietors and chefs John and Denise Pearson welcome you to this historic turn-of-the-twentieth-century school building. There's also a restaurant and a country inn on the five acres of land.

As you wander the grounds, stop to admire the herb and vegetable gardens that produce foods for the restaurant. Other native Virginia products are used in the restaurant whenever possible. More than forty selections of Virginia wines are included in the collection of more than 400 from California, the Pacific Northwest, France, and Italy. The restaurant is open for lunch and dinner Thursday through Tuesday. It is closed on Christmas Day. And if you're a Cheesehead (Greenbay Packers football fan), this is the place to be during football season.

Two overnight suites are upstairs, each with a queen-size bed and private bath. The two rooms share a sitting room and service kitchen. Flint Hill Public House is located at 675 Zachary Taylor Highway on Route 522 in Flint Hill. Call (540) 675–1700 for reservations and information; www.flinthillpublichouse.com.

Winchester

Farther west on Route 50 or Route 7 in Winchester, you can discover the **Shenandoah Valley Discovery Museum,** which lets you explore the Shenandoah River watershed, experiment with laws of physics, and uncover the relationship among the service, manufacturing, and business sectors of the town. Art materials are available, as are small appliances that you can take apart. And if those muscles need a little stretching, try the 8-foot-high (25-foot-long) climbing wall.

Those who think museums are stuffy should have been here when six original Andy Warhol prints were on display, along with a silkscreen studio where visitors could try their hand at this art form. A fairly permanent (it's there indefinitely) exhibit is entitled Reflections on Mirrors, which explores the nature of them, be they convex or concave, one-way, or otherwise. There are also make-and-take activities.

grayandblue

The remains of 3,000 Confederate and 4,500 Union soldiers killed in nearby battles were laid to rest at the **Confederate & National Cemeteries** in Mt. Hebron, 305 East Boscawen Street, Winchester; (540) 662–4868.

Based on the motto "To touch is to explore, to explore is to discover, to discover is to learn," there's lots to explore, discover, and learn here. In the natural history section there are "discovery drawers," and one can dig for fossils in the fossil pit or visit a Burmese python named McGuyver. In the Our Town section there's a hospital with an emergency room and ambulance. Children can learn about an integral part of Winchester's history and industry in the apple-packing shed, which also helps teach about physical sciences and mathematics. The handicap obstacle course brings to life the realities and frustrations of navigating in a walking-person's world. The aforementioned climbing wall isn't just a place for exercise; it's an enjoyable way (one hopes) to learn about gravity.

The museum is at 54 South Loudoun Street on the Downtown Walking Mall, Winchester (540–722–2020; www.discoverymuseum.net), and is open 9:00 A.M. to 5:00 P.M. Monday through Saturday and 1:00 to 5:00 P.M. Sunday. Admission is $5.00 per person.

Virginia's Country Classic

Winchester's most famous daughter, Virginia Patterson Hensley Dick (September 8, 1932–March 5, 1963), was buried at the Shenandoah Memorial Park following her plane-crash death in Tennessee. You may know her better as award-winning country singer Patsy Cline. A bell tower has been erected here in her memory. Enter the north gate and take the first right to the bench on the left.

Other places of Cline history include her Winchester home, at 608 South Kent Street; the home where she married Charlie Dick on September 15, 1957, at 720 South Kent Street; Gaunt's drug store, where she was a waitress at the soda fountain, at the corner of South Loudoun and Valley Avenue; G & M Music, at 38 West Boscawen Street, where she recorded; WINC Radio 520 on North Pleasant Valley Road, where Patsy often performed; Handley High School on Valley Avenue, where she attended high school; and the Kurtz Cultural Center at the corner of Cameron and Boscawen, where a memorabilia case is on display.

In addition to Patsy Cline Boulevard in Winchester, the 7-mile stretch of U.S. Highway 522 running south out of Winchester is known as the Patsy Cline Memorial Highway. It was dedicated in November 1986. For a brochure highlighting Cline landmarks and historic sites, contact Celebrating Patsy Cline, Inc., P.O. Box 3735, Winchester, VA 22604; (540) 665–0079; www.patsycline.com.

Frederick County

Now, turning south, along Route 11, 5⅓ miles north of Stephens City, is the site of the **Battle of Kernstown,** the only battle in which Stonewall Jackson was defeated (8,000 Federals against Jackson's 3,500 Confederates). Ironically, two years later, in June 1864, the Second Battle of Kernstown was the last Confederate victory in the Shenandoah Valley (540–662–1824). Although there are buildings on the road in front of the property, you can see the back portions where the battle of March 23, 1862, took place, and historic markers relate the events of the battle. Contact the Kernstown Battlefield Association for scheduled events; www.kernstownbattle.org.

America's oldest motor inn, Middletown's **Wayside Inn,** has been in operation since 1797, when it was known as Wilkerson's Tavern, and it has always been a marvelous place to dine and to stay, with twenty-four rooms. The furnishings make the place an antique-lover's paradise. There are seven dining-room options, but a meal in the Lord Fairfax Room or the Old Servant Kitchen (both favorites), a walk through the inn, or an extended stay is always a pleasure. The inn is located at 7783 Main Street in Middletown (540–869–1797 or 877–869–1797; www.alongthewayside.com). To reach the Wayside from I–81,

OTHER PLACES WORTH SEEING

Dayton
Shenandoah Valley Folk Art and
Heritage Center (540) 879–2616
www.heritagecenter.com

Front Royal
Skyline Caverns (540) 635–4545 or
(800) 296–4545;
www.skylinecaverns.com

Lexington
George C. Marshall Museum
(540) 463–7103
www.marshallfoundation.org

Roanoke
To the Rescue Museum
(540) 776–0364

Staunton
Staunton/Augusta Arts Center
(540) 885–2028
www.saartcenter.org

Waynesboro
Shenandoah Valley Art Center
(540) 949–7662

take the Middletown exit (exit 302) and follow signs to the inn.

Like stepping back in time to the 1890s, the *Hotel Strasburg* (213 Holliday Street, Strasburg; 540–465–9191 or 800–348–8327; www.hotelstrasburg .com) combines Victorian history and charm to make a special place for lodging and dining. Tastefully decorated with many antique pieces of period furniture and an impressive collection of art, the inn's dining rooms and quaintly renovated sleeping rooms invite you to wander through them. Do arrive early so that you can peek into the rooms to view the varied quilts and furniture pieces. There are no elevators and no dedicated staff to take your luggage to your room; that means a steep set of stairs to navigate, so pack light.

Shenandoah County

If you'd really like to drive through a covered bridge, then head toward the *Meems Bottom Covered Bridge* between Mount Jackson and New Market over the north fork of the Shenandoah River. It was built in 1893 of materials hewn and quarried nearby and was nearly destroyed by fire in 1976. It was reopened in 1979 and then closed again due to structural problems. It has since reopened. Mount Jackson says the bridge is 191 feet long; the Virginia Department of Transportation says it's 204 feet. In any case it's the longest covered bridge in the state and the only one still open for vehicular use.

This single-span Theodore Burr truss, built under the supervision of F. S. Wisler, succeeded at least two other bridges. Records show that one was burned in 1862 as Stonewall Jackson went up the valley ahead of General John C. Fremont prior to the battles of Harrisonburg. Another was washed away during a flood in 1870. ("Up the valley" here is southward, since the river flows northward to join the Potomac at Harpers Ferry.)

The bridge is easily reached by taking exit 269 from the south or exit 273 from the north off I–81 to Highway 11 and turning west on Route 720. Call (540) 459–2332 for information.

It's amazing what a little fame will do, or more important, what a great reputation will do to garner that little bit of fame. So goes the story with the **Route 11 Potato Chip Factory.** It's been covered in the *Washington Post, New York Times, Winchester Star, Bon Appetit, Gourmet,* and *Southern Living. Today, Good Morning America,* and *The Early Show* have had segments about the yummy place, and perhaps most important it's been featured on the *Food Finds* show on the Food Network.

With all that publicity, you know these spudmasters are doing their job. You can watch them do it on Friday and Saturday, between 9:00 A.M. and 5:00 P.M., with early morning to early afternoon the best time. If you've never tried making potato chips (or chips from other veggies), this is the place to visit. Of course, you can shop at the retail store or through their Web site. As they say, the "best things in life are still made by hand."

The Chip Factory and retail store are on Main Street, U.S. Route 11 (just south of the only traffic light in town), Middletown (the first exit north of the I–81/66 merge); (800) 294–SPUD (7783) or (540) 869–0104; www.rt11.com.

skylinecamping

Shenandoah National Park has more than 600 campsites open between spring and October at Loft Mountain (mile 79.5), Lewis Mountain (mile 57.5), Big Meadows (mile 51.3), and Mathews Arm (mile 22.1). There are 200 sites that can be reserved up to ninety days ahead at Big Meadows, but the rest are first-come, first-camped. There are camp stores and flush toilets, and all accept recreation vehicles; however, there are no hookups. Call (800) 365–2267; www.nps.gov/shen.

Do stop by the **Shenandoah Valley Travel Association Center** (277 West Old Gross Road), just off I–81 at exit 264 New Market, and talk with the marvelously friendly and competent staff, who will help lead you to your specific interests. The center is open daily from 9:00 A.M. to 5:00 P.M. Write to the Shenandoah Valley Travel Association, P.O. Box 1040, Department CE88, New Market 22844; call (540) 740–3132 or (800) VISIT–SV; www.svta.org.

Shenandoah Caverns, at exit 269 off I–81, has a large elf statue welcoming you to one of the many caverns available for touring in this part of the state. The tour descends a staircase into the fifty-six-degree cavern system, or you can take the elevator—the only cavern system in Virginia that has one. The caverns open daily at 9:00 A.M., with the last tour time varying by season. Admission, which includes the American Celebration Parade and Main Street or Yesteryear, is $18.00 for adults, $16.00 for seniors, and $8.00 for children six through fourteen; 261 Caverns Road, Shenandoah Caverns; call (540) 477–3115. The caverns' Web site is located at www.shenandoahcaverns.com.

The *American Celebration on Parade* is where you can see, pose by, and even climb on some of the most extensive and glorious parade floats that have graced such events as the Presidential Inaugural, Mardi Gras, Rose parade, Miss America Pageant, and Thanksgiving parade. You are guaranteed to be amazed at their beauty, complexity, and size. They come from the shop of Hargrove, Inc., a Maryland company that started in the 1940s. The company has been decorating the National Christmas Tree in Washington, D.C., since the Pageant of Peace was established in 1954, and some of the lights and decorations from the trees are included in the holiday exhibit. The 40,000-square-foot facility has changing exhibits, and the Shenandoah Jubilee singers perform about a dozen concerts a year at the facility.

Admission is $17.50 for adults and $7.00 for children ages six to fourteen for American Celebration on Parade, Main Street of Yesteryear, and Shenandoah Caverns. The exhibits are open daily at 9:00 A.M. Closing time and the last tour vary seasonally; 397 Caverns Road, Shenandoah Caverns; (540) 477–4300; www.shenandoahcaverns.com.

Page County

The *Jordan Hollow Farm Inn* (326 Hawksbill Park Road, Stanley) is a 200-year-old working horse farm on 150 acres, not too far from Luray Caverns, with Gail Kyle and Betsy Anderson as your innkeepers.

There are fifteen suites and rooms at the inn (each with sunporch and rocking chair, private bath; some with a whirlpool bath and fireplace) in several buildings. A large community room features a fireplace, television, books, and games.

Breakfast is a real treat and might be a maple/walnut/apple bake with fruit and sausage, or a large Greek omelette with homemade bread, sausage, and fruit. The restaurant is open in the evenings by reservation.

An assortment of animals populates the property (including fifteen cats, give or take a few), and horseback riding is available (bring your own horse, or use one of theirs). If riding isn't your pleasure, try some hiking. Besides offering a great getaway for two, the inn has a conference room for up to thirty-five people, and some rooms suitable for families. Rates are from $143 to $250, including breakfast. Call (540) 778–2285 or (888) 418–7000 for more information; or visit www.jordanhollow.com.

Reportedly the largest bell at the Luray Singing Tower, **Luray Caverns** (a few miles east of Mount Jackson, on Route 211, Luray) weighs 7,640 pounds. The world's largest musical instrument is the Great Stalacpipe Organ in the Cathedral Room of Luray Caverns; (540) 743–6551; www.luraycaverns.com. The caverns open daily at 9:00 A.M., with the

funfacts

Two turkey statues, one at each end of Route 11, welcome you to Rockingham County, the top poultry producer of Virginia.

last tour time varying by season. Admission, which includes a visit to the Car and Carriage Caravan Museum, is $19.00 for adults, $16.00 for seniors, and $9.00 for children six to thirteen.

West of Mount Jackson is Orkney Springs, where the **Shenandoah Valley Music Festival,** one of the outstanding events of its type, is held every summer. First opened in 1962, the festival offers programs that vary from the great masterworks for orchestra to light classical music, lilting pops, vocal music, and big band sounds. You could not ask for a more beautiful setting in which to hear beautiful music (and it's mountain informal to boot). William Hudson, director of the Fairfax Symphony, is the artistic director and administrator for the nonprofit festival.

Of course you're invited to bring your own picnic to eat on the lawn before the concert. Tickets range from $16 to $23 depending on the event and seating choice. To get there take exit 283 off I–81 and go east on Route 703; then turn right onto Route 11 through Mount Jackson and turn right onto Route 263; follow Route 263 (going west) for 15 miles. For more information or discount subscription tickets, write to the Shenandoah Valley Music Festival, P.O. Box 528, Woodstock 22664; call (540) 459–3396 or (800) 459–3396; or visit www.musicfest.org.

Harrisonburg

The **Daniel Harrison House** (Old Route 47/North Main Street, Dayton), southwest of Harrisonburg and just north of Dayton, also is known as Fort Harrison. The front part of this sturdy stone structure was built in about 1748, with the rest of the house constructed in the 1850s. When the nonprofit organization formed by the Harrisonburg-Rockingham Historical Society purchased

TOP ANNUAL EVENTS

March
Highland Maple Festival, Highland
(540) 468–2550
www.highlandcounty.org

April
Easter Sunrise Service, Natural Bridge
(540) 291–2121
www.naturalbridgeva.com/events
Historic Garden Week, statewide
(804) 644–7776
www.vagardenweek.org

June
Hall of Fame Jousting Tournament, Mt.
Solon (540) 350–2510
www.nationaljousting.com

October
Shenandoah Hot Air Balloon Festival,
Long Branch Plantation (Clarke County)
(540) 837–1856
www.historiclongbranch.com

the property in 1978, it immediately began restoration, including dismantling and rebuilding the east and west stone walls.

Within the past few years, the organization has repainted the interior and exterior and redone the floors. Some original cedar shingles were found in the attic and replicated. A group of local archaeologists has searched for the hidden tunnel that supposedly connected the house to the nearby spring and that reportedly was used as protection from marauding Indians. That search has not been completed, and the society hopes to continue it.

The house is open 1:00 to 5:00 P.M. Monday through Saturday. Tours are available for school groups and others by calling (540) 879–2681 or (540) 879–2616. $5.00 admission fee. Visit their Web site at www.heritagecenter.com.

Opened in 1947, the *L&S Diner* in Harrisonburg says its pan-fried chicken is the most popular item on the menu. Seems natural, as this is one of Virginia's big poultry centers. If you'd like to stop and try some, the diner is open from 5:30 A.M. to 8:00 P.M. Monday through Saturday. It's located in an authentic railway car at 255 North Liberty Avenue, Harrisonburg; (540) 434–5572.

Quilting is a favorite pastime, whether for the wonderful historical patterns created over the years, the heirloom quality, or the physical and mental warmth they create, and you can explore all these facets at the *Virginia Quilt Museum.* Here you'll discover the roles and significance of quilts in American society and be amazed and delighted at the ingenuity, the creativity, and just the beauty of all the quilts on display. You can take lessons, perhaps learn about that beloved quilt that's been handed down in your family for generations, or stop in the gift shop.

The museum is open from 10:00 A.M. to 4:00 P.M., Thursday, Friday, Saturday, and Monday, and 1:00 to 4:00 P.M. on Sunday, and is housed in the historic Warren Sipe House, 301 South Main Street, Harrisonburg. Admission is $5.00 for adults, $4.00 for seniors, and $3.00 for students. For information, call (540) 433–3818; or visit www.vaquiltmuseum.org.

The **Natural Chimneys** regional park area in Mount Solon is the home of some towering limestone structures, impressive scenery indeed. Does your mind see 120-foot chimneys or massive castle turrets? Two annual jousting tournaments have been taking place here since 1833. The first jousting happened in 1821 between two men deciding who should have a certain damsel for his wife. You can view the drama of medieval competition during the Hall of Fame Joust on the third weekend in June. An August weekend features local crafters as well as the tournaments, and it draws a larger crowd. A few thousand people turn out for the one-day event, a combination of horsemanship, balance, and marksmanship. Some jousters use lances a hundred years old.

Tour the **Jousting Hall of Fame Museum** at Natural Chimneys, featuring the history of the sport of ring jousting and about fifty exhibits on the best and most important men and women in the sport. Trophies, brass plates with the names of champions engraved on them, and testimony of the jousters' accomplishments fill the displays. To qualify, a member must have a minimum of twenty years' involvement in jousting and must have promoted jousting on a national level, made special contributions, and won titles.

Natural Chimneys is open March 1 through October 31. Camping (145 sites with water and electricity) is available for $20 for local residents and $21 for others from Labor Day to Memorial Day and $23 and $24, respectively, during the summer. That includes your admission into the chimneys area. Admission to the chimneys and museum is $3.00 for one person or $6.00 per car. You can't see the chimneys from the jousting grounds, but they're only 100 yards away. Natural Chimneys is just north of Mt. Solon on Route 721. Call (540) 350–2510 or (888) 430–CAMP or visit www.uvrpa.org.

Staunton

It's said that the **Frontier Culture Museum** (near Staunton, which is pronounced Stanton) is the only one of its kind in the world.

The museum shows four working nineteenth-century farmsteads. Two of them were brought to the site from European nations—Northern Ireland and Germany—and the English farm was reconstructed (it couldn't be removed because of English preservation law). It is said that although the countless stones that made up the Irish farmhouse were numbered in place, somehow they multiplied like so many wire hangers, and quite a few were left over after it was reassembled here in the United States.

The fourth farmstead was donated by Phyllis Riddlebarger of Botetourt County, Virginia, reflecting the melding of European influences. Her late husband's grandparents bought the farm in 1884. You can see the adaptations in the German V-notched log barn construction, and the A-frame roofed smokehouse has English derivations. The center will also amass and preserve archival and genealogical collections and artifacts. Historical research, academic outreach, intern programs, and the preparation of appropriate materials and publications will play a vital role in the museum programs.

The museum is located at the junction of I–64 and I–81 (1250 Richmond Avenue, Staunton); admission is $10.00 for adults and $6.00 for children ages six to twelve. Visiting hours are 9:00 A.M. to 5:00 P.M. mid-March through November and from 10:00 A.M. until 4:00 P.M. the rest of the year. For more information write the museum at P.O. Box 810, Staunton 24402, call (540) 332–7850, or visit www.frontiermuseum.org.

On display in the **Staunton firehouse** at 500 North Augusta Street is Jumbo, a 1911 Robinson fire engine lovingly restored by Billy Thompson's White Post Restorations. Stop by during the day and the firefighters on duty will show you into the room; or if you come at night, you can look through the windows. Souvenir tumblers are available, and because it cost $143,000 to restore the fire truck, they'll accept donations. Call (540) 332–3884 for further details; www.stauntonfire.com.

Wright's Dairy Rite is not the last curb-service (where you order from the speaker on a "Servusfone" at your parking place) hamburger joint in the state (a few Sonic Burgers, at several locations, offer the same service), but it's probably the most historic. F. A. Wright opened this eatery in 1952 and insisted that only the highest-quality and freshest ingredients be used in his kitchen. Mr. Wright created a tradition in Staunton that has existed for more than fifty years. To this day Wright's is still family-owned (Wright's son-in-law James E. Cash and his son, James R. Cash). This is where the Statler Brothers used to hang out and perhaps where they began composing one or more of their songs. Although the '50s have remained here, Wright's now offers free wireless Internet service. Wright's is at 346 Greenville Avenue, Staunton; (540) 886–0435; www.dairy-rite.com.

Staunton has a different festival every month, so there's almost always something happening in this very vibrant town. Check with the **Staunton–Augusta County Travel Information Center,** 35 South New Street, for detailed tourism information and a Visitor Appreciation Card, good for merchant discounts and more. (540) 332–3972 or (800) 342–7982; www.staunton.va.us.

It's time to brush up your Shakespeare, your Ben Jonson, and your Tom

Stoppard at the ***Blackfriar Playhouse, Shenandoah Shakespeare*** in Staunton. Hoping to duplicate, or go several levels higher than, the annual Shakespeare Festival in Ashland, Oregon, Ralph Cohen has directed the fund-raising ($4 million worth) and construction of the world's only replica of the Bard's favorite theater (the Globe was an outdoor theater; the Blackfriar an indoor facility). It's oak and has wooden benches for about 300 (you can rent a cushion and backrest), and the house lights don't go down when the acting starts so you have a much more intimate relationship with the cast, who can see who the audience is and how you're reacting. And it's jaw-droppingly beautiful.

The Blackfriar Playhouse has productions daily except Monday, with matinees on Tuesday, Wednesday, Thursday, Saturday, and Sunday. Tickets start at $10 and go to $28, and shows will be in repertoire, so you can catch two or three days or a full weekend of great theater; 11 East Beverley Street, Staunton; (540) 885–5588; www.shenandoahshakespeare.com.

When you want that perfect Virginia souvenir, travel Route 250 east out of Staunton, toward Waynesboro, to visit the ***Virginia Made Shop,*** owned by Terry and Ginger LeMasurier, featuring a wide collection of Virginia products, including Pruden's hams and bacon, wines, crafts, Colonial gifts and accessories, and souvenirs. They do a particularly good Christmas-craft business.

Many of the crafts appear more modern than old-timey, but there is a variety of things, such as cornhusk dolls, cornhusk flowers, grapevine and pinecone wreaths, and cotton rugs, the best-selling item in the shop. Everything promotes Virginia, and almost everything is made in Virginia except some souvenirs made elsewhere in the United States (they couldn't find Virginia manufacturers for some of these items). Nothing is foreign-made, and about half the artists are from the Staunton area.

This shop has been open since early 1984. 54 Rowe Road, Staunton; (540) 886–7180 or (800) 544–6118.

Rockbridge County

Captain Joseph Kennedy constructed what is now called ***Wade's Mill*** some time around 1750, and his family owned it for more than a century. James F. Wade, hence the name, purchased it in 1882, and his family operated it for the next four generations. The four-story mill is powered by a 21-foot waterwheel from a nearby stream (known originally as Captain Joseph Kennedy's Mill Creek) and is one of the few remaining mills still producing a wide variety of flours on millstones. On your free self-guided tour, you can see all the gears and pulleys used to grind the wheat. It's listed on the National Register of Historic Places.

Jim and Georgie Young now carry on the tradition of the miller and his wife with fresh, old-fashioned, stone-ground grains and mixes. Then they take things a step further with cooking classes, catered dinners for your special occasions, and more. Check for such events as wine tastings; special dinners with guest chefs; an apple butter festival with music, crafts, and great foods and wines; Friday luncheons (and occasionally on Saturday, too); picnics; and special menus featuring international cuisine like that of Spain, Provence, and New Zealand. Check their Web site for some mouthwatering recipes that will have you ordering from the catalog immediately, if you don't decide you really want to stop by in person.

Wade's Mill is open Wednesday through Saturday from 10:00 A.M. to 5:00 P.M. and Sunday 1:00 to 5:00 P.M., from April through the middle of December. It's closed on Sunday from June through August and on July 4 and Thanksgiving Day. The mill is located at 55 Kennedy-Wade's Mill, Raphine (4 miles west of I–81 at the Raphine exit); (800) 290–1400 or (540) 348–1400; www.wades mill.com.

One of the more spectacular sights on the eastern side of the Continental Divide is **Natural Bridge.** It's more than one hundred million years old, 215 feet high, and 90 feet wide. It was surveyed by George Washington in 1750 (you can see his initials carved on the wall of the bridge) and once owned by Thomas Jefferson (he bought it and 157 acres of land from King George III of England for twenty shillings in 1774). Seeing the bridge, hiking through nature, stopping in the Wax Museum and taking the self-guided tour of the museum factory, viewing the "Drama," and touring the caverns means you can spend an hour or two here or an entire day.

The nightly illumination of Natural Bridge is a tradition that started on May 22, 1927, when President Calvin Coolidge pressed the start button for the first time. Musical accompaniment was added to this Drama of Creation.

Colonel Henry Parsons explored the caverns in 1889–1891, and when modernization took place, some tools, a ladder, a lantern, and rope were found where they had been left almost a hundred years before.

Scenes of Virginia and Natural Bridge history are included in the Wax Museum, with highlights from the lives of such notables as George Washington and Thomas Jefferson.

A combination ticket to Natural Bridge, the caverns, the Wax Museum, and toy museum is $28 for adults, $14 for children. Other ticket packages are available, and hotel guests receive a discount on the ticket price.

The Natural Bridge complex is on U.S. Highway 11, Natural Bridge; (540) 291–2121 or (800) 533–1410; www.naturalbridgeva.com.

Nelson County

It's always nice to find a good, well-recommended down-home diner, and the **Blue Ridge Pig** (Rockfish Valley Highway, Nellysford; 804–361–1170), on Route 151 northeast of Waynesboro, seems to fit that description to a T. On the be-sure-to-try list are home-smoked pork and beef barbecue (sliced or chopped), ribs, and smoked turkey, all done in a large wood-burning smoke-house behind the restaurant. Even the homemade lemonade and limeade, spicy baked beans, and potato salad rate raves. The Pig is popular with locals, skiers from the nearby Wintergreen resort, and truckers going up and down the coast. There's carryout as well as dining in. It's open from 11:00 A.M. to 8:00 P.M.

When you want to golf and snow ski in the same day, learn to mountain bike, be pampered in a spa, kayak, rock climb, fish, boat, horseback ride, have some good food, enjoy Blue Ridge Mountain scenery, or just do nothing at all, the place to do it is the **Wintergreen Resort.**

One of the more fascinating programs offered at Wintergreen is OWLS, the Outdoor Wilderness Leadership School, where you can enjoy the historic and magnificent Blue Ridge Mountains while developing your biking proficiency with Wintergreen guides to lead you. The OWLS center rides take you through the George Washington National Forest, Walnut Creek Park, or Panorama Farm on their Gary Fisher full-suspension bikes. They provide the rentals, trail maps, and shuttle service—you provide the muscle power. Four-hour tours are offered daily, starting at 10:00 A.M. and 2:00 P.M. Reservations are required. www.owlsadventures.com

You can also take a course in rock climbing and rappelling, and enjoy a fly-fishing retreat. Yes, there are options for those who are more domestic and indoors-oriented.

Wintergreen Resort, P.O. Box 706, Wintergreen, VA 22958; (434) 325–2200 or (800) 926–3723; www.wintergreen resort.com.

Be sure to stop by Nelson County's **Crabtree Falls,** just off the Blue Ridge Parkway near the Wintergreen Resort, which has 3 miles of cascading water-falls. It is touted as the highest waterfall east of the Mississippi River, with a ver-tical drop of 1,200 feet. You can hike the

famousresidents

Among the famous who live or have lived in the Rappahannock County area are painter Ned Bittinger, former columnist James Kilpatrick, former Pittsburgh Symphony director Lorin Maazel, former senator Eugene McCarthy, and sculptor Frederick Hart.

Oh Tannenbaum

The folks from Monterey were rightfully proud in 2004 when a 70-foot red spruce tree traveled through thirty-four Virginia communities on its way to the Capitol in Washington, D.C. Prior to that, schoolchildren were taken to see the tree while it was still growing, then there was a party with music and refreshments. Several buses, filled with most of the Monterey population, accompanied the tree on its trek. Souvenir shirts, tree ornaments, key chains, and cuddly stuffed bears were sold to mark the occasion. The Capitol holiday tree comes from a national forest, and this was the first time a Virginia forest was chosen. You can visit the Department of Forestry's online shop at www.capitolholidaytree2004.org for more information.

2-mile trail along the cascading waterfall, and there are several lookout points; Route 56, Lovingston; (434) 263–7015 or (800) 282–8223.

Change direction, and drive about 4 miles west of Staunton on Highway 250 to visit the Jennings Beach Valley, around ***Churchville*** (named because of all the churches). This is the area where John Trimble, an early Irish settler, was killed in 1764 in the last Indian raid in Augusta County. Visit www.high landcounty.org.

A few more miles westward and you'll pass the scene of the ***Battle of McDowell*** (540–396–6169), where you can view Confederate breastworks (low barriers to protect gunners). A forest-walk entrance leads to an area where, in 1862, a military action brought Confederate troops to this mountain-top to build fortifications that would block Union advances into the Shenandoah Valley. So effective were these fortifications that it would be 1864 before Union troops would try again to enter the valley. More than a century later, the trenches of these wartime fortifications are visible. A short ³⁄₁₀-mile loop trail (about a twenty-minute walk that's a little steep and rocky in places) is marked. Travel on the forest walk is one-way and is for the foot traveler only. Three exhibit points along the way tell the story of this small part of Civil War history.

Once you've driven through Highland County, you understand what it means to be the third-least-populated county east of the Mississippi. There's an estimated ratio of five or six sheep to every person living here. Monterey, the county seat, is 50 miles and four mountains away, via winding, twisting Route 250, from Staunton.

This is maple sugar country, as testified to by the ***Highland Maple Museum*** (540–468–2550) on the outskirts of Monterey. Take a clockwise trip around this open-air museum to learn the history of maple syrup and sugar making and the tools, equipment, and processes used to make them. The museum was created in 1983 by the Highland County Chamber of Commerce and is open 9:00 A.M. to 6:00 P.M. daily. Come spring, particularly the last two weeks in March, it's time for buckwheat cakes and maple syrup, and you can find them in any restaurant in the area. For information write P.O. Box 223, Monterey 24465; www.highlandcounty.org.

Bath County

Now, you can head down Route 220 and along Route 39 for some real solitude.

On one of my exploratory trips I took off from Hot Springs toward West Virginia on Route 39, a designated scenic byway, and just marveled at this pristine area. A tape of Vivaldi's *The Four Seasons* (what else?) was cranked up fairly high to serenade the woodland creatures through the car's open windows, whether or not they wanted to be entertained. There was no one else on the road for miles. In fact, other than the road, there was barely a sign that a human had happened by this way.

This is Bath County, where the population boasts that there are no traffic lights in the county, no billboards (there are advertising signs on the roads, but no "billboards"), and, because the weather is cool enough, no mosquitoes. I must admit that, in traveling through this area, I have never met a mosquito in Bath County. What Bath has to offer is lots of pretty scenery, some of the oldest rock formations known to geology, and a few pleasant ways to spend some time.

Suddenly, as though from a scene from the movie *Close Encounters of the Third Kind,* I turned a corner, and stretched out below me were the workings and company town of Virginia Power's **Bath County Pumped Storage Project.** As I recall, there were about 3,000 people working on this facility. There was on-site housing for 1,000. This meant that another 2,000 were commuting daily, some from as far as 90 miles away. I must have just missed rush hour.

It was my introduction to the waterpower concept. Virginia Power took two streams, the Big Back Creek and the Little Back Creek, and dammed both, creating huge reservoirs. During the day, water is released from the upper storage area to the lower storage area via 1,000-foot-high pipes that are nearly 29 feet in diameter. Water gushes through the turbines, generating electricity. When evening comes, the turbines and the procedure are reversed, and the water is sent back up to the original reservoir area. Why? you might ask. For several reasons. One, the procedure works as both a flood- and drought-prevention program. The water's recycled, so there's no fear of a dry season, and the downstream farmers and residents are assured of a constant supply of water and power. The only water loss is from evaporation. Second, it's a relatively inexpensive means of power generation. Approximately one kilowatt is lost (in the return water process) for every four generated.

You can visit the pump station, but you can't use the two lakes because they can fluctuate in level up to 60 feet in a very short time. There is, however, a 325-acre recreational lake, a thirty-site RV campground, a group/family picnic shelter, a sandy beach with swimming area and bathhouse, a hiking trail, and other recreational facilities. The campground doesn't have individual electric hookups (I've always thought that strange), but there is a comfort station with hot-water showers, flush toilets, and a dumping station.

A stocked trout stream, also occupied by smallmouth bass, is available, and the ponds have largemouth bass (18 inches is about the record), red-eared sunfish, bluegill, and channel catfish enjoying the habitat. There's a charge of $1.00 per vehicle for day-use activities.

Free project tours are available by appointment for groups or on the second Thursday of each month for individuals. You see the upper reservoir and dam, lower reservoir and dam, the second and third floors of the powerhouse, the generating bay, and the control room. Reservations are requested a couple of weeks in advance. The minimum number is one person; the maximum is forty. For reservations and more information, call (540) 279–3289; or visit their Web site located at www.dom.com/about/stations/hydro/bath.jsp.

Arlene and Luca DiCecco, violinist and cellist, respectively, operate **Garth Newel** (Welsh for "new house") **Music Center** (Route 2, Box 565, Warm Springs 24484), Virginia's only center for studying and performing chamber music. Arlene is from South Africa and was educated in London. Luca is from Connecticut; they met in Rome when he was there as a Fulbright Scholar. Between Warm Springs and Hot Springs, on 114 acres, with the Allegheny Mountains as a background, you can hear concerts featuring string quartets or a piano trio or sometimes as many as an octet, with Paul Nitsch as pianist and harpsichordist in residence.

Concerts are performed every Sunday at 3:00 P.M. and almost every Saturday evening at 5:00 P.M. from July 4 through Labor Day. Lighter compositions are performed at the Fourth of July and Labor Day events. In summer the performances are held on the stage of Herter Hall. Students sometimes participate in these programs and can also be heard throughout the area at other events in local churches. In winter the venue moves to the manor house living room, and guests enjoy gourmet meals, country lodging, and fireside concerts.

Several spring and fall holiday music weekends are scheduled, and guests can stay for the entire weekend or may obtain lodging elsewhere in the vicinity. Reservations are sometimes made up to a year in advance, particularly for Thanksgiving weekend, but they definitely should be made at least two months ahead (540–839–5018 or 877–558–1689; www.garthnewel.org). Garth Newel is a nonprofit operation, sponsored by contributions, donations, and matching grants from arts organizations.

Jean Randolph Bruns runs **Anderson Cottage Bed-and-Breakfast** in a 200-year-old log tavern with nineteenth-century additions. It is closed in winter except for a two-bedroom housekeeping cottage available year-round. Rates range from about $70 to $125 per night (Old Georgetown Road, Warm Springs; 540–839–2975; www.bbonline.com/va/anderson).

If you're a movie buff, the hills may look familiar because Jodie Foster and Richard Gere filmed *Sommersby,* a movie about the struggles of a couple following the Civil War, in these beautiful Allegheny Mountains. **Hidden Valley Bed-and-Breakfast** was used in the film. Ron and Pam Stillham are the innkeepers of this bed-and-breakfast with three rooms and eighteenth- and nineteenth-century antiques. For reservations write to them at Hidden Valley Road, Warm Springs 24484, call (540) 839–3178, or visit www.bbonline.com /va/hiddenvalley/.

Head east from here to continue on Route 39, one of Virginia's **scenic byways,** heading eastward to Lexington. This byway goes through Goshen Pass, 3 miles of impressive turns and twists and views (hard to keep your eyes on the road) with jagged cliffs towering a thousand feet on either side. It's necklaced by dogwood, ferns and mosses, hemlock, laurel, maples, mountain ash, pines, and rhododendron. A scenic overlook (built during the repairs from the flood of November 1985) has plenty of parking places, and a picnic area is just yards away.

Head south out of Bacova, and you'll come to what Bath County may be best known for, **The Homestead** at Hot Springs (U.S. Highway 220 North, Hot Springs), one of those venerable resorts dating back for what seems forever. It's set on some 15,000 acres, offers three golf courses (one designed by Robert Trent Jones), numerous tennis courts, warm baths, swimming pools, bowling, skiing, ice skating, horseback riding, carriages, stream fishing, children's activities, and countless other amenities.

Playing golf in this area can be devastating to your ego. The courses are tough, but some people say it's the magnificent view (which tends to add a few strokes to your average score) that's so distracting to your concentration.

Although not inexpensive (no one would expect it to be), you can sometimes book into packages—such as golfing, wine tasting, tennis, or skiing—that will reduce the overall price. You can stay at the nearby Cascades, which is owned by The Homestead, for a little less and pay a nominal premium to dine at The Homestead or use some of its facilities. As can be expected, fall foliage is a busy time, and you can have trouble getting a shadow in this place without prior reservations. Occupancy is light in July and August. Call (540) 839–1766 or (866) 354–4653 for reservations and more information or visit www .thehomestead.com.

Pick up Route 220 going south, where you'll see **Falling Springs,** a leaping cascade of about 200 feet noted by Thomas Jefferson in his book *Notes on Virginia,* written in 1781. The Westvaco Corporation, which owns the land on which the falls and the wayside are located, recently completed extensive renovations to the overlook, so you can more safely stop and enjoy the view. Take your camera and maybe look for some afternoon sun or early-morning mist. It's beautiful. Not far away are two natural areas where you might want to stay awhile. (540) 962–2178.

Thomas M. Gathright Sr., a landowner, farmer, and avid sportsman, and Benjamin C. Moomaw Jr., executive director of the Covington–Alleghany County Chamber of Commerce, championed the cause for the construction of a water-control project on the Jackson River to protect Covington and other downriver communities from flooding. In their honor are **Lake Moomaw** and **Gathright Wildlife Management Area.** The 12-mile-long lake, with its 43½ miles of shoreline, was created by a dam that is 1,310 feet long and rises 257 feet above the Jackson River bed. The dam's appearance is misleading, particularly if you've seen such monumental projects as Hoover Dam. It's a clay and rock structure that you can drive over, and it looks like just another piece of shoreline. Many people ask, "Where's the dam?" It isn't until you go into the visitor center and see the display and then go outside to the overlook that you realize the water at the dam is 150 feet deep (the lake has an average depth of 80 feet). The visitor center, open from 8:30 A.M. to 3:30 P.M., has some interesting information.

The 2,530-acre stocked lake created by the Gathright Dam has year-round boating, boat ramps, lighted docks, water sports, sandy beaches, fishing, camping, picnicking, hiking, and hunting (in season). There are wheelchair-accessible fishing decks. The area is abundant with wildlife, including bald eagle, white-tail deer, and turkey. You must possess a valid fishing license and a free permit from the Gathright Visitor Center.

Camping in the Gathright Dam and Lake Moomaw area is available in several USDA Forest Service camping areas on a first-come, first-served basis. Furnished cabins are available and reservations can be made by calling (800) 933–PARK. Obviously, there are some peak times when the whoosh of a dog's wagging tail couldn't squeeze into the campgrounds, particularly during fall foliage time. The Morris Hill camping area (with fifty-five campsites and a dump site, potable water, and restrooms), about a forty-five-minute drive from recreational facilities at Lake Moomaw, doesn't always fill up when the leaves are changing.

For additional information write to the James River Ranger District, 810–A South Monroe Avenue, Covington 24426, or call (540) 962–1138. The dam and lake are about 10 miles north of Covington. Take Route 220 to Route 687, to Route 641, to Route 666, which will bring you to the facilities.

The other nature area is **Douthat State Park** in Millboro. Some of the cabins and campgrounds that surround the oval-shaped Douthat Lake—as well as the roads, trails, dams, and picnic areas at Douthat State Park—were built by the Civilian Conservation Corps between 1932 and 1942.

Although (or because) it's off the beaten path, more than 180,000 people visit here annually. The 4,493-acre park has some incredible scenery, twenty-four trails that cover 40 miles of wooded hiking trails (easy to strenuous), waterfalls, boating, camping, environmental center, sandy beach, swimming, and a visitor center. Overnight reservations can be made online or by calling (800) 933–PARK; www.dcr.state.va.us/parks/douthat.htm.

The **Lakeview Restaurant** in Douthat State Park is one of only three in the state park system, and the view competes with the food. Call or check the above Web site for operating hours. From the screened-in porch, you can see the lake, canoes, paddleboats, and rowboats. Fishing is a major activity, with trout stocked twice a week from April through September. Check at the camp store for fishing permits. For more information call (540) 862–5856. The restaurant is on Route 629; (540) 862–8111.

Clifton Forge

If you can't get enough of regional fine arts and handcrafted products, then stop by the **Alleghany Highlands Arts and Crafts Center** in Clifton Forge. This not-for-profit volunteer organization has exhibits, displays, and sales of jewelry, needlework, pottery, quilts, stained glass, woodenware, other fiber arts, and framed and unframed watercolors, oils, and graphic arts. The center is open 10:00 A.M. to 4:30 P.M. Monday through Saturday. The center is at 439 East Ridgeway Street, Clifton Forge; (540) 862-4447; www.alleghanyhighlands .com/arts.

Now, just before you reach civilization, stop for a moment or two by the **Humpback Covered Bridge** in Humpback Bridge State Wayside Park (Midland Trail and Route 60 West, Covington), a graceful, arched span erected in 1835 just west of Covington. It is said to be the only existing bridge of this type in the country and perhaps in the world, although apparently three of

Humpback Covered Bridge

them were originally built within a mile of one another. The bridge received its name because of a rise of 8 feet from the ends to the center. It has no center support. Reportedly, eighteen-year-old Thomas Kincaid, using an ax as his principal tool, cut the hand-hewn timbers and made the locust pins that join the timbers. No nails were used.

The structure was part of the 200-mile-long James River/Kanawha Turnpike and, when completed, linked the head of bateau navigation on the James River from Covington with the Ohio River at the Kentucky line. Apparently it was saved from destruction by an unwritten agreement between the Confederate and Union soldiers during the Civil War.

The 100-foot, single-span walled structure over Dunlop Creek carried traffic for nearly one hundred years before being abandoned in 1929 and, for nearly a quarter of a century, stood derelict near its then modern successor. Since 1954 it has been maintained as a part of a five-acre highway wayside 3 miles west of Covington on Highway 60. At the wayside are several picnic tables, barbecue grills, and two portable toilets, and you can wade through the creek for a better, or at least a different, view of the bridge. Several Civil War cannonballs have been found in the creek and along its banks, as both Union and

funfacts

Cyrus McCormick, the inventor of the mechanized reaper, was born in Steele's Tavern. Visit his farm to discover his achievements through a museum, restored blacksmith shop, and gristmill. **Cyrus McCormick Farm** is located on Route 606 (exit 205 off I–81), Steele's Tavern (540–377–2255).

Confederate troops moved across the bridge with cannons. Graffiti artists have used the walls and roof of the bridge as their canvas, but none of the words seems too objectionable, being mostly love notes from the young at heart and the young in mind.

Unlike most other covered bridges in the state, which take a detailed map to find, this one is easy to locate: There are signs off I–64 at exit 3 (the Callaghan Interchange) directing you to the Humpback. You can also get there by traveling west out of Covington for about 3 miles (540–962–2178; www.virginiadot.org/infoservice/faq-covbridge5.asp).

Lexington

Now, it's east to Lexington. First stop is the *Lexington Visitors Bureau,* located in the Centel Telephone Company building (106 East Washington Street, Lexington). Tour counselors are waiting in the welcome center to assist you and provide brochures, directions, and a warm welcome. Sofas and chairs are available, so you can sit awhile and review the material you've received. Displays and exhibits describe the area attractions, and a slide show highlights the events of the area. For more information call (540) 463–3777 or (877) 453–9822; www.lexingtonvirginia.com.

Sam Houston was born in a cabin just north of downtown Lexington on March 2, 1793. As commander-in-chief of the Texas army, he won the battle of San Jacinto, which secured Texan independence, April 21, 1836. He was president of Texas, 1836–1838, 1841–1844; U.S. senator, 1846–1859; and governor, 1860–1861. He died in July 1863. A 38,000-pound piece of Texas pink granite marks the spot at the *Sam Houston Wayside.* Route 11 North, exit 195 off I–81 or exit 55 from I–64, Lexington; www.lexingtonvirginia.com/houston.htm.

The *Virginia Horse Center* (Route 39, Lexington), said to be the largest facility of its type in the East, is fascinating regardless of how much you know (or don't know) about horses. Every weekend, from spring through fall, there are horse sales, 4-H horse-judging competitions, Grand Prix jumping, dressage exhibitions, breed shows, and much more. There's a covered grandstand with seating from which to watch the events in the main rings, or you can stand around the rail and talk to contestants, participants, or others related in a peripheral or major way. Even when the horses and riders are being led through some basic riding events (similar to school figures in ice skating), you can feel the excitement charging through the audience. A 4,000-seat coliseum allows year-round operation and houses an exhibit area, concession concourse, offices, and meeting rooms. For more information call (540) 464–2950 or visit www.horsecenter.org.

That delicious aroma you smell comes from the **Cocoa Mill Chocolate Company,** started in 1993. They handcraft their chocolates with premium chocolate, natural flavors, fresh cream and butter, and authentic liqueurs. Chocolates are prepared in small batches because they believe freshness contributes as much to flavor as quality ingredients, with each piece hand dipped, hand decorated, and hand packed so that careful attention is paid to every detail. During some times of the year—not around Valentine's Day—you can watch the operation and then buy your favorites after watching them being made. The store is open from 10:00 A.M. to 5:00 P.M. Monday through Saturday. Call Bob Aimone, the owner, for more tour information; 115 West Nelson Street, Lexington; (800) 421–6220 or (540) 464–8400; www.cocoamill.com.

On display at the **George Marshall Museum** is the Nobel Peace Prize bestowed on Marshall and the Oscar won by General Frank McCarthy, an aide to Marshall, as producer of the movie *Patton.* Also in the museum are exhibits tracing Marshall's life and an electric map tracing the significant events of World War II. The museum is open daily from 9:00 A.M. to 5:00 P.M. Admission is $3.00 for adults and $2.00 for seniors. On Virginia Military Institute grounds, Lexington; (540) 463–7103; www.marshallfoundation.org.

About 4 miles east of the visitor center, out Route 60 east at the **Ben Salem Wayside Park** (U.S. Highway 60/106 East Washington Street, Lexington) are the remains of the James River and Kanawha Canal. Conceived by George Washington as part of the "Great Central American Waterway from the Rockies to the Atlantic Ocean," this was the earliest canal system in the Western Hemisphere. The wayside is a delightful place for a picnic or a quiet afternoon spent watching the waters frolic over the river rocks. Call (540) 463–3777 for information.

If your idea of a bed-and-breakfast place is an early Victorian setting, furnished with antiques, wraparound verandas on the first and second floors, with breakfast served on antique Meissen china, a fireplace to relax in front of as you listen to classical music, and a wide trout stream defining the property line, then you might want to stop at the **Hummingbird Inn** in Goshen.

Pam and Dick Matthews are the innkeepers for these four individually decorated rooms, each with its own bathroom, two with a whirlpool bath, and one with a working fireplace. An overnight stay comes with a tasty breakfast. A four-course dinner, with wine, is

who'sburiedin lee'stomb?

Robert E. Lee, Confederate general, is buried in the campus **Lee Chapel** (**and Museum**) at Washington & Lee University in Lexington; (540) 463–8768.

Rolling, Action!

Should you go to see the Robert Duvall, Stephen Lang, Jeff Daniels, and Mira Sorvino film *Gods and Generals,* you'll no doubt recognize the VMI campus because part of the film was shot there in the fall of 2001. Ronald F. Maxwell chose the locale for the 1860s historical movie to shoot two scenes in the life of Confederate General Thomas J. "Stonewall" Jackson (Lang), who taught at VMI for ten years prior to the War. The first scene is when Jackson is leading the VMI cadets to war in 1861, and the second is when his body was returned two years later. *Gods and Generals* is a prequel to Maxwell's 1993 movie *Gettysburg* and is based on the 1996 novel by Jeff Shaara. Duvall portrays Robert E. Lee.

available on Saturday at 7:00 P.M. The basic rates are from $120 to $165 per night. Write to the inn at 30 Wood Lane, Box 147, Goshen 24439, or call (540) 997–9065 or (800) 397–3214; www.hummingbirdinn.com.

About halfway between Lexington on the south and Staunton on the north is Steele's Tavern. The **Sugar Tree Inn** sits about five minutes off the Blue Ridge Parkway, half a mile high and surrounded by its own hardwood forest. It was built and designed as an inn (not a readaptive use of an old barn, etc.), by local people using hand-hewn chestnut, oak, and poplar timbers taken from original buildings throughout Rockbridge County. Logs as much as 200 years old were mortised and pegged together without nails, just as in pioneer days.

Its twelve rooms (each with its own woodburning fireplace) in four buildings are spacious, "with human-size private baths and generous chairs in which to rock or relax." For those who like luxury when they "rough it," some of the rooms have a whirlpool bath, ceiling fan, air-conditioning, and VCR. A full breakfast is provided in an on-premises glass-walled dining room, and dinner is available Thursday through Saturday if you just can't bring yourself to leave these woods. Sugar Tree Inn is at 145 Lodge Trail on Highway 56, Steeles Tavern. Call (800) 377–2197 or (540) 377–2197 for additional information; or visit www.sugartreeinn.com.

Craig County

In a Craig County valley is the town of **Paint Bank,** nestled between Peter's Mountain and Pott's Mountain, on the banks of Pott's Creek, not too far from Covington and Roanoke. It consists of a general store (said to have "the most ambitious worms in the county"), post office, volunteer fire department, mill (with hopes for restoration), hotel, fish hatchery, and the creek. The folks at

Hollow Hill Farm, about a mile from town, are working toward a major resurgence of the town. There's a definite synergy there. The general store, open from 6:00 A.M. to 9:00 P.M. Monday through Saturday and 7:00 A.M. to 9:00 P.M. on Sunday, provides for the needs of the area residents, and Hollow Hill Farm provides the mounted buffalo heads, buffalo skulls, and buffalo meat that tourists seem to want. The farm covers about 4,000 acres and is home to 300 head of the purest-bred American bison (buffalo) and 75 head of Scottish Highlander cattle (said to be the shaggiest and strangest-looking cattle in the county). Drive along Route 600 and see the cattle grazing alongside the road.

In 1907 a train depot was constructed to serve the Norfolk and Western Railway that had just been extended to Paint Bank. The depot has been refurbished and is now available for lodging for hunters, hikers, birders, and others who want to get really off the beaten path. The *Depot Lodge* has five rooms, each with private bath and a cast-iron free-standing gas stove. Lodge guests can take a private tour of Hollow Hill Farm and see the beasts up close and personal.

Stephen Cutler, a New Yorker, owns the Depot Lodge (540–897–6000 or 800–970–DEPOT), the General Store (540–897–5000), and Hollow Hill Farm (540–897–5786) and sounds really excited about all the improvements to the area; www.depotlodge.com.

Roanoke

Roanoke (at one time, possibly Rawrenock or Roenoak, an Indian word meaning "white shell beads" or "money") is the largest Virginia city west of Richmond. A huge neon star atop *Mill Mountain,* reportedly the country's largest manufactured star, was erected by the chamber of commerce in 1949. You can see this star from 60 miles away (at least from the air—quite a sight when you're flying into town on a foggy night and 17,500 watts of neon light beams through the mist). It is 88½ feet high (1,045 feet above sea level) and weighs 10,000 pounds. There are 2,000 feet of neon tubing, and several color combinations are possible. There are two good times to visit the star: first, in the daytime for an overview of Roanoke; second, at dusk, when the star is lit and crackling with electricity. It is illuminated every night until midnight, and it's almost as though Roanoke is saying, "Come on by, we'll leave the star on for you." Mill Mountain is within the city limits, and it's said to be the only mountain in Virginia, and perhaps east of Phoenix, that's located inside a city.

Start your tour at the *Roanoke Valley Convention & Visitors Bureau* at 101 Shenandoah Avenue NE, Roanoke (800–635–5535 or 540–342–6025; www.visitroanokeva.com), where they should have the answers to all your tourism questions, and even some you didn't know you had.

Across the street and around the corner are several interesting shops (all Roanoke), including the ***Roanoke Farmers' Market*** (the oldest in continual use in Virginia) at 310 First Street, (540) 342–2028; the Patrick Henry Hotel (Roanoke's restored landmark hotel) at 617 South Jefferson Street, (540) 345–8811 or (800) 303–0988; www.patrickhenryroanoke .com; and an Orvis outlet store at 19-B Campbell Street, (540) 345–3635. Orvis is America's oldest mail-order company, maker of fine fishing and hunting equipment and classic country clothing and gifts.

funfacts

Although statistics just don't seem to be available for an accurate account, it's been said that the best and perhaps the most popular place to propose in Roanoke is at the Mill Mountain Star.

Then venture to the ***Center in the Square*** complex at One Market Square, Southeast Roanoke (540–342–5700; www.centerinthesquare.org), and plan to spend some time here. Within this renovated 1914 warehouse building are the Science Museum of Western Virginia and Hopkins Planetarium, the Art Museum of Western Virginia, the Roanoke Valley History Museum, and the Mill Mountain Theatre. Some 400,000 people visit this unique complex annually; it received an award in 1996 at a United Nations awards forum showcasing the best in urban development.

Start at the ***Science Museum of Western Virginia*** and ***Hopkins Planetarium*** on levels four and five. This is a hands-on place where children and adults can play to figure out how things work. You can broadcast a weather forecast, explore things in the touch tank, or stop by the Tot and Parent Learning Center. Learn how the body works at BodyTech or explore how color, sound, and light work. And when earthly bounds no longer can contain you, see the show at the planetarium. The Mega Dome shows such IMAX films as *Lost Worlds* and *Wildfire.*

Almost as much fun as the exhibits, demonstrations, and programs is the gift shop. There's no admission fee to get in here, but it could cost a bunch to get out. And it will be worth every penny, too. The museum is open 10:00 A.M. to 5:00 P.M. Tuesday through Saturday and 1:00 to 5:00 P.M. on Sunday (540–342–5726; www.smwv.org). Admission is $8.00 for adults, $7.00 for senior citizens, and $6.00 for children ages three to twelve. Combination tickets, which include the MegaDome or the Planetarium, or both, are available.

For those who prefer the visual arts, it's off to the ***Art Museum of Western Virginia*** on levels one and two. Here you'll see an emphasis on nineteenth- and twentieth-century art, with selections from the Hudson River school, works by Rodin, folk art of the Southern mountains, and contemporary American painters, printmakers, and photographers. A fairly recent addition includes an excellent Japanese print collection. Family activities abound, with classes, films, lectures, workshops, rainy-day projects, and an interactive art center for children in ArtVenture.

A new 75,000-square-foot, Randall Stout-designed building is due to open in 2007, on Salem Avenue.

The museum is open 10:00 A.M. to 5:00 P.M. Tuesday through Saturday and 1:00 to 5:00 P.M. Sunday. ArtVenture is open 10:00 A.M. to 2:00 P.M. Saturday. Admission is $3.00 for exhibits, $2.00 for ArtVenture; (540) 342–5760; www.art museumroanoke.org.

Can't get enough of history? Then, it's off to the **History Museum and Historical Society of Western Virginia** on level three. This is where you'll learn about the background of Roanoke, from prehistoric artifacts through frontier and Colonial days, through the heyday of the Norfolk & Western Railroad, up to World War II and current times. Examples of almost three centuries of fashion are displayed, and there's a country store to oooh and aaah over and explain to the younger generation (after you've said, "I have one of those in my attic" or "I remember my grandparents using one of those things"). In the History Museum gift shop, you can buy books, a handmade quilt, maps, genealogical charts, and vintage toys.

The museum is open 10:00 A.M. to 4:00 P.M. Tuesday through Friday, 10:00 A.M. to 4:30 P.M. Saturday, and 1:00 to 5:00 P.M. Sunday. Admission is $3.00 for adults and $2.00 for senior citizens and children ages six to twelve (540–342–5770; www.history-museum.org).

If performing arts are what you crave, then plan on catching a show at the **Mill Mountain Theatre,** which has been characterized as "New York quality in the Blue Ridge." Known as one of the best regional theaters in the country, it offers year-round presentations of new and original works, musicals and classics, children's plays (including a family musical each winter holiday season), and a new playwright's competition. In addition to new works and local talent, the theater has attracted nationally acclaimed and award-winning performers. Call (540) 342–5740 or (800) 317–6455 for their schedule and ticket prices. www.millmountain.org.

One of my favorite stopping places is the **Hotel Roanoke** and Conference Center, now managed by the Doubletree Corporation. Built for $45,000 in 1882 on a ten-acre knoll overlooking the city, it was constructed in the Tudor style, with hand-rubbed English walnut, carved oak, cherry, and ash woods, gaslight chandeliers, and floors polished to shine like glass. Much of the original Honduras mahogany remains. As with many wooden structures, part of the hotel burned in 1898. Through its history it has celebrated many firsts. It was the first hotel in Roanoke to have bathrooms with a porcelain or zinc tub, and the first sewer line in town ran from the hotel.

Telephones with multiple plugs (so you could move the telephone around the room) were installed in 1931. It also featured closets with lights that turned on automatically when the door was opened, electric fans, full-length mirrors, and running ice water. In 1937 it became one of the first hotels in the world to be air-conditioned. In 1940 Fred Brown, the hotel's chef, created peanut soup, an item that is still on the menu.

Extensive renovations and additions have been done in the past years, and in the entranceway you can see personalized bricks purchased by local citizens in a fund-raising effort to help the restorations. The hotel is at 110 Shenandoah Avenue, Roanoke; (540) 985–5900; www.hotelroanoke.com.

The *Harrison Museum of African American Culture* is the only repository of African-American culture in western Virginia. It is "a haven for the arts and treasures of a strong and mighty race." The museum is on the ground floor of the first public high school for blacks in western Virginia. Each year it presents a minimum of eight art exhibits and two performing-arts presentations. Art and history lectures, demonstrations, and workshops are offered. The book/gift shop has Afrocentric art, books, cards, and jewelry.

The Harrison Museum is open 1:00 to 5:00 P.M. Tuesday through Sunday. There is no admission charge. It's located at 523 Harrison Avenue NW. For more information write to the museum at P.O. Box 12544, Roanoke 24026, or call (540) 345–4818; www.harrisonmuseum.org.

The *Virginia Museum of Transportation,* the official transportation museum of Virginia, holds the South's largest collection of steam locomotives, cars, boats, airplanes, and missiles. What might excite your imagination is the H-O–gauge railroad, with 1,400 feet of track, one hundred turnouts, and assembly yards and structures set on 1,200 square feet. It's all computer controlled. You can board a three-car passenger train on a 7½-gauge track for a half-mile ride through the museum grounds. There's a gift shop on the premises with railroad memorabilia including hats, goggles, belt buckles, handkerchiefs, patches, pins, recordings, photographs, books, puzzles, train sets, whistles, mugs, decals, and postcards.

The Virginia Museum of Transportation, at 303 Norfolk Avenue SW, Roanoke (540–342–5670; www.vmt.org), is open 11:00 A.M. to 4:00 P.M. Monday through Friday, 10:00 A.M. to 5:00 P.M. on Saturday, and 1:00 to 5:00 P.M. on Sunday. Admission is $7.40 for ages twelve and over, $6.40 for seniors, and $5.25 for ages three to eleven.

When is learning about history a lot of fun? When you can be a participatory member, as you can at Virginia's *Explore Park.* This is a living-history museum, classroom, and nature center located near Milepost 115 on the Blue Ridge Parkway. Wander through a German double-crib "bank" barn, a blacksmith/wheelwright shop, homes, a one-room schoolhouse, and other buildings, all gingerly moved to this location. Interpreters will help you understand, and maybe even try to get you to participate, all in the name of learning what life was like for Native Americans and nineteenth-century settlers. You can actually comprehend what it was like to pump a blacksmith's bellows, cook in a fireplace, harvest a garden, weave on a loom, and make furniture. And if you remember these things, then you can show your children and grandchildren "how to do it right." And when it's really time to stretch your legs, there are 6 miles of mountain hiking trails to entice you.

Know what a courting candle is? It's a candle, naturally, placed in a spiral wrought-iron holder. Daddy, usually, would know how long it would take for the candle to burn, and determine how long a gentleman might visit. Daddy would then extend the candle over the top of the holder for the appropriate amount of time. When the candle stopped burning, it was time for the gentleman to leave. You can buy one at the gift shop that offers a variety of crafts, gifts, books, and games, including items made at the blacksmith shop.

Events are scheduled regularly at the park, which is open on weekends in April and then Wednesday through Sunday through October. The admission fee is $8.00 for adults, $6.00 for seniors, and $4.50 for children ages six to eighteen. The park is at 3900 Rutrough Road, Roanoke; (540) 427–1800 or (800) 842–9163; www.explorepark.org. Hours vary by season. Call the park for more information.

Where to Stay in Western Virginia

BASYE

Bryce Resort
1982 Fairway Drive
(540) 856–2121 or (800) 821–1444

COVINGTON

Cliff View Golf Club & Inn
410 Friels Drive
(540) 962–2200 or (888) 849–2200

Milton Hall
207 Thorny Lane
(540) 965–0196

FRONT ROYAL

Killhavlin Bed and Breakfast
1401 North Royal Avenue
(540) 636–7335

Lackawanna Bed and Breakfast
236 Riverside Drive
(540) 636–7945 or (877) 222–7495

Woodward House on Manor Grade
413 South Royal Avenue
(800) 635–7011

GOSHEN

Hummingbird Inn
30 Wood Lane
(540) 997–9065 or (800) 397–3214

HARRISONBURG

Hearth n' Holly Inn
46 Songbird Lane
(540) 434–6766 or (800) 279–1379

Stonewall Jackson Inn
547 East Market Street
(540) 433–8233 or (800) 445–5330

Village Inn
4979 South Valley Pike
(540) 434–7355 or (800) 736–7355

HOT SPRINGS
The Homestead
1766 Homestead Drive
(540) 839–1766

KEEZLETOWN
Old Massanutten Lodge
3448 Caverns Drive
(540) 269–8800

Stonewall Jackson Inn
(540) 433–8233 or (800)
445–5330

LEXINGTON
Applewood Inn & Llama Trekking
Buffalo Bend Road
(540) 463–1962 or (800)
463–1902

Brierley Hill Country Inn
985 Borden Road
(540) 464–8421 or (800)
422–4925

House Mountain Inn
455 Lonesome Dove Trail
(540) 464–4004

Stoneridge Bed and Breakfast
246 Stoneridge Lane
(540) 463–4090 or (800)
491–2930

LURAY
Bluemont Bed & Breakfast
1852 South Route 340
(540) 743–1268 or (888)
465–8729

South Court Inn
160 South Court
(540) 843–0980 or (888)
749–8055

Woodruff Inns & Restaurant
138 East Main Street
(540) 743–1494 or (855)
937–3466

MCGAHEYSVILLE
Massanutten Resort
1822 Resort Drive
(540) 289–9441 or (800)
207–6277

NEW MARKET
Apple Blossom Inn
9317 North Congress Street
(540) 740–3747

PORT REPUBLIC
Grandma's Cottage
8570 Main Street
(540) 249–8113 or (877)
241–8133

STANLEY
Whitefence Bed & Breakfast
275 Chapel Road
(540) 778–4680 or (800)
211–9885

Jordan Hollow Farm Inn
326 Hawksbill Park Road
(540) 778–2285 or (888)
418–7000

STAUNTON
Belle Grae Inn
515 West Frederick Street
(540) 886–5151 or (888)
541–5151
www.bellegrae.com

Frederick House
18 East Frederick Street
(540) 885–4220 or (800)
334–5575

Inn at Old Virginia
1329 Commerce Road
(540) 248–4650 or (877)
809–1146

Stonewall Jackson Hotel and Conference Center
28 South Market Street
(540) 885–4848 or (866)
860–0024

STRASBURG
Hotel Strasburg
213 South Holliday Street
(540) 465–9191 or (800)
348–8327

WARM SPRINGS
Anderson Cottage Bed and Breakfast
Old Germantown Road
(540) 839–2975

WINCHESTER
George Washington
103 East Piccadilly Street
(Wyndham) (407)
895–2557

WOODSTOCK
Inn at Narrow Passage
Route 11 South
(540) 459–8000 or (800)
459–8002

Where to Eat in Western Virginia

CATAWBA

Homeplace
4968 Catawba Valley Drive
(540) 384–7252

HARRISONBURG

Village Inn
4979 South Valley Pike
(540) 434–7355

LURAY

Parkhurst Restaurant
2547 U.S. Highway 211
West
(540) 743–6009

ROANOKE

Alexander's
105 South Jefferson Street
(540) 962–6983

All Sports Café
2326 Grandin Road
Southwest
(540) 725–5155

Angler's Café
310 Second Street
Southwest
(540) 342–2436

Arzu International
213 Williamson Road
Southeast
(540) 982–7160

**Bratcher's Ice Cream
Parlor**
3436 Orange Avenue
Northeast
(540) 344–4030

Carlos Brazilian
4167 Electric Road
(540) 776–1117

Coach & Four
5206 Williamson Road
Northwest
(540) 362–4220

Double Dragon
7232 Williamson Road
(540) 265–0393

Famous Anthony's
2221 Crystal Spring
Avenue Southwest
(540) 981–0200

Green Dolphin Grille
127 Campbell Avenue
Southeast
(540) 857–0688

Howard's Soup Kitchen
24 Church Avenue
Southwest
(540) 342–9439

**Kabuki Japanese Steak
House**
3503 Franklin Road
Southwest
(540) 981–0222

Lew's
7707 Williamson Road
(540) 563–5332

Library
3117 Franklin Road
Southwest
(540) 985–0811

Nawab
118 Campbell Avenue
Southwest
(540) 345–5150

ROCKY MOUNT

Hub
245 North Main Street
(540) 483–9303

Ippy's
1760 North Main Street
(540) 489–5600

Longview
11445 Virgil H. Goode
Highway
(540) 483–1658

Olde Virginia Barbeque
35 Meadow View Avenue
(540) 489–1788

SALEM

Blue Jay
3648 Ellen Drive
(540) 380–2311

**East of Chicago Pizza
Company**
115 East Main Street
(540) 389–7070

International Dynasty
1941 West Main Street
(540) 389–6055

Mac "n" Bob's
316 East Main Street
(540) 389–5999

Sakura Japanese
2171 Apperson Drive
(540) 772–0168

Salem Ice Cream Parlor
404 West Main Street
(540) 389–2373

Salem Sports Grill
912 East Main Street
(540) 375–0971

STRASBURG

Hotel Strasburg
(540) 465–9191 or (800)
348–8327

WHITE POST

L'Auberge Provencale
13630 Lord Fairfax
Highway
(540) 837–1375

Southwestern Virginia

Ah, southwestern Virginia. This is where the skyscrapers take the form of mountains, not buildings; where canyons are really canyons (the deepest this side of the Mississippi), not the canyons created by structures.

You will note that interstate highways here are more serpentine than ironed-ribbon straight. If you're observant, you'll even notice that one stretch of Interstate 77 and Interstate 81 overlap and you can be going south on one and north on the other and still be on the same side of the road.

Enjoyable scenery notwithstanding, this span of I–77 includes two tunnels, one through East River Mountain and the other through Big Walker Mountain. Each tunnel is about a mile long and saves the traveler from 10 to 20 miles of meandering and hilly roadway along Route 21. On the other hand, if you're interested in off-the-beaten-path options, saving time and miles may not interest you.

This is where Mother Nature's awe-inspiring works are yours for the looking and hiking and exploring. You will find the frontier spirit and revitalizing natural beauty. You will be able to take time for camping, fishing, and swimming in numerous state and national parks. You will find quaint old mills and summer outdoor dramatic offerings that retell the history and life of mountain days decades and centuries ago. And you will find

SOUTHWESTERN VIRGINIA

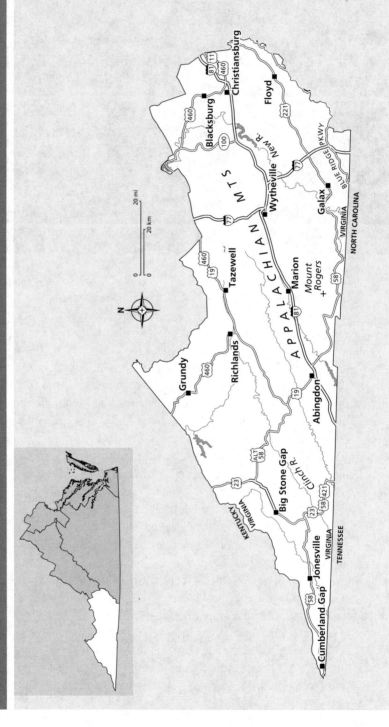

unusual ways to enjoy yourself, including trekking via llama.

Virginia has thirty-four *state parks,* thirty-three natural areas, more than 1,400 campsites, 180 cabins, and hundreds of miles of trails throughout the state, all available for your outdoor pleasure.

The southwestern section has more than a dozen parks, preserves, and management areas, including Breaks Interstate Park (276–865–4413), Buffalo Mountain Natural Area Preserve (276–676–5673), Claytor Lake State Park (540–643–2500), Clinch Mountain Wildlife Management Area (276–944–5024), Grayson Highlands State Park (276–579–7092), Hungry Mother State Park (276–781–7400) with the Hemlock Haven Conference Center (276–781–7425), Natural Tunnel State Park (276–940–2674) and the Cove Ridge Center (276–940–2696), Pinnacle Natural Area Preserve (276–676–5673), Shot Tower and New River Trail State Park (276–699–6778), Southwest Virginia Museum Historical State Park (276–523–1322), and the Wilderness Road State Park (276–445–3065).

For more information about these facilities, call the Virginia Department of Conservation and Recreation, (804) 225–3867 or (800) 933–PARK; or visit the Web site at www.dcr.state.va.us.

We'll start our tour after leaving Salem and Roanoke to the northeast and head southwest along I–81, then along Route 460 back down to Radford and Wytheville, then north and south on I–77 up to Bluefield and down to Galax, over to Bristol, and just weave back and forth until we arrive at Cumberland Gap, a truly spectacular and amazing place to end any trip.

Montgomery County

The history of a place helps us see how the people of today arrived here and understand what they think, how they act, and where they're going. A good place to visit might be the *Montgomery Museum and Lewis Miller Regional Art Center.* It focuses generally on southwestern Virginia, particularly

Montgomery County, and the works of primitive and nineteenth-century country folk artist Lewis Miller as well as contemporary art displays. There's also a genealogical research area.

The museum is housed in a mid-nineteenth-century Presbyterian church manse of American and Flemish bond brick, made with local materials and hand-hewn oak beams and rafters. Admission is $1.00 for adults and 50 cents for children under twelve. The museum is open 10:30 A.M. to 4:30 P.M. Monday through Friday, and is located at 300 South Pepper Street, Christiansburg; (540) 382–5644; http://montgomerymuseum.org.

In the center of Christiansburg, the county seat, at 2 East Main Street, is a 1936 post office with a **WPA mural** by John DeGroot entitled *Great Road.* This 1939 Rural American Art painting is one of about two dozen post office murals and sculptures created in Virginia in the late 1930s and early 1940s as part of the Works Projects Administration, Roosevelt's New Deal program established to keep unemployed artists working.

funfacts

In May 1808, Thomas Lewis and John McHenry were involved in the first duel with rifles known to have taken place in Virginia. Both men died. This duel led to the passage of the Barbour Bill in January 1810, which outlawed dueling in Virginia. Dr. John Floyd was the attending physician and later went on to become governor of Virginia and a member of Congress. A marker in Christiansburg at Routes 11 and 460 designates the site of the duel.

The Oaks Historic Bed-and-Breakfast Country Inn in Christiansburg comes with a recommendation from the Smithfields of Redwood City, California (and a four-diamond rating from AAA), who rave about "one of the most exquisite bed-and-breakfast places we've seen anywhere. Wonderful food. The owners and hosts are warm, fascinating, and fabulous, and they are great tour guides."

The Oaks is the focal point of the East Main Street Historic District in Christiansburg. Construction began in 1889 and was completed in 1893. Modern bathrooms and other amenities have been added, and the original floor plan and elegant interior have been carefully restored and preserved. At 311 East Main Street, Christiansburg. The Oaks is operated by Lois and John Ioviero; (540) 381–1500 or (800) 336–6257; www.bbhost.com/theoaksinn.

Floyd County

South of Christiansburg is Floyd and **Floyd Country Store,** where, every Friday evening at 7:00 P.M., folks bring their banjos, fiddles, guitars, and harmonicas, their old-timer's memories, and the music of Floyd County. Floyd's is

All Roads Lead to Floyd or Away from it

If you're looking for a particular place in the town of Floyd, directions will start with "Begin at 'the stoplight'" in the center of town at the intersection of Route 8 and Route 221. It's the only traffic light in the county. You should also note that there's no turn on red. If you go north on Route 8, you're aiming toward Interstate 81 and Christiansburg. Go south and you head toward Stuart. Go west on Route 221 to Interstate 77 toward Galax, or east toward the south side of Roanoke. Because they are all long and winding roads, you need a good map, a GPS system, or a sense of adventure because using the sun for a compass just won't work. www.visitfloyd.org/about/tour.

located at 206 South Locust Street in Floyd; (540) 745–4563; www.floyd countrystore.com.

To learn about the political, geological, and natural history of this area, head north of Christiansburg on Route 460 to Blacksburg, to stop at *Virginia Tech,* home of the Hokies and the largest university in Virginia. There are a number of interesting places to see, the first of which is *Smithfield Plantation* (1000 Smithfield Plantation Road, Blacksburg). When Colonel William Preston constructed it back in 1772, it would have been difficult to predict the influence he would have on the area. Let it suffice to say that the Preston family was a founding family of Blacksburg and Montgomery County. William Preston, born in 1730, arrived here from Ireland in 1738, and served in the militia in the French and Indian and Revolutionary Wars. He then went on to serve in the House of Burgesses, representing several different counties. He built Smithfield in the Tidewater Plantation style and named it in honor of his wife, Susanna Smith.

The plantation is open from 10:00 A.M. to 5:00 P.M. Monday, Tuesday, Thursday, Friday, and Saturday, and 1:00 to 5:00 P.M. on Sunday, April 1 through the first weekend of December. Admission is $5.00 for adults, $3.00 for students thirteen and up or with college identification, and $2.00 for children ages twelve and under (540–231–3947; www.smithfieldplantation.org).

Driving through this country could stir your interest in the earth sciences, and fortunately, Virginia Tech has a *Museum of Geological Sciences* to satisfy your curiosity. Included in its collection is a full-scale model of an allosaurus (a huge carnivorous North American theropod dinosaur of the Later Jurassic period, about 150 million years ago). And if that means nothing to you, just check with the children; they're sure to know. It also has fossils, gemstones, a seismograph, and the largest display of Virginia minerals in the state.

funfacts

In Lee County you can:

- be farther west than Detroit
- be farther west than all of West Virginia
- be closer to eight other state capitals than to Richmond
- see five states at once
- see "black diamonds" (coal)
- walk the "Trail of the Lonesome Pine" (see Big Stone Gap)
- sleep in Virginia's smallest city (Norton, population about 3,900)
- visit the University of Virginia's College at Wise, a place that grew from a home for indigents and the homeless into the only branch of the University of Virginia.

The museum is in 4044 Derring Hall, Blacksburg (540–231–6521; www.geol.vt .edu) and is open 8:00 A.M. to 4:00 P.M. Monday through Friday. There is no admission charge.

Head northwest out of Blacksburg and you're touring through Giles County. Near Newport are located two of the seven remaining *covered bridges* (Sinking Creek and C. K. Reynolds) that are accessible to the public in Virginia. They are modified William Howe truss bridges (in 1840 he combined iron uprights with wooden supports, creating the forerunner of the steel bridge) and cross Sinking Creek. The first is a 55-foot bridge, which used to be along the Appalachian Trail near Route 700 (Mountain Lake Road) but was bypassed by a realignment of the trail. The bridge was left in place so that the property owner could use it when a new bridge was built in 1949. The second, a 70-foot span, was left in place when a new bridge was constructed in 1963. The bridge indicates it was constructed in 1912; the state says circa 1916. (540) 921–5000.

Farther up Route 700 in Pembroke is the *Mountain Lake Hotel Resort* (115 Hotel Circle, Mountain Lake), which has been catering to summer visitors for years. Although former manager Joseph "Mac" McMillin used to say that people would tell him they or their relatives stood on the fire line fighting the blaze that destroyed the old (1850s) wooden structure, in fact it was torn down and rebuilt in 1936 with stone cut from the property.

Even if you have never visited Mountain Lake, you may feel you know the place, for it was featured in the 1986 movie *Dirty Dancing,* with Patrick Swayze and Jennifer Grey.

The dining room offers gracious service, a pleasant house wine, and fairly good food. Of course, after a day of fresh air and exercise, anything is likely to taste good. About twenty-five non-hotel guests can be seated in the dining room, but reservations are essential.

Mountain Lake is the highest lake in Virginia (4,000 feet), one of only two natural lakes, and the highest inhabited mountain in the state. Activities

The Preston Dynasty

Virginia Tech's original name was Preston and Olin Institute; named for William Preston.

Colonel William Preston and his wife, Susanna, of Smithfield Plantation (Blacksburg) fame, raised and educated their twelve children at Smithfield.

Smithfield Plantation was the birthplace of two Virginia governors, James Patton Preston and John Buchanan Floyd, and briefly home of a third, John Floyd Jr. (grandson of William). Their progeny and other relatives would go on to serve in Congress and achieve positions of high rank through various state governments. Among the relatives was Montgomery Blair, the postmaster of the United States in President Lincoln's cabinet.

abound, including fishing on the 250-acre lake (the chef will cook your catch of the day, which might be a largemouth bass, rainbow or palomino trout, or even a 4-inch bream), tennis, and golf in summer. Photography is marvelous all year, with wild azaleas and rhododendrons in spring, blazing leaves in fall, and crystal snow scenes as winter starts its visit. The resort is open from the first Friday in May to the last Saturday night in October with weekends and Thanksgiving in November. For more information call (540) 626–7121 or (800) 346–3334; or visit www.mountainlakehotel.com.

The *George Washington* and *Jefferson National Forests* blanket 1.8 million acres across Virginia, West Virginia, and Kentucky, and an entire book could be compiled on the various trails and activities within the system. As a sampling I'll use the part of the forest in the area around Giles County that is supervised from the New River Valley ranger district. A visit or call (540–552–4641; www.southernregion .fs.fed.us/gwj) to the Blacksburg office will find the rangers eager to help you with all your questions and suggest things you'll enjoy doing.

Among the activities is a 2-mile hike to view the *Cascades,* a spectacular 60-foot waterfall. The approach is via Little Stony Creek (stocked with trout), past a steam boiler from an old sawmill (1918–1922) and an awesome look at Barney's

coolwaters

Mountain Lake (near Blacksburg) is one of only two natural freshwater lakes in Virginia; it was formed when a rock slide dammed the north end of the valley. Debris of organic matter filled around the rocks to form a watertight seal. The lake is fed by underground streams that rarely allow the water temperature to rise above 72 degrees.

Lake Drummond in the Great Dismal Swamp is the other natural lake in Virginia.

190 Off the Beaten Path

OTHER PLACES WORTH SEEING

Floyd
New Mountain Mercantile Here and Now
Gallery (540) 745–4278
www.fin.org

Gate City
Homeplace Mountain Farm and
Museum (276) 386–6300
www.scottcountyva.org

Meadows of Dan
Mabry Mill (276) 952–2947
www.blueridgemtns.net

Rural Retreat
Cedar Springs Trout Farm
(276) 686–4505

Wall (a sheer bluff rising from the creek bed to a height of 3,640 feet) from the bottom of the bluff. The hike along this easy-to-moderately-difficult trail should take three and a half hours (round-trip).

Up from Mountain Lake is **Minie (or Minnie) Ball Hill,** a great place to find Civil War souvenirs. According to legend, General George Crook, pressed by Confederate troops and bogged down by muddy trails, was forced to abandon an extra weight of ammunition and perhaps even a cannon full of gold (which some say is at the bottom of Mountain Lake). Lead bullets, or "minié balls," left behind on May 12, 1864, are still found by those who search this area. Actually, minié balls do not refer to size, but to French army captain Claude Étienne Minié, who developed the bullet-shaped projectile that could be shot from the muzzle-loading rifle.

Take a hike along **Sinking Creek Mountain,** named for a streambed that tends to dry up in summer months, or go up to **Hanging Rock** for a 360-degree look at the world. An old fire tower is good for watching the spring (April) and fall (mid-September to mid-October) migration of redtail, broadwing, and sharpshinned hawks.

Go with the Flow

The Eastern Continental Divide runs through the Christiansburg and Blacksburg areas. All the water to the east of this divide flows through the Roanoke River into the Atlantic Ocean. The water to the west runs into the New River and eventually to the Ohio and Mississippi Rivers and on to the Gulf of Mexico before spilling into the Atlantic. Unfortunately, there are no signs indicating the location of this ridge. Look instead for where the New River (which runs south to north, by the way) has etched through limestone, leaving spectacular towering formations hundreds of feet tall.

A Sportsman's Map of Jefferson National Forest is available from the ranger station for about $1.00.

Audie Murphy, the most decorated United States soldier of World War II, died in an airplane crash on May 28, 1971, on Brush Mountain. You can visit the **Audie Murphy Monument** (540–552–4641; www.audiemurphy.com/ roanoke.htm); placed on the crash site by Post 5311 of the Veterans of Foreign Wars.

The monument's plaque reads:

AUDIE LEON MURPHY
JUNE 20, 1924–MAY 28, 1971

BORN IN KINGSTON, TEXAS. DIED NEAR THIS SITE IN AN AIRPLANE CRASH. AMERICA'S MOST DECORATED VETERAN OF WORLD WAR II. HE SERVED IN THE EUROPEAN THEATRE, 15TH INFANTRY REGIMENT, 3RD INFANTRY DIVISION, AND EARNED 24 DECORATIONS INCLUDING THE MEDAL OF HONOR, LEGION OF MERIT, DISTINGUISHED SERVICE CROSS, AND THREE PURPLE HEARTS.

Radford City

Driving back down Route 460 and then I–81, you come to Radford, the home of **Radford University.** Assuming it's a nice day, or if you're too early or too late for other attractions to be open, stop by the **Burde Outdoor Sculpture Court,** which features contemporary pieces in metal, wood, and cement by artists from the entire region; (540) 831–5754; www.runet.edu.

At the **Flossie Martin Gallery,** also at the university in Powell Hall 200, you most likely will see something different each time you visit, with works representing regional and national artists. Among the more famous names represented are John Cage, Christo, and Dr. Jehan Sadat (widow of the former president and Nobel Peace Prize recipient Anwar el-Sadat of Egypt) with her own Egyptian art collection.

The gallery is open Monday through Friday 10:00 A.M. to 5:00 p.m (4:00 P.M. during summer session) and on Saturday and Sunday from noon to 4:00 P.M. The gallery is closed during university breaks. Call (540) 831–5754.

funfacts

Pearisburg, named for George Pearis, who donated the land for the Giles County seat, is one of only two towns located on the Maine-to-Georgia Appalachian Trail. In 1992 a portion of the town was listed as a National Registry Community, designated as a Historic District.

Pulaski County

A mile or less off I–81 and away from the rush of today's traffic is *Newbern,* a town from yesterday. The entire 1-mile-long linear town, basically located on the Olde Wilderness Road, was declared a historic district in 1979. The land was granted to early settlers by King George III in 1772, and it was founded as a town in 1810, acting as the Pulaski County seat from 1839 to 1893. At an altitude of 2,135 feet, the town, with its beautiful sunsets and surrounding mountains, reminded the settlers of Bern, Switzerland.

Daisy Williams, born in 1905, was a major force in bringing the past to our present in the form of the *Wilderness Road Regional Museum* (5240 Wilderness Road, Newbern; covering Floyd, Giles, Montgomery, and Pulaski Counties and the city of Radford), which includes rooms furnished in period style and several outbuildings. A log kitchen has been constructed behind the museum, on its original foundation. The museum committee is always looking for such artifacts as paintings, letters, photographs, and documents from 1810 to 1865 to further document the growth and development of the area. The museum fee is $2.00 for adults and $1.00 for children, and it is open from 10:30 A.M. to 4:30 P.M. Monday through Saturday and 1:30 to 4:30 P.M. on Sunday. Call (540) 674–4835.

The historic district contains original log and wooden buildings, including a jail, hanging house, store, churches, private residences, and an inn that served as a stagecoach stop. You also can see the waterworks, a slave-built flagstone sidewalk, a pre–Civil War church, the community center, and other points of interest. The original *Newbern Reservoir,* constructed in 1870, also remains. The water system, more than 110 years old, is still intact, and a piece of the original pipe is shown as part of the reservoir display. Various fires destroyed the courthouse in 1893, the Methodist church in 1912, and eleven of the original houses in 1924, but fifty-one of the original landmarks constructed between 1810 and 1895 still stand. Tours are $1.00 for adults and 50 cents for children.

A walking-tour brochure about Pulaski County and Newbern (listing accommodations, restaurants, campgrounds, entertainment, a calendar of events, maps, tours, and attractions) is available from the Pulaski County Chamber of Commerce, P.O. Box 169, Pulaski 24301; (540) 980–1001.

Newbern Reservoir

In 1965 ***Ruritan National,*** called the only rural American civic organization, opened its headquarters in Dublin. According to Curtis Graham, coordinator of expansion development of new clubs, Ruritan organized in rural Holland, Virginia, in 1928, and for many years didn't have a national office. Directors wanted a place in Virginia, relatively near an interstate highway and an airport, but in a semirural area. With access to I–77 and I–81, the local club in nearby Dublin submitted a proposal for land donated by Burlington Industries, and so the Ruritans made this area their home. There's a small history room with pictures of past presidents and other memorabilia. You're invited to visit weekdays between 8:30 A.M. and 5:00 P.M. (540–674–5431; www.ruritan.org).

The ***Fine Arts Center for the New River Valley,*** in Pulaski, offers music shows, exhibitions, poetry and literary readings, lectures, and private collections, and shows by amateur and professional artists. The Virginia Historic Landmark building, constructed in 1898, is considered an excellent example of Victorian commercial architecture. Free concerts are presented at Pulaski's Jackson Park throughout the summer.

The center is open 1:00 to 4:00 P.M. Tuesday through Sunday. There is no admission charge. A gift shop is on the premises. The center is located at 21 West Main Street, Pulaski (540–980–7363).

The ***Pulaski Railway*** was erected by the Norfolk & Western Railroad in 1886 when passenger service existed here and Pulaski was one of the major stops along its route. The railroad donated the station, a remarkable example of railway stations of the late 1800s, to the town in 1989. It was restored in 1994 and now houses the ***Raymond F. Ratcliffe Memorial Museum.*** You're invited to stop by to see the model railroads and local historical artifacts. The station is at 124 South Washington Avenue, Pulaski (540–980–2055). There's no

funfacts

admission charge, and it's open 8:30 A.M. to 5:00 P.M. Monday to Friday.

Colonel John Chiswell discovered lead and zinc deposits in this area about 1757 while he was hiding from the Cherokees. From those deposits shot was made for firearms for frontiersmen and settlers at the shot tower, now part of the ***Shot Tower and New River Trail Historical State Park,*** Route 1, Box 81X, Austinville 24312; (276) 699–1791. This is one of only three such towers in the United States. Thomas Jackson built the tower around 1807 (although the date is disputed in some circles). The walls are 2½ feet thick, with a 20-foot square base. Inside the tower you'll see how lead was dropped from the pouring kettle sieve at the top of the 70-foot tower to a kettle of cold water 75 feet below ground. The 145-foot fall and cold-water dunking formed the shot into hardened round balls, and the size of the shot depended on the size of the mesh in the sieve it was poured through.

The shot tower was designated a National Historic Mechanical Engineering Landmark in 1961 by the American Society of Mechanical Engineers. There are seventy-seven steps up the winding staircase. The tower is open noon to 5:00 P.M. Monday through Friday and 10:00 A.M. to 6:00 P.M. weekends, Memorial Day through Labor Day. There is a $2.00 parking fee. Guided tours are $2.00 for adults and $1.00 for children (twelve and under). Call (276) 699–6778 for the schedule or visit www.dcr.state.va.us/parks/newriver.htm.

The state park itself is a linear park paralleling for the most part the Norfolk & Western Railway bed. It winds 57 miles along the New River, through four counties, Carroll, Grayson, Pulaski, and Wythe. You're invited to use the trail for hiking, biking, horseback riding, cross-country skiing, and access to the river. (*NOTE:* Some parts of the trail are quite steep, and most of the trail is isolated. Check at one of the stations for information about water releases during the rainy months.)

Galax

Head out of the Fort Chiswell area and you're on your way to Galax (which also is the name of a mountain evergreen, by the way), passing by Hillsville on your way.

TOP ANNUAL EVENTS

April
Historic Garden Week, statewide
(804) 644–7776 or (804) 653–7141
www.vagardenweek.org

June
Grayson County Fiddler's Convention,
Elk Creek (276) 773–3711

July
Fairview Ruritan Old Fiddler's
Convention, Galax (276) 773–3711

September
Virginia Mountain Crafts Guild Claytor
Lake Fair, Dublin (434) 299–5874
Virginia Highlands Festival
(800) 435–3440 or (276) 676–2282

October
White Top Mountain Molasses Festival,
White Top (276) 773–3711

In Galax the place for crafts is the **Rooftop of Virginia Craft Center.** Housed in a cathedral-type setting, it is part of Rooftop of Virginia CAP, a community action agency that hosts senior citizen activities as well as Head Start programs. The center offers for sale such authentic handmade items as pottery, wood carvings, quilts, and needlework, and the work is done by native craftspeople. If you're stopping at either Grayson Highlands State Park or the Mount Rogers National Recreation Area during summer, you'll find some of these crafts available as well. The center is open 9:00 A.M. to 5:00 P.M. Monday through Saturday. It is at 206 North Main Street, Galax; call (276) 236–7131; www.rooftopcrafts.com.

The **Jeff Matthews Memorial Museum** is housed in two pioneer cabins (one built in 1834). Among the things you'll see are more than 1,000 different knives collected by Matthews, newspapers dating to January 4, 1800, covering George Washington's burial, and forty mounted heads and animal rugs from other parts of the country collected by Gleen Pless.

With today's ever-more-painless dentistry, you might want to notice a collection of old dental equipment from local dentist Dr. Paul Katt, who was still practicing dentistry at the age of eighty when he died in 1988. Among the equipment are his chair, an X-ray machine, and tools of the trade from an

funfacts

Word has it that the *Hillsville Diner,* established in 1946, now in Hillsville about halfway to Galax, was transported from Mt. Airy, North Carolina, and that a young Andy Griffith worked there, when it was in Mt. Airy, of course. The diner is at 525 Main Street, Hillsville (276-728-7681).

funfacts

In 1948 pharmacist John Hope built a large playhouse (about 15 feet by 25 feet, estimated by the current owner) for his children out of about 10,000 medicine bottles. You may call (540) 728–9205 for an appointment to see the *Bottle House,* which is on North Main Street in Hillsville.

earlier generation. A Confederate soldier display in two rooms shows pictures of all the men they could locate from Galax, Grayson, and other nearby towns, who fought in the Civil War.

The museum is open 1:00 to 5:00 P.M. Wednesday through Friday, 11:00 A.M. to 4:00 P.M. Saturday, and 1:00 to 4:00 P.M. Sunday. It's closed on Monday and Tuesday. The visit is free, but donations are accepted. It is located adjacent to the Vaughan Memorial Library at 606 West Stuart Drive in Galax. For more information call (276) 236–7874.

On October 6, 2001, the $5.2 million *Blue Ridge Music Center,* an outdoor stage and amphitheater just off the Blue Ridge Parkway, about 12 miles east of Galax, enjoyed its first concert. To be located at Milepost 213 on the Blue Ridge Parkway, an interpretive center is planned by the National Park Service to preserve, interpret, and present the unique American music tradition of the Blue Ridge Mountains. The complex will include an interpretive center, a 500-seat hillside amphitheater, informal music areas, an instrument makers'

independence

Located 15 miles west of Galax, the town of Independence came into being in 1850 over a dispute between residents of two towns about where to locate the county seat. In a Solomonesque decision, adjacent county commissioners chose a site favored by a group of "independents."

shop, a picnic area, and hiking trails. The visitor center is open daily from 9:00 A.M. to 5:00 P.M. (276) 236–5309; www.blueridgemusiccenter.org.

The center will be operated cooperatively by the National Park Service and a nonprofit foundation, the National Council for the Traditional Arts. This will tie in nicely with the annual Old Time Galax Fiddlers Convention held every August, which draws 10,000 musicians and 40,000 attendees.

If you're a miniature railroad fan, then you must see the *Twin County Railroad.* It is said to be the largest model railroad in southwest Virginia open to the public. Located 3 miles south of Galax on U.S. Highway 89, off State Route 821 (276–236–3876), the model railroad was constructed by the Twin County Railroad Club and depicts the Norfolk & Southern Railroad line from Foster Falls to Lambsburg. The exhibit is open Sunday 2:00 to 5:00 P.M. www.tcrrclub.swa-biz.com.

Grayson County

West of Galax is Independence, the Grayson county seat. There, at the *1908 Courthouse,* is the art and cultural center of Grayson County. The former county courthouse also houses the *Vault Museum,* formerly the court clerk's vault room, and has a display of an early mountain home, barn, and blacksmith shop, complete with tools and farm implements. There's also the Grayson County Tourist Information Center and an arts and crafts shop featuring Grayson County artists and artisans. The building is open from 9:00 A.M. to 5:00 P.M. Monday through Friday and 10:00 A.M. until 4:00 P.M. on Saturday. For more information stop by at 107 East Main Street, Independence, call the Grayson Tourist Information Center at (276) 773–3711, or visit www.historic 1908courthouse.org.

Wytheville

It's back north now to Wytheville, where you can see exhibits from the old mining camps, Civil War artifacts, and antique farm machinery at the (Colonel) *Thomas J.* (Jefferson) *Boyd Museum,* the Father of Wytheville. Its collection includes Boyd's surveyor's instruments, Wytheville's first firefighting equipment, minerals, paintings, tools, musical instruments, antiques and clothing, books, and racks of photographs of early people from and places in the county. Large items, including a buggy, a moonshine still, and business equipment, are in the basement.

The Boyd Museum is on 295 Tazewell Street, Wytheville, and is open 10:00 A.M. to 4:00 P.M. Tuesday through Friday and noon to 4:00 P.M. on Saturday. Admission is $3.00 for adults and $1.50 for children ages six through twelve. For more information call (276) 223–3331; http://visit.wytheville.com/boyd.htm.

Next to the Thomas J. Boyd Museum is the *Haller-Gibboney Rock House Museum,* an old Pennsylvania gray limestone house that has seen a lot of history. The home was built in 1824 and served as a hospital to both Confederate and Federal troops. Included in its exhibits are furnishings that were transported by oxcart from Pennsylvania, possessions of the Haller, Gibboney, and Campbell families, who

trivia

Elizabeth Brown Memorial Park (276–223–3355) is the site of the largest festival in Wytheville, the annual *Chatauqua Festival in the Park,* attended by thousands.

lived in the house from 1820 until 1967. Dr. John Haller, the second occupant of the Rock House, was Wytheville's first resident physician.

The furnishings are displayed in a parlor, dining room, reception room, and some bedrooms. There are also displays of coins, rocks, and Indian relics of the area, among other regional artifacts. Another Rock House souvenir of the Civil War time is a bullet hole in the wall of the front parlor. The museum is located at 205 Tazewell Street, Wytheville. The museum is open from 10:00 A.M. to 4:00 P.M. Tuesday through Friday and noon to 4:00 P.M. on Saturday April through October. Admission is $3.00 for adults and $1.50 for children. A combination ticket to both museums is $5.00 for adults and $2.50 for children. Call (276) 223–3330 for additional information; http://visit.wytheville.com/museums.htm.

Beagle Ridge Herb Farm and Environmental Education Center, operated by Gregg and Ellen Reynolds, includes a formal walled herbal display garden; a lavender walk; thyme, oregano, and lavender collections; a pergola that shades the medicinal herbs; nursery beds; a water garden; and a shrub border with rugosa roses. Other special areas are being added. They grow organic garlic and herbs to make delicious herbal vinegars and seasonings and manufacture a line of herbal bath products. You can take a workshop, hike, or talk with Gregg and Ellen about your garden and theirs.

Ellen reports exciting news that's almost obvious with their new, longer name. They have started FAWN Inc., a nonprofit foundation for environmental education on a part of their property. "We believe being a good steward to the land begins at a young age and as environmental educators it is our mission to give back to the community."

Yesterday upon the stair, I saw a man who wasn't there

So, George Wythe, for whom Wytheville is named, never visited the town. He did, however, sign the Declaration of Independence and design the original great seal of Virginia. It's circular, with a figure of Virtus, the goddess of virtue, dressed as a warrior in the center. She holds a spear in her right hand, with its point held downward touching the earth. In her left hand is a sheathed sword pointing upward. Her left foot rests on the chest of the figure of tyranny, who is lying on the ground. Above the figure is the word "Virginia," and under the figures is the state motto "Sic Semper Tyrannis" or "Thus Always to Tyrants." The seal was adopted in 1776 and modified in 1930.

Wythe also was the first professor of law in an American college, the College of William and Mary in Williamsburg.

Self-proclaimed as "Your Outdoor Classroom in the Blue Ridge," the programs they offer vary from pre-K to high school, women in the outdoors, and just about everything in between.

Beagle Ridge Herb Farm is open from 10:00 A.M. to 5:00 P.M. Thursday through Sunday from May through October and by appointment. Call (540) 962–2247 during the week and (276) 621–4511 on weekends; 1934 Matney Flats Road, Wytheville; www.beagleridgeherbfarm.com.

When you head north out of Wytheville, you come to Big Walker Mountain, and the *Big Walker National Scenic Byway* and *Big Walker Lookout,* at an elevation of 3,405 feet, in the Big Walker National Forest. The Appalachian Trail goes through this area, affording many vistas of the farmland below to the north and mountain wilderness to the south. The lookout, with a 100-foot tower, is at the halfway point of the byway.

There also are a commercial tourist shop and a swinging bridge to a chair lift (the first and tallest in Virginia), a snake pit, and other "attractions." Of course, the main attraction is the view. In spring it's highlighted by the newborn blossoms; in fall, by the flaming foliage. There's a beginners hiking trail, *Monster Rock Trail,* that begins behind Big Walker Lookout and follows the ridge of the mountain.

The chair lift is open daily during the summer and weekends-only in spring and fall. The byway is open year-round; the lookout is open 10:00 A.M. to 6:00 P.M. daily from Memorial Day to Labor Day. The overlook is free. The tower and swing bridge (8711 Stoney Fork Road, North Wytheville) are $4.50 for adults and $3.50 for children ages three to eleven (540–228–4401; www.scenicbeauty.va.com).

skeeterdogs

Since 1920, Skeeter's E. N. Umberger store (165 East Main Street, Wytheville) has been serving its self-proclaimed "world-famous hotdogs" or "skeeterdogs." More than seven million have been sold so far "without a dissatisfied customer." They've been shipped to customers from Singapore, Amsterdam, Germany, and Great Britain. By the way, Edith Bolling Wilson, a descendant of Pocahontas and wife of President Woodrow Wilson, was born in the residence above the store. Call (276) 228–2611; www.geocities .com/Area51/4667/skeeters.html.

Bland County

For an unusual activity you certainly can write home about, try trekking with the *Virginia Highland Llamas* (Route 1, Box 41, Bland 24315). With advance reservations, Bob and Carolyn Bane will lead you and your party, along with a herd of llamas, up Big Walker's old Appalachian Trail section. On special saddles the llamas will carry a picnic lunch you can enjoy after hiking through lush green meadows up to a beautiful vista.

The hike, which costs about $60 per person, is about three hours up and two and a half hours down. All you need are sturdy footwear, a camera, and film. Everything else is furnished. Llama treks are available April through October. For more information or reservations call (276) 688–4464; www.llamaweb.com/llfarms/vhl/vhl.html.

Continuing north on I–77, you'll come to Bastian and the **Wolf Creek Indian Village and Museum** (exit 58, 1,000 feet north on Route 52, Bastian). The living-history museum is a twenty-four-and-a-half-acre re-creation of an American Indian community with a population of about a hundred persons that existed nearby approximately 800 years ago.

The remains of the original village site came to the attention of state archaeologists in 1969 after highway workers began excavating the area to build I–77. Archaeologist Howard MacCord mapped the area before it was flooded by the rerouting of Wolf Creek, and the catalog of artifacts includes fourteen Indian skeletons, signs of eleven wigwams, and several storage pits.

The reconstructed village includes wigwams, fire pits, a perimeter fence, and other facilities. Costumed interpreters help you understand the skills that these Indians probably used and how they created their pottery and weavings.

A picnic area with fourteen tables and grills, a shelter, and hiking trails are available.

Wolf Creek is open 9:00 A.M. to 5:00 P.M. daily. It is closed Thanksgiving, Christmas, and New Year's Days. The admission fee to the museum and the Indian Village is $8.00 for adults and $5.00 for children ages five through sixteen; a family pass costs $30.00; (276) 688–3438; www.indianvillage.org.

Tazewell County

The **Historic Crab Orchard Museum and Pioneer Park** (U.S. Highway 19 and Route 460 at Crab Orchard Road, Tazewell) displays photographs, multimedia presentations, and artifacts dating from millions of years ago to the present in a 110-acre area near Tazewell (it's a short "a") designated as a prehistoric and historical archaeological area. Among the regular exhibits are a leg bone and teeth of a huge mastodon that roamed the area millions of years ago, the

Cuz . . .

Find your way to Pounding Mill and **Cuz's Uptown Barbeque, Cabins and Resort,** located in a renovated dairy barn. Since 1979 they've been fixing huge steaks, smoked prime rib, fresh fish, Thai curry, and pit-smoked barbecue. Stop in on weekends and listen to live bluegrass music. There are two hand-hewn cedar cabins, each with a fireplace and a two-person hot tub, and one brightly colored beach-style bungalow. Enjoy breakfast served on your porch, play tennis on the clay court, take a dip in the pool, or just relax.

Open from 3:00 to 9:00 P.M. Wednesday through Saturday from March through December. U.S. 460, Pounding Mill; (540) 964–9014; www.cuz.us.

double palisades (protective fortification wall of tree trunks) of the Native Americans, and relics from the Revolutionary and Civil Wars. Many of these "souvenirs" of the past were uncovered during the construction of Routes 19 and 460.

A "lepidodendron tree," which is really sandstone rock, might be the first thing you see as you enter the museum. The lepidodendron was a popular growth item about 300 million years ago and grew in the water that then covered the area. Eventually the trunk would break off, and water would rot the interior, which would then fill with sand and form a cast of the inside of the tree trunk. Some of the wood would adhere to the stone, carbonize, and form bituminous coal. You'll also see "Old Hitler," the remains of a fairly huge black bear who dined on the sheep of the area. Great for a kid's imagination! I'll admit it, the Historic Crab Orchard Museum and Pioneer Park in Tazewell is one of my favorites, no qualifiers attached. If *Beverly Hillbillies* brainwashed us into believing that hillbillies are stupid, I like Crab Orchard because it is here to disavow us of that impression.

So, what is Crab Orchard? Well, it's a collection of buildings and exhibits that lets you see how things were over the last 350 years so that you can realize how much they have changed. Around the main museum are thirteen historic buildings, including three of stone. Another point I find fascinating is the difference in log-house building, depending on whether the settlers' origins were Scotch-Irish, English, or German. The Lincoln Logs form of construction is not the only way. There's a horse-drawn equipment barn (which houses old buggies), a hearse, one of two known early models of the McCormick reaper (the other's at McCormick's place in Steele's Tavern), a 1917 Model T, and various saddles. There are two cabins with reproductions or antiques that won't deteriorate easily because there's no heat or cooling in the buildings. You can also see a kitchen, lard house, and loom house (with a 150-year-old operational loom and a volunteer in the process of making a very large rug that eventually will go on exhibit).

Crab Orchard, however, is more than what's past and gone. There's a new exhibit every quarter: perhaps photographs, a history of railroading, German Expressionistic art, or the paintings of local artist Tracy Ratliff. Another exhibit featured a collection assembled by Kathleen Harman, a curator of textiles from Abingdon. She's been collecting antique woven coverlets and oral histories from all over southwest Virginia. These coverlets were made at home by slaves or housewives to decorate their homes. She's also compiling the oral histories that go with them, such as "how fast Grandma could shear a sheep."

The activities calendar is filled with such items as a May Civil War reenactment and, on July 4, a community festival that's attended by several thousand people with crafts and home-baked goods. In September there's a storytelling festival. Crab Orchard is open 9:00 A.M. to 5:00 P.M. Monday through Saturday (but there are no Saturday hours from Christmas through March) and 1:00 to 5:00 P.M. Sunday (Memorial Day through Labor Day). It's closed Thanksgiving, Christmas, and New Year's Days. Admission is $8.00 for adults and $4.00 for children six through twelve; the family rate is $22.50. Event day demonstrations may have an extra charge. There are a slew of discount opportunities if you're a member of AAA, AARP, or a special group. For more information call (276) 988–6755; or visit www.craborchardmuseum.com.

Not too far from Tazewell is **Burkes Garden,** which was surveyed in 1748 and is now designated a Virginia **Scenic Byway.** This beautiful valley is unique

And the waters came and came and came

The town of Grundy, Buchanan County seat, lies along the Levisa Fork River and has been the victim of a number of floods, often with fatal results. Years have passed since the idea was proposed to move the town, build a new highway, create a floodwall with that highway, and revitalize the town. Now, in a project through the auspices of the town, the Virginia Department of Transportation, and the U.S. Army Corps of Engineers, the $100 million (or more) project seems to be under way. Among the things moved, to be moved, or replaced are the old railroad depot, the police and fire stations, the town hall, the community college, and a mountain. So, take a look, watch the construction, and realize when you come back, perhaps a decade from now, all will be different.

because it is surrounded by only one mountain. It's also the highest, coldest, greenest, and maybe the prettiest in Virginia. James Burke discovered the area in the 1740s when he followed a wounded elk there. Legend says he planted the potato peelings that provided food for the Irish surveying party that came through in 1749, who jokingly named the place "Burkes Garden." To get there, take Route 623 east and south out of Tazewell for about 15 miles; (276) 988–5091.

Smyth County

The *Smyth County Museum,* located at 109 West Strother Street in Marion, originated with a schoolhouse built in 1838. One small room is a restored 1800s schoolroom, complete with blackboard, bench seats, water bucket, and switches. Other collections include Civil War memorabilia, household items, a photograph gallery, and the Hall of Fame of notable Smyth Countians. The museum is open on Friday and Saturday from 2:00 to 5:00 P.M. There is no admission fee. For more information call (276) 783–7067; www.marionva .org/attractions/museums/scm.htm.

Just as your back (or whatever) is about to give out from hours of driving and riding while you're exploring the back roads and beautiful mountain scenery, along comes *Saltville,* the Salt Capital of the Confederacy. Suddenly, out of what appears to be almost nowhere, is the Saltville Fitness Trail, running along the railroad tracks to help you work on your tired muscles and brain cells. The first salt mine in America opened here in 1795. Apparently it wasn't really a "mining" operation, as the salt was removed from the ground in liquid form, but it produced four million bushels of salt in 1864. You can see examples of the big salt kettles around the town.

Time in Saltville goes back a long way. Each summer a dig is conducted by the Virginia Museum of Natural History and the Smithsonian Institution for prehistoric bones, and finds have included a musk ox skeleton and the track of a giant ground sloth. It's possible they've also found evidence of human life in our hemisphere from 14,000 years ago. The floor of the Saltville valley has a flat layer of mud, which is why so many artifacts and fossils have been preserved and not washed away.

The town continues this prehistoric

funfacts

The soft drink Dr Pepper was created in Rural Retreat. It didn't exactly put the town on the map, but it helped. Dr Pepper's Drug Store closed a few years ago, and then the building burned down. But talk to the locals for the real story about Dr Pepper.

theme during the Labor Day celebratory parade, which includes a gigantic (man-made) wooly mammoth and a baby mammoth, complete with trunks that blow water. In addition to the annual dig in the Well Fields, a visit to Saltville could include a tour through the town, where you can learn more about the history of this "salt town." Self-guided tour brochures can be picked up at the Chamber of Commerce of Smyth County at 124 West Main Street in Marion or at the Saltville Town Hall.

A tour of Saltville begins at the **Museum of the Middle Appalachians** at the **Saltville Museum Park,** which contains memorabilia of Saltville's rich history and of the industries that manu-factured salt and salt by-products for almost 200 years. The museum is housed in what was an office of one of the early salt companies. The park includes two 1890s steam locomotives that were used by local industry; tramway buck-ets that were part of a 7-mile tramway used to carry limestone; and huge iron kettles, used during most of the nineteenth century for boiling down salt brine. In the museum's main hall, you can see an interactive model of the Valley with historical and geological points of interest, fossils from the late Pleistocene Epoch, Woodland Indian artifacts, relics from the two battles that occurred in the Saltville Valley, and other items of historic importance. The museum is open from 10:00 A.M. to 4:00 P.M. from Monday through Saturday and from 1:00 to 4:00 P.M. on Sunday. Admission is $3.00 for adults and $2.00 for seniors and children six to twelve. Call (276) 496–3633 for further information.

Next to the **Madam Russell Methodist Church** is the **Madam Russell House.** The church and home are named after Elizabeth Henry Campbell Russell, sister of Patrick Henry. She was a leader of the Methodist Church in the region. Construction of the church was begun in 1898, using local sand-stone. Her home, at 725 Mathieson Road (276–496–4934; www.saltville.org), is open 9:00 A.M. to 5:00 P.M. daily in summer.

To become more intimately acquainted with the town, call (540) 496–5342 for historic tour information at the town hall, and obtain an informative book-let on the town's historic attractions.

Washington County

Probably the best-known historic and tourist area in Washington County is Abingdon, the oldest incorporated town west of the Blue Ridge Mountains. One of the better-known attractions in Abingdon is the world-famous *Barter Theatre* (open February through December), with such comic and lightly serious traveling company presentations as the marvelously funny *Greater Tuna* by Jaston Williams and Joe Sears. Bob Porterfield gathered the first production company together during the Depression, when they bartered their presentations in exchange for food and services from area residents. The seats—taken from the closed Empire Theatre on Broadway and installed in the 1950s—served well but have been replaced with "new" seats from the closed Jefferson Theatre in Falls Church, Virginia. The Barter Theatre is at 133 West Main Street, Abingdon; (276) 628–3991; www.bartertheatre.com.

The *Historic District of Abingdon* is about 20 square blocks of restored 100- to 200-year-old homes and buildings, each with its own story. As examples, on East Main Street are the Cave House Craft Shop (where about 150 crafters from within 50 miles of town sell their quilts, pottery, gourmet food, sculpture, fine art, and other items) and the *William King Regional Arts Center* (415 Academy Drive, Abingdon; 276–628–5005; www.wkrac.org), with a gallery and eight studios of artists and crafters. www.abingdon.com.

Stop by the *Fields-Penn 1860 House Museum,* at 208 West Main Street, Abingdon (276–676–0216 or 800–435–3440), which shows how a typical family lived in the pre–Civil War period. It's filled with period furniture, and a

bartertheatre

Gregory Peck, Ernest Borgnine, Patricia Neal, Ned Beatty, Hume Cronyn, Gary Collins, and Larry Linville are among more than one hundred well-known stars of stage, screen, and television who launched their careers at Barter Theatre in Abingdon.

The sculptures surrounding the lighting fixtures were created by Mary Filapek, in the Barter production building. Payton Boyd designed the seat covers, based on the Charles Vess design of the Barter logo. There are about forty thousand stitches on each embroidered pattern, with the embroidery donated by Lebanon Apparel. The lobby drapers were designed by Amanda Alridge, Pat Van Horn, and Amy Fansler of the costume shop, and the stained glass circular window on the building's facade was crafted by Abingdon artist Allen Boyd; 163 West Main Street, Abingdon; (276) 628–3991; www.bartertheatre.com.

trivia

You'll see "Black Diamonds" around this area a lot. It's a nickname for coal that came into popular use during the 1970s Middle East oil crisis. So, you'll see the Black Diamond Savings Bank and the Black Diamond District (a high school sports conference). The coal is mined in pits and inside mountains, just as regular diamonds are, and the coal is the heart of the far southwest Virginia economy.

guided tour will take you through the museum, which is open 1:00 to 4:00 P.M. Wednesday through Saturday.

Pick up the pamphlet on the house at the Abingdon Convention and Visitors Bureau at 335 Cummings Street, Abingdon, or call (276) 676–2282 or (800) 435–3440.

It's said that on the night of the full moon, haunting violin melodies can be heard from the third floor of the *Martha Washington Inn* in Abingdon. Traditional lore says that during the Civil War, Captain John Stoves, a Union officer, was captured near the inn, which was a girls' finishing school at the time. As he lay dying, a "Martha Girl" who was known as Beth played a comforting melody on her violin. Soon after he died, she came down with typhoid fever and died. They're both buried in Abingdon's Green Springs Cemetery. More cheerful times at the Inn could include a visit to the natatorium, the Spa at the Martha, the annual jazz festival, or other events. 150 West Main Street; (276) 628–3161. The Web site is at www.marthawashingtoninn.com.

The towns of Abingdon and nearby Damascus have opened a 3-mile hiking and biking trail as part of the *Virginia Creeper Trail.* The 34 miles of the VCT run along an old railroad bed from Abingdon to the North Carolina state line. A shuttle service is available for those who only want to go one way. This portion of the trail begins near the corner of Green Springs Road and A Street and continues to the Watauga Road (State Route 677).

There is an abundance of beautiful scenery as the trail passes through farmland, a small mountain range, and over creeks and gullies. Thanks to the assistance of the Jacobs Creek Job Corps and the Seabees, there are four trestle bridges, which have been floored for pedestrian use and are provided with handrails. Motorized vehicles, firearms, and alcoholic beverages are not permitted. The trail passes through private property, and you are asked to remain on the trail itself and not trespass. For additional information contact the Mount Rogers National Recreation Area, Route 1, Box 303, Marion 24354; (540) 783–5196; www.vacreepertrail.org.

Russell County

With a fairly recent restoration, the old *Russell County Courthouse* (276–762–7254) at Dickensonville on Copper Creek became the first landmark in Russell County to be nominated to the National Register of Historic Places. The courthouse was used from late 1799 to 1818, when a new county seat was designated. To see the courthouse, take Route 58/19 out of Abingdon to the Hansonville split and follow Route 58 to the left about 4 miles to Dickensonville; (540) 762–7254; www.virginiaheritage.org/russell.co.htm.

Bristol

Going south out of Abingdon, you come to *Bristol,* the "twin cities" whose State Street is the dividing line between Tennessee and Virginia. The famed BRISTOL—A GOOD PLACE TO LIVE sign, with arrows pointing to the Virginia and Tennessee sides of State Street, is right outside the train station.

The *Birthplace of Country Music Alliance Museum* (BCMA) is based in Bristol, where it focuses on the history of country, bluegrass, and other music that's such a vital part of this area, its influences, and how it has affected the local and national population. The BCMA works to help preserve and promote this musical heritage by showing historically significant artifacts and teaching about the history of country music. Although there's information from colonial days, it mostly concentrates on the period starting in 1927 through the mid-1970s.

There's no admission charge to the BCMA museum and gift shop that is open all year during mall hours. It's located on the lower level of the Bristol Mall, 500 Gate City Highway (U.S. 58/421), Bristol; (276) 645–0035; www.birthplaceofcountrymusic.org.

Scott County

West of Bristol, near Duffield, is the *Natural Tunnel,* an 850-foot-long tunnel that's as high as a ten-story building, which was carved over thousands of years through the limestone rock of Powell's Mountain by Stock Creek's persistence. It's large enough for trains to go through, as well as people and the creek. A visitor center sits atop the mountain, with a chairlift to take visitors down to the tunnel, and is accessible to the disabled. The lift is $2.00 each way (or $3.00 round-trip), so you can walk down and lift back or walk or lift both ways. It's about a thirty-minute walk versus a seven-minute lift ride. The exhibits in the historical railroad museum emphasize the natural history of the area and the impact of railroading.

A real "wow" is the view of a wide chasm between steep stone walls bordered by several pinnacles or "chimneys." There are also camping and picnicking facilities, an amphitheater, and a swimming pool. The park is open from dawn to dusk for day use, and the campground and cabins are available from March 1 through December 7. The visitor center gift shop, set up to look like a railroad station, is open 10:00 A.M. to 5:00 P.M. on weekdays and 10:00 A.M. to 6:00 P.M. weekends from Memorial Day through Labor Day; it's also open 10:00 A.M. to 4:00 P.M. weekends in April, May, September, and October. For additional information on cabin and camping fees, call (276) 940–2674 or (800) 933–PARK; www.dcr.virginia.gov/parks/naturalt.htm.

Nashville, Tennessee, may claim to be the home of country music, but the Carter Family fold claims that A. P. Carter, his wife, Sara, and her cousin Maybelle (mother of June, Helen, and Anita Carter) were the pioneers of this music form. The Carter Family recorded 300 songs between 1927 and 1942, 100 of them written by A. P.

Now the ***Carter Family Museum, Memorial Music Center,*** and ***Music in the Fold*** on Saturday nights at 7:30 show what country music, clogging, and buck dancing are about in a rustic country setting. A 1,000-seat music "shed" is the site for traditional country music every Saturday night.

The museum, open an hour prior to show time, displays the role the Carter Family played in developing and promoting traditional bluegrass and country music, shown through instruments, original records, photographs, and personal family items. The museum is their old home, and A. P. Carter's general store is "the fold" where the shows are held. There is a 50-cent admission charge.

An annual festival, with only acoustic music, celebrating the first recordings by the Carter Family, is held the first weekend in August.

You'll find the Carter Family Fold in Hiltons (Route 614, 3 miles east of Weber City). For more information call (276) 386–9480. Call (276) 386–6054 for a recorded schedule of upcoming performances; www.carterfamilyfold.org.

Wise County

The ***University of Virginia's College at Wise*** (540–328–0102) is the only branch of the University of Virginia. It was founded in Wise in 1954 after local citizens petitioned UVA to build a college here. Until then, access to public higher education in far southwest Virginia was minimal, limited to a few extension courses.

Wise County donated the land and two old stone buildings (still standing and in use) that had served as the Wise County Poor Farm, a home for the indigent. The state offered up a total of $5,000 in appropriations for the first year. Local citizens contributed twice that to furnish and equip the school. One hundred students entered the first class in 1954.

funfacts

This area may look familiar to those of you who've seen the movie *Coal Miner's Daughter*. Some filming for the movie was done in Bee, Haysi, and Wise (fairground scene).

Until 1968 the school was a two-year "feeder college" for UVA (and other universities). Many of our area's most prominent citizens got their start at Clinch Valley College (CVC) during its two-year phase.

CVC is now the only four-year state college in Virginia west of Radford (the college became a four-year school in 1968; it was never a community college). Ties with UVA have strengthened considerably in past years.

As mentioned above, coal mining is a major industry in this southwest corner (in Lee, Scott, and Wise Counties), with some fourteen million tons of coal mined by about 4,500 miners in 300 different mines.

Dickenson County

Northeast of Wise (north on Route 23, east on Route 83) is Clintwood, the Dickenson County seat. This is where Ralph Stanley, noted bluegrass and mountain singing legend, grew up, lives, and has helped establish the **Ralph Stanley Museum and Traditional Mountain Music Center**. The $1.4 million complex is at one end of a heritage trail that starts in Floyd, goes by Galax, through Grayson County, Bristol, Hiltons, and then to Clintwood. Stanley donated old musical instruments and memorabilia collected since he started in the business as a teenager. The museum is open Monday through Saturday from 10:00 A.M. to 5:00 P.M. (closed Monday from November through April) and 1:00 to 5:00 P.M. on Sunday. Admission is $12 for adults and $10 for seniors, students, and Dickenson County residents. www.ralphstanleymuseum.com.

Big Stone Gap

The **Harry W. Meador Coal Museum** at East Third Street and Shawnee Avenue in Big Stone Gap is operated by Big Stone Gap Department of Parks and Recreation. The museum exhibits artifacts collected by the late Harry

Meador Jr., who went from being a union laborer to the vice president of coal development for a local coal company. Other items have been painstakingly assembled from private homes and public buildings, which illustrate the coal-mining heritage of the area and coal mining's profound effect on the local lifestyle.

Among the more interesting exhibits are photographs, mining equipment and tools, and coal company items. There's also a 1900s dentist office tucked in there.

The museum is open 10:00 A.M. to 5:00 P.M. Wednesday through Saturday and 1:00 to 5:00 P.M. Sunday; also open by appointment. There is no admission fee. For more information call (276) 523–9209; www.bigstonegap.org/attract /coal.htm.

For the longest continuing outdoor drama in the United States, see **The Trail of the Lonesome Pine** (the official outdoor drama of Virginia), telling the story of the romance of a mountain girl during the development of the coal industry. The drama is adapted from a book by John Fox Jr., which was the nation's first million-selling novel (and was later made into a movie), and it has been presented every year since 1963. Performances are given at 8:00 P.M. Thursday, Friday, and Saturday, June through August (Clinton Avenue, off Alternate 58W, Big Stone Gap). Ticket prices are $15.00 for adults, $12.00 for seniors, and $8.00 for students. Call the June Tolliver House and craft shop at (276) 523–1235 or visit the Web site at www.trailofthelonesomepine.org.

June Tolliver was the heroine of Fox's book, and her home is open for tours from 10:00 A.M. to 5:00 P.M. Tuesday through Saturday and 2:00 to 6:00 P.M. on Sunday during the spring and summer, and 10:00 A.M. to 5:00 P.M. Thursday through Saturday in the fall and winter. Fantastic local craft offerings from the gift shop, again open only until the last week before Christmas, are a must. The June Tolliver House is on Highway 23, Big Stone Gap; (800) 362–0149 or (276) 523–4707; www.bigstonegap.org/attract/june.htm.

The Big Stone Gap welcome center, **Interstate 101 Car and Visitor Center** is located in a 1870 Pullman Company passenger train car. It had two staterooms, a dining area, kitchen, and an observation room. The president of the Interstate Railroad company used it when they purchased it in the 1920s. The car was retired in 1959 and used as a hunting cabin on Dorchester Lake on Black Creek in Wise County. Eventually, it was donated to the Gap Corporation in 1988 when it was restored. Stop by the center to learn about sights and activities in this area and about the car's history. 619 Gilley Avenue, Big Stone Gap; (276) 523–0115 or (276) 523–2060; www.bigstonegap.com.

To see authentic Fox family furnishings, visit the *John Fox Jr. Museum* at 2747 Shawnee Avenue East in Big Stone Gap. The house was opened in 1970, and afternoon tours are given in June, July, and August by appointment (closed Monday). Dinner for groups of up to forty people is available by pre-arrangement. The museum is open from 2:00 to 5:00 P.M. Wednesday through Sunday from the Wednesday after Memorial Day until the Sunday before Labor Day. Admission is $3.00 for adults, $2.00 for seniors, and $1.00 for students. For more information call (276) 523–2747; www.bigstonegap.org/attract/john fox.htm.

The *Southwest Virginia Museum* is in a four-story mansion bequeathed in 1946 by Congressman C. Bascom Slemp. Opened in 1947, it strives to preserve a picture of the early southwest Virginia pioneer lifestyle. The museum is located at the corner of 16 West First Street and Wood Avenue (Route 58), just off U.S. Route 23 in Big Stone Gap. It is open from 10:00 A.M. to 4:00 P.M. Monday through Thursday, 9:00 A.M. to 4:00 P.M. on Friday, 10:00 A.M. to 5:00 P.M.

choo

Supposedly the Bee Rock Tunnel, at 47 feet, 7 inches, is the second shortest railroad tunnel in the world. At one time the town of Appalachia was the center of eight coal camps; many of the camps and the railroad buildings constructed by the Louisville & Nashville Railroad and the Southern Railroad created a junction here. Appalachia; (276) 565–3900.

on Saturday, and 1:00 to 5:00 P.M. on Sunday from Memorial Day through Labor Day. It is closed on Monday the rest of the year. Admission is $2.00 for adults and $1.00 for children (six to twelve). Call (276) 523–1322 or (800) VA–BYWAYS for more details; www.swvamuseum.org.

Cumberland Gap

Our tour will end in Lee County, the most southwestern of Virginia's counties, where Virginia borders Kentucky and Tennessee at Cumberland Gap. Getting there along Route 58 is an experience that can just about make you forget there's a highly industrialized civilization just a few miles away. Once you leave Duffield (Scott County), it's a pleasant drive past serene, checkerboarded pastures, little towns, white churches of assorted denominations, vent-sided barns filled with drying burley tobacco, closed-sided barns for livestock, wild-flowers, and cemeteries. Norman Rockwell couldn't have painted anything more idyllic.

Historical markers along the road relate the comings and goings of Indians, such as the June 1785 massacre by a notorious Native American known as Benge. Two miles west of Rose Hill is an Indian burial mound, most likely Cherokee.

Once you reach the Gap, you have to go into Kentucky to reach the visitor center (open from 8:00 A.M. to 6:00 P.M. Memorial Day through Labor Day and until 5:00 P.M. the rest of the year) where there are displays on the Civil War and about Daniel Boone and the thirty axemen who cut the Wilderness Trail in 1775. The Cumberland Gap is both a scenic wonder of the world and a lesson in the significance of geography to history. From 1775 to 1800 some 300,000 settlers traveled this way to get to the other side of the Appalachian Mountains as the Gap evolved into the primary track of an immense trans-Allegheny migration.

Leaves start turning in this neck of the woods as early as 125 days before Christmas, but the peak is late fall. During fall you're likely to find the view fogged much of the time, but at the visitor center you can buy slides of what the view would look like on a clear day.

Although major industrialization has not invaded this area, it is far from being the " 'Boone'-docks." By 1792 Kentucky had a population of 100,000 people; it was admitted to the Union as the fifteenth state, the first west of the Allegheny Mountains, and mostly we have Daniel Boone to thank. He was no Prince Charming accidentally coming upon a one-hundred-year-old forest growth around Sleeping Beauty's castle. He didn't one day push aside a bush and say, "Oh, here's a way to get across the mountains," but that's getting ahead of the story.

Rather, the trail was an evolving process. Deer and buffalo migrated across the Gap, and Indians followed their path. The Cherokees, leading strategic battles against other tribes, had made the trip on foot from their native North Carolina. An occasional courageous person wandered through, and there was talk of the marvelous bluegrass country and the riches of food, livestock, and logging trees. Eventually coal would be discovered here as well.

Gabriel Arthur went through the Gap, then called the Warrior's Path, as a captive of the Indians in 1673. He escaped to tell the tale. It was another seventy-seven years before Dr. Thomas Walker went through the Gap in 1750 and documented his travels.

That's when the excruciatingly slow wheels of progress were put in motion. Walker was there for a real estate company looking for the bluegrass territory for a future development. He came close, but he never found it. He did name the Gap though, after the Duke of Cumberland, son of King George II.

Then, Richard Henderson, a lawyer and land speculator, formed the

Transylvania Co. to establish trade with the Indians. Daniel Boone and thirty axemen were hired to cut and mark the trail known as Boone's Trace, or the Wilderness Road, between areas now known as Kingsport, Tennessee, and Fort Boonesborough, Kentucky. It wasn't very wide in places: In some areas it was barely a horse path; in others just large enough for a wagon to get through. Some say it was littered with the bleached skeletal bones of history.

Then the Revolutionary War began, and the Gap just wasn't on anyone's front burner for a while. In fact, because the British stirred up the Indians against the settlers during the American Revolution, Kentucky was a downright dangerous place at the time.

The Wilderness Road eventually became a two-way thoroughfare. As some settlers trekked westward, others brought cattle, sheep, pigs, and turkeys eastward to the markets along the Atlantic Ocean. At the turn of the century, other means of transportation were developed, including the Erie and Chesapeake and Ohio canals, the Pennsylvania Main Line, and even steamboats up the Mississippi. The Gap was of extreme strategic value during the Civil War and changed hands a few times, but mostly it languished.

On June 11, 1940, the area was declared a National Historical Park, and no matter how many people are visiting the park when you're there, you're bound to think you're one of the first to discover its rugged beauty. It's the second largest of fifteen historical parks in the National Park system. Modestly put, the National Park Service says that it's one of the "lesser-used" areas in the system and therefore offers an above-average park experience.

Fast-forward to today, and when you visit the park's 20,000-plus acres straddling the crest of the Cumberland Mountains, you'll be greeted at a visitor center with films, exhibits, overnight camping passes, and general information. There are 70 miles of hiking trails (from 1 mile to the scenic 21-mile Ridge Trail), a developed campground and primitive camp areas with summertime campfire programs and daytime activities, Hensley Settlement, caves, and the *Pinnacle Overlook.*

The Pinnacle is reached via a 4-mile drive from the visitor center. The drive is off-limits to trailers and vehicles more than 20 feet long because the road can give a new meaning to the term *hairpin turn*. Depending on available staff, a shuttle runs to the overlook; the charge is $5.00 per person.

On a clear day at the Pinnacle you can easily see the three states of Kentucky, Tennessee, and Virginia, and, of course, the Gap, approximately 1,000 feet below you. On exceptionally clear days you can see the Great Smoky Mountains of North Carolina, and possibly even South Carolina and Georgia. More likely, you'll see a lot of mist and will have to rely on purchasing slides and pictures of the spectacularly sweeping vistas.

The plants and wildlife here are seldom seen elsewhere, and they abound in much the same setting as when the gap was first described. There are hardwoods (majestic virgin hemlock, oak, and magnolia) and pines. There are clumps of mountain laurel and rhododendron, so spring and early summer fill the eyescape with fragrant wildflowers and brilliant redbud and dogwood. Although you'll periodically come across some rocky outcroppings, the area is fully clothed in greenery because the glaciers never came this far south, so the hilltops weren't denuded of valuable plant-supporting dirt. Because of the various elevations, each season's exotic blooms last a very long time, and you need only climb up or descend a few feet for a different botanical view.

From 1903 to 1951 the Hensley and Gibbons families (who intermarried) occupied the **Hensley Settlement.** It was unreachable by our current standards of accessibility. Everything had to be made or grown there or carted in on mule-drawn sleds or by hiking. They lived without roads, electricity, or other conveniences. Sherman Hensley was the last to depart. The Park Service has been re-creating this last settlement, and several buildings and farms have been restored.

It's a 3½-mile hike to the Hensley Settlement, or during summer you can take a park-operated shuttle bus. There's a charge for the interpretive ride, but if you want to miss the historical notes and hike to the settlement, there's no charge. Figure on about three hours to tour the property, the homes and outbuildings, the schoolhouse and outhouses, and the farmland and cemetery. Perhaps thirty-five burials were held here, most of them for children.

The biggest change to come to Cumberland Gap National Historical Park is the completion of two two-lane, nearly 1-mile-long tunnels that cut off $3\frac{2}{10}$ miles of curving, dangerous winding roads and will allow the old Wilderness Road (now U.S. Highway 25E) to be restored roughly to the way it was in Daniel Boone's days. First, it will be narrowed down to a 10-foot wagon trail. Native seeds of grasses, shrubs, and trees have been collected and propagated to be used to restore the gap. This method is less expensive than buying nursery stock and is a lot more natural. It probably will be well into the twenty-first century before the area looks the way it did 200 years ago, but the work is providing a major head start.

Cudjo Caverns, which may be the longest cave system in Virginia (although not completely navigable by humans) with reportedly the world's largest stalagmite, have been under commercial operation for years. Lights were installed, as were wooden handrails and steps and asphalt trails and other "modern" conveniences that don't go well with successful cave life. As an example, the asphalt releases hydrocarbons, which leach into the ground and destroy the cave's ecology. The caverns were purchased from Lincoln

Memorial University by the Park Service and are now closed for inventory and cleaning (trash, graffiti, and algae) and will remain closed so that they can once again become "wild." Tours will be resumed in a couple of years, led by lantern and natural light. (Other caves in the area are open for exploration.) There is no admission charge into the park.

For additional information call (606) 248–2817, or write P.O. Box 1848, Middlesboro, KY 40965; www.nps.gov/cuga.

Where to Stay in Southwestern Virginia

ABINGDON

Inn on Town Creek
445 Valley Street Northeast
(276) 628–4560

Martha Washington Inn
150 West Main Street
(276) 628–3161

Summerfield Inn Bed and Breakfast
101 Valley Street Northwest
(276) 628–5905 or (800) 668–5905

Victoria and Albert Inn
224 Oak Hill Street Northeast
(276) 676–2797 or (800) 475–5494

BIG STONE GAP

Country Inn
627 Gilley Avenue
(276) 523–0374

FANCY GAP

Inn at Orchard Gap
4549 Lightening Ridge Road
(276) 398–3206

FLOYD

Inn at Hope Springs Farm
6847 Floyd Highway South
(540) 789–3276

MEADOWS OF DAN

Primland Resort
5537 Busted Rock Road
(276) 952–3492

PEARISBURG

Inn at Riverbend
135 River Ridge Drive
(540) 921–5211

PEMBROKE

Mountain Lake Hotel
115 Hotel Circle
(540) 951–1819 or (800) 346–3334

RADFORD

Nesselrod on the New
7535 Lee Highway
(540) 731–4970

SMITH MOUNTAIN LAKE

Manor at Taylor's Store
8812 Washington Highway
(540) 721–3951 or (800) 248–6767

WOOLWINE

Mountain Rose Inn
1787 Charity Highway
(276) 930–1057

Where to Eat in Southwestern Virginia

ABINGDON

Alison's
1220 West Main Street
(276) 628–8002

Huddle House
986 East Main Street
(276) 628–1900

The Tavern
222 East Main Street
(276) 628–1118

CHRISTIANSBURG

Farmhouse
285 Ridinger Street
Northwest
(540) 382–4253

Gables
9 Radford Street
(540) 382–6100

Giovanni's Gourmet
95 College Street
(540) 382–7218

HOT SPRINGS

Sam Snead's Tavern
1766 Homestead Drive
(540) 839–7666

General Index

Entries for Museums and WPA Murals appear in the special indexes on pages 223 and 225.

MUSEUMS

WPA MURALS

About the Author

Judy Colbert travels frequently in Virginia and its neighboring states, searching for the unique and unusual. Her greatest pleasure is talking to local residents who've read her book and say, "I've lived here all my life and never knew that!" Next is when people say, "I did what you suggested in your book and had a marvelous time." What could be more satisfying?

An award-winning author and photographer, Judy Colbert has had articles and photos appear in *Washingtonian, McCall's, AAA World, Latitudes, Maryland Life, Marketing Review, USA Today,* and more than 500 other national and local publications. Judy has talked about travel on hundreds of radio and television shows including *Good Morning America.* In 1991 she was honored as the Travel Writer of the Year by the Maryland Office of Tourism.

Judy is the author of *Maryland Off the Beaten Path*®, published by The Globe Pequot Press; *Places to Go with Children in Washington, D.C.,* for Chronicle Books; and *Country Towns of Maryland and Delaware* for Country Roads Press. She also has authored the *Divorce Common Sense Handbook,* and *Super Bowl Trivia* (under the name J.M. Colbert), and co-authored *Big Bang Marketing for Spas,* all for Tuff Turtle Publishing.

Judy is a regular contributor to several Internet sites, writing about spas, business travel and etiquette, and museums for children.